Space-Time and the Proposition

The 1944 Lectures on Samuel
Alexander's Space, Time and Deity

by

John Anderson

Edited and with an introduction by Mark Weblin

SYDNEY UNIVERSITY PRESS

SYDNEY UNIVERSITY PRESS
Print on Demand Service
SETIS at the University of Sydney Library
University of Sydney
www.sup.usyd.edu.au

The publication of this book is part of the University of Sydney Library's electronic texts initiative. Further details are available at www.sup.usyd.edu.au
© 2005 Sydney University Press

Reproduction and Communication for other purposes
Except as permitted under the Act, no part of this edition may be reproduced, stored in a retrieval system, or communicated in any form or by any means without prior written permission. All requests for reproduction or communication should be made to Sydney University Press at the address below:

Sydney University Press
Fisher Library
University of Sydney
NSW Australia 2006

E-mail: info@sup.usyd.edu.au

ISBN 1 920898 08 5

For current information see
http://purl.library.usyd.edu.au/sup/1920898085

Designed and Printed in Australia at the University Publishing Service
University of Sydney

Table of Contents

Editorial Prefaces   6

Introduction   11

Lecture 1: Reading list and introduction: Plato and Kant the great guides to the categories; Hegel's multiplication of the categories 'reactionary'; Alexander as a 'realistic Kantian'   30

Lecture 2: Realism assumed in this course but empiricism the theme: connection between empiricism and realism; the problem of proof in logic and the doctrine of the 'self-refuting'; the problem of 'conditions of existence' - categories have no significant opposite; how, then, is a situational logic possible?; Alexander doesn't begin with a propositional approach - his theory of predication; the problem articulated and the solution proposed.   33

Lecture 3 Connection and Distinction: Alexander - Space as the form of togetherness and Time as the form of distinctness; these come together in Space-Time; Hume's 'rationalism'; rationalism and monism; Rationalism defined; Empiricism defined; James and 'vicious intellectualism'; Kant as the answer to Hume; Alexander as the answer to Kant.   40

Lecture 4 Rationalism treats relations as identities; Idealism as monism; objective and subjective Idealism; the problem of unity and diversity; the problem of causality; predication.   45

Lecture 5 The 'necessity' of mathematical truths; Leibnizian theory of analysis; predication as a form of identity; clarity and vagueness; empiricism – the proposition is not derived from anything - problem of 'essences'; Alexander on the mental and the neural; his evolutionism.   50

Lecture 6 Question of mental quality: Alexander's evolutionism – the doctrine of levels; Space-Time as a 'stuff' – Alexander's substantialism or materialism; criticism of materialism - how could qualitative things ever arise from pure Space-Time?; – Spencer – criticism of substantiality – mind not 'higher' than body.   56

Lecture 7 Alexander's treatment of quality unempirical and unpropositional; propositional theory – the mental and neural occur in same place; identity of the spatio-temporal and the propositional; 'stuff' theory inconsistent with propositional theory; criticism of 'Time is the mind of Space' (mind is the Time of body); Space as togetherness or continuity - Time as distinctness or structure; criticism of physical Space-Time.   61

Lecture 8 Criticism of Alexander's substantialist view that Space-Time is a 'stuff'; rejection of levels of qualities and compresence – problem of theory of perspectives; general theory of Space-Time; Space as togetherness – Time as distinctness; how can we advance a theory of Space-Time?; things as spatio-temporal.   66

Lecture 9 The difficulty of speaking about Space and Time; lack of concreteness in Hegelian Idealism; Alexander's debt to Kant; the spatio-temporal as conveyed by the propositional form; the medium of things cannot be Space alone nor Time alone; the argument from repetition; the characters of Time and Space.   72

Lecture 10 Alexander's contention that mind and body are genus and species - general characterisation of genus and species; the 'mutual necessitation' of Space and Time; importance of the proposition; successiveness and one-dimensionality; analogical character of the statement.   77

Lecture 11 Motions: the problem of definition of a straight line; empirical grounds for geometry; irreversibility and transitiveness; criticism of 'point-instants'.   82

Lecture 12 Alexander's confusion of transitiveness and irreversibility; discussion of pendular motion; difference of direction fundamental to transitiveness in Time and two dimensionality in Space; absolute difference of direction fundamental to irreversibility in Time and three dimensionality in Space.   87

Lecture 13 Successiveness, transitiveness and irreversibility in Time and one, two and three dimensionality in Space; problem of abstraction; the intractability of qualities.   95

Lecture 14 Bradley on a) qualities and relations b) Space and Time; the problem of ultimate 'units'; rationalism of Leibniz and Russell; the problem of absolute terms; situational logic and spatio-temporal logic; Heraclitus and his all inclusive system – rejection of the 'universe' or 'cosmos'; belief in ultimates and the desire for security.   99

Lecture 15 Situational logic recognises externality everywhere; cf Leibniz and the Pythagoreans; internality in Leibniz, Berkeley and Kant; empiricism and mind.   104

Lecture 16 Transition to the categories: Alexander treats Space-Time as an infinite whole; his failure to treat the question in terms of the proposition; Space and Time and the propositional form; subject and predicate of the proposition; 'paradoxes' of the situational logic.   107

Lecture 17 Problem of the 'historical'; Alexander's treatment of the categories as predicates - categories must also be subjects; categories as relations; categories have no obverse   110

Lecture 18 Identity: as a relation; as coextension; the problem of coextension; the doctrine of unlimited intension.   114

Lecture 19 Identity: in a narrower sense; Alexander's debt to Hegel; Kant: the categories and the forms of the proposition; categories as involved with the form of the proposition; identity as being a subject.   119

Lecture 20 Difference or diversity: as being a predicate; involved with the subject; identity embodies difference; identity embodies all other categories; the copula as occurrence – existence and truth the same; the category of existence; the copula as a relation; positive and negative copula; existence involves relation; the five categories of the proposition   124

Lecture 21 The five categories of the proposition (cont.) - Relation: possible distinction between predication and relation; the function of the predicate - the qualitative predicate and Time - the predicate as activity.   128

Lecture 22 Relation: problems of Russellian logic; relational arguments; conjunctive and disjunctive arguments.   132

Lecture 23 Quantification of the predicate – relational arguments.   138

Lecture 24 Relational arguments (continued).   143

Lecture 25 Predicative logic: the distinction of quantity   *150*

Lecture 26 Universality: there are no universals nor particulars; 'system' in Hegel; optimism in Idealism; the 'concrete universal'; the notion of system; the systematic thinker.   *155*

Lecture 27 Notion of the 'term': both particular and universal; the universal as concrete or abstract (Moore-Russell view); universals as governing principles – connection with social activity; Cornford and 'Moira' – criticised by Taylor and Burnet; Parmenides on the Pythagoreans; Heraclitus   *160*

Lecture 28 Alexander on Universality as a plan: synthetic character of the proposition; the categories as universals.   *165*

Lecture 29 No pure particulars: colour; plans; the concrete universal.   *169*

Lecture 31 Stout's theory of universals criticised.   *178*

Lecture 32 Order of the Categories: Quality and Quantity; Universality and Quantity; the category of Number - begins with integers; integers characteristic of groups.   *182*

Lecture 33 Rejection of category of 'whole and part': Alexander's haphazard treatment of categories.   *187*

Lecture 34 General remarks about the categories: Alexander has no method of discovering the categories; the natural order of the categories; criticism of Hegel.   *192*

Lecture 35 Alexander's theory of number: enumeration; Alexander's rationalistic treatment of mathematics; Alexander's discussion of Russell-Frege theory of cardinal number.   *197*

Lecture 36 Ordinal numbers: category of order.   *202*

Lecture 37 Transition between categories: logical, mathematical, physical; category of quantity - from mathematical point of view as real number - from physical point of view as solidity; category of intensity – number dependent on quality – confused conceptions of degree.   *206*

Lecture 38 Measurement of sensation: Weber's law; 'threshold of consciousness'; cognitionalism in psychology.   *212*

Lecture 39 Category of substance outlined; category of intensity continued.   *218*

Lecture 40 The categories related to the proposition: Idealism as a philosophy of degrees: category of Substance.   *222*

Lecture 41 Alexander confuses substance with identity: the three groups of categories – and the transitions between them; substance continued – as the constitution of a thing.   *228*

Lecture 42 Substance as constitution or composition – structure as harmony: Heraclitus; category of causality – Alexander emphasises spatial side – Kant emphasises temporal sequence – concomitance.   *234*

Lecture 43 General points on the order and grouping of the categories; causality continued.   *240*

Lecture 44 Another grouping of the categories – causality continued – Alexander neglects the universality of causal connection.   *245*

Lecture 45 Alexander neglects the causal field: Alexander's immanentism; thinghood/individuality; reciprocity.   *250*

Lecture 46 The source of the categories as the form of the proposition: the physical categories; structure and aesthetics; category of individuality.   *256*

Index   *262*

Editorial Prefaces

John Passmore once wrote that to hear John Anderson's lectures of Samuel Alexander's *Space, Time and Deity* was to be taken to the heart of Anderson's own philosophy. These lectures provide the justification for that assertion. However, while recognising the significance of these lectures for understanding Anderson's philosophy, it is also important to note Jenny Anderson's comment that no two courses of Anderson's were ever the same and arguments often arose among his students as to which one was best.[1] His work, as she said, was never stereotyped. It is this observation that explains the relative delay in the publication of these lectures.

After the death of the Anderson's only child, Sandy, in 1996, the University of Sydney received a substantial bequest to establish an archives of material belonging to the Anderson family and to employ an editor to publish any material deemed to be of intellectual or philosophical importance. The Professor John Anderson and Family Archives were established in 1998 and the position of John Anderson Senior Research Fellow was advertised and filled in February 1999. The John Anderson Archives is 13 shelf metres in length of which his lectures occupy 1.5 metres. There are one hundred sets of Anderson's lectures on varying subjects, although only one third of these are in Anderson's own hand. Shortly after the establishment of the Anderson archives, the Scholarly Electronic Text and Image Service (SETIS) in Fisher Library had all of his handwritten manuscripts typed and placed on the John Anderson web site (http://setis.library.usyd.edu.au/oztexts/anderson.html). John Anderson lectured twice on *Space, Time and Deity*, once in 1944 and again in 1949 and in the Anderson Archives there is one manuscript of the 1944 lectures in Anderson's own hand and several records of the 1949 lectures taken by students. Only the 1944 manuscript has been typed for inclusion on the John Anderson website.

---

[1] Cullum, G. and Lycos, K. (Ed.) *Art and Reality* (Sydney: Hale and Ironmonger, 1982) p 3

The first John Anderson Research Fellow, George Molnar, from his appointment in February 1999 until his unexpected death in August of the same year, comprehensively edited Anderson's manuscript of the 1944 lectures, although no attempt was made to refer to or integrate any of the material from the 1949 lectures.[1] Since George's death, I have received several requests to complete his work and publish the 1944 lectures. However given the substantial differences between the two sets of lectures and the possibility that only one set of lectures on Alexander might ever be published, I did not believe that the high cost of commercial publication could warrant an edition of the 1944 lectures appearing which did not integrate material from the 1949 lectures. This difficulty has now been rectified by the enterprise shown by the University of Sydney Library in relaunching Sydney University Press as a print-on-demand publisher. Thanks to this innovation, it is now possible to publish these lectures with some confidence that the 1949 lectures can be published at a later date.

The editorial work performed by Mr Molnar was extensive and is explained in his own editorial preface. All of Mr. Molnar's editorial notes, diagrams and equations have been retained with some minor additions and alterations. It should be noted that Mr. Molnar reproduced the lectures *verbatim* and this leads to an occasional heaviness of style throughout the manuscript.

My own contributions to this volume over the last eight weeks have been the choice of a title, the creation of a table of contents and index, the inclusion of an occasional editorial note (designated by 'ENMW') and writing the introduction to the work. Regarding these contributions, the choice of title is intended to reflect the main theme of the course – that Alexander's 'neglect' of the proposition is the cause of his errors and confusions on Space-Time and the categories – and while the analytical table of contents is intended to assist the reader follow

---

[1] George Molnar's own philosophical work was edited by Stephen Mumford and published as *Powers: A Study in Metaphysics* (Oxford: Oxford University Press, 2003).

the main lines of the discussion, these descriptions were not used by Anderson himself and have been taken from the content of each lecture. Further the intention behind the introduction is to provide a brief account of the intellectual context of the 1944 lectures, the origin and structure of Alexander's *Space, Time and Deity*, Anderson's introduction to *Space, Time and Deity* and his subsequent research on it, and a general outline of the structure and argument of the lectures. However the introduction is not intended to provide a detailed examination of the arguments used in the lectures. There can be no substitute for thinking through these issues and the interested reader is referred to the table of contents and the index for further detail in the work. It should also be noted that the division of the lectures into groups such as Space-Time, the Logical Categories, the Mathematical Categories and the Physical Categories, do not correspond neatly to the lectures themselves although they do follow Anderson's own classification and grouping of the categories. This results in a certain 'fluidity' in the classification of the lectures in terms of these various groupings.

I would like to thank Paul Crittenden, James Packer, Creagh Cole, Ross Coleman, Tim Robinson, Julia Mant, Professor Richard Waterhouse, Dr. John Grumley and the staff of the Philosophy department for their assistance in the production of this work.

Mark Weblin
John Anderson Senior Research Fellow
Department of Philosophy
University of Sydney
July 2005

mark.weblin@arts.usyd.edu.au

Preface

In 1944 Professor John Anderson gave a course of lectures on Alexander's *Space Time and Deity*[1] to a class of Fourth Year Honours students at the University of Sydney. The course comprised forty-six lectures delivered over three terms.

The lectures as originally given were based on notes, some of which are extant. Subsequently Anderson wrote up his lectures, with the help of notes taken by three students: A.J. Baker, P.C. Gibbons, and T.A. Rose. The complete manuscript, with marginal notes and corrections, takes up 145 pages of closely written text (approximately 73,000 words). An edited version of this manuscript is reproduced here.

The pagination of the manuscript text is indicated by square bracketed numbers in bold, inserted at the point where each page of the *ms* begins. So, for example, the material in the edited version that occurs *between* '**[10]**' and '**[11]**' reproduces *page 10* of the manuscript.

Anderson did not use footnotes in his manuscript. The edited version uses three kinds of footnotes, marked 'MN', 'NT', and 'EN', respectively. Their significance is as follows:

> I. *MN*: these are *marginal notes* by Anderson. They are reproduced here verbatim, except that brackets enclosing the whole of a marginal note have been omitted. The footnote has been placed in the approximate position in the text to which the marginal note refers. All marginal notes are reproduced as footnotes, except for (a) those that were crossed out or obliterated, (b) those that deal with the order of presentation of the material in lectures, and (c) those that deal with the transcribing of the students' notes.
>
> II. *NT*: these are Anderson's notes, and asides, and references, that occur *in the text*. They are invariably separated from the

---
[1] Samuel Alexander, *Space Time And Deity, The Gifford Lectures At Glasgow 1916-18* 2 vols. (London: Macmillan and Co. Limited, 1920).

rest of the sentence by bracketing which has *not* been reproduced. They are frequently introduced by "cf.". I have relegated this material to footnotes to improve the flow of the main text.

III. *EN*: these are editorial notes. *All* changes to the text are noted in editorial notes.

Punctuation.

Anderson used underlining for emphasis. This has been changed throughout to italics.

Bracketing: round and square brackets are used by Anderson, first, as punctuation, second, as a sort of guide in the spoken delivery of lectures. When brackets that occur in the manuscript are omitted from the edited version, the change is indicated in an EN.

References: in the edited version the titles of works cited in the text have been either italicised (books or classics such as Platonic dialogues), or placed in inverted commas (articles in periodicals or chapters in books). The titles of works in the NTs or MNs are italicised only if they are underlined in the manuscript, and the inverted commas in NTs and MNs are as in the original.

The illustrations are hand drawn in the manuscript, but have been redrawn for publication. "AJPP" throughout stands for *The Australasian Journal of Psychology and Philosophy*.[1]

G. P. Molnar,
John Anderson Senior Research Fellow,
School of Philosophy, University of Sydney   August 1999

---

[1] The editor is grateful for help and information provided by A.J. Baker, and P. Coleman.

Introduction

The origin and context of the 1944 lectures.

The 1944 lectures on Alexander's *Space, Time and Deity* occupy an important place in John Anderson's corpus of lectures. From the time of his arrival at Sydney University in 1927 to 1937, the year before his departure overseas on sabbatical leave, Anderson's lectures to students were concerned with Logic, Ethics, Greek Philosophy and Modern Philosophy. However Anderson's controversial public and political life during the thirties, coupled with the atheistic character of his philosophy, led to moves during the thirties to appoint a second professor, specialising in moral philosophy, who would be more sympathetic to theism and the appointment of A.K. Stout, son of the famous Idealist G.F. Stout, in 1938 was intended to stymie Anderson's growing influence.[1] While this move failed, with Stout becoming a close friend and colleague of Anderson, this appointment did appear to give Anderson more time to develop his theoretical position in more detail and during the war years he lectured on a wide range of new subjects. Apart from returning to old favourites such as Plato and Logic, he now discussed in his lectures subjects as varied as Scientific Method, Ethics and Aesthetics, Political Philosophy, Socialism, and, in 1941, a set of lectures on 'Dialectic', where he traced the development of dialectic from the Eleatics through to Hegel. At the end of these lectures, Anderson briefly discussed the introduction to *Space, Time and Deity* but did not complete an extended examination of the book. This fuller examination first occurred in 1944 and then again in 1949.[2]

---

[1] See Department of Philosophy Archives, Sydney University Archives, Fisher Library, Sydney University.

[2] Apart from these lectures, from 1939 Anderson had also begun to give discuss Alexander's philosophy in meetings to the Sydney Branch of the Australasian Association of Psychology and Philosophy (A.A.P.P.). However these addresses were outlines and sketches of the main features of Alexander's philosophy and did not discuss in detail the nature of Space-Time and the categories.

In examining the intellectual context of Anderson's life during these years, it is important to note that during the war, Anderson was engaged on some of his most important intellectual and philosophical work. His 'The Servile State', published in the Australasian Journal of Psychology and Philosophy (A.J.P.P.) in 1943, is still regarded as one of his finest articles and the 1945 'Prospects of Democracy' is an important statement of his theory of liberal democracy.[1] He also wrote several important articles on ethics and social theory for the A.J.P.P. including 'The Meaning of Good', 'The Nature of Ethics' and 'Freudianism and Society'.[2] During this period Anderson was also leading an active intellectual life on the university campus. In his addresses to the Sydney University Literary Society he discussed Joyce and Ibsen, while in his addresses to the Sydney University Freethought Society, he covered issues as varied as obscenity, mythology, Christian credulity, Freethought and sex, totalitarianism and liberal education. Further Anderson's censure by the N.S.W. Parliament after his 'No Religion in Education' address in 1943 is an instructive example of how he could galvanise public opinion on the questions of education, religion and academic freedom.[3] Anderson was not merely sitting in his armchair pondering the esoteric question of the nature of Space-Time, but was actively engaged in the public controversies of his day.

The development and structure of Alexander's <u>Space, Time and Deity</u>.

Samuel Alexander was born in Sydney in 1859 and moved at a young age to Melbourne where he gained his secondary

---

[1] See Anderson , J. *Studies in Empirical Philosophy* (Sydney: Angus and Robertson 1962) – hereafter *Studies* – pp 328 - 339 and Anderson, J. *A Perilous and Fighting Life: From Communist to Conservative – The Political Writings of Professor John Anderson* (Melbourne: Pluto Press 2003) pp 215 - 220.
[2] See Anderson *Studies* pp 248 – 267, 268 – 278 and 340 - 358 respectively.
[3] See Baker, A. J. *Anderson's Social Philosophy: The Social Life and Political Thought of Professor John Anderson* (Sydney: Angus and Robertson, 1979) pp 118 – 122, Kennedy, B. *A Passion to Oppose* (Melbourne: Melbourne University Press, 1995) p 159 and Franklin, J. *Corrupting the Youth: A History of Philosophy in Australia* (Sydney: Macleay Press, 2003) pp 17 - 22.

education at Wesley College. Alexander studied briefly at Melbourne University before travelling to England in 1877 where he won a scholarship to Oxford University.[1] In 1887 he won the Green Prize in Moral Philosophy with his dissertation on ethics which became the basis of his Moral Order and Progress and in 1893 gained the position of Professor of Philosophy at Manchester University, becoming one of the leading Absolute Idealist's of the time.[2] Alexander's thinking remained comfortably within the confines of Absolute Idealism for the remainder of the century, until he was disturbed by the publication in 1903 of G. E. Moore's 'The Refutation of Idealism'.[3] Alexander now began a critical re-examination of his attachment to Absolute Idealism and by the time he was invited to deliver the Gifford lectures at Glasgow University between 1917 and 1918, he had formed and developed the position which he subsequently published as *Space, Time and Deity*.[4]

In brief, *Space, Time and Deity* is an attempt to explain the nature and origin of the universe itself. The volume is divided into four separate books – Space-Time, The Categories, The Order and Problems of Empirical Existence and Deity – and is preceded by

---

[1] Alexander, S. *Philosophical and Literary Pieces* (London: Macmillan and Co. 1939) p 1ff
[2] Alexander, S. *Moral Order and Progress* (London: Trubner and Co.1889). D. G. Ritchie in his *Darwin and Hegel* (London: Swan Sonnenschein, 1893, pp 66 - 67) argued that Alexander's analysis of punishment in *Moral Order and Progress* was one of the best examples of the reconciliation of evolutionary theory and Absolute Idealism.
[3] Alexander, S. *Space, Time and Deity* (London: Macmillan and Co. Limited, 1920) Vol. 1 p xxxi. Moore, G.E. 'The Refutation of Idealism' in *Philosophical Studies*, (London: Routledge & Kegan Paul Ltd, 1922), pp.1-30.
[4] The key articles in Alexander's intellectual development after 1903 were: 'Ptolemic and Copernican Conceptions of The Place of Mind In the Universe' *Hibbert Journal* Vol. VIII, Oct. 1909.; 'The Method of Metaphysics; and the Categories' *Mind* Vol. XXI, 1912; 'The Basis of Realism' *Proceedings of the British Academy* Vol. VI 1914.

an Introduction which explains his philosophical orientation.[1] In his Introduction, Alexander rejected the terms Idealism and Realism as adequate descriptions for his philosophy, preferring Empiricism as a better term for the enterprise he described as metaphysics, 'the empirical study of the non-empirical'.[2] In this introduction, Alexander acknowledges his debt to Moore and the conclusion that he derived from Moore's refutation viz. that there is a distinction between the act of mind or consciousness and the thing of which it is conscious or aware. For Alexander, consciousness and object are "..together or compresent in the world".[3] This compresence of mental activity and the object itself was in turn the basis for his epistemological distinction between contemplation and enjoyment – that the mind contemplates its objects but enjoys itself. While many philosophers in the Realist and phenomenological traditions in the early decades of the twentieth century discussed this distinction between mental activity and object, Alexander's unique contribution was to recognise that this relation of compresence between mind and object is not unique to mind, but is the most basic relation between any two objects existing in Space and Time.[4] Indeed it is this distinction between mind and body which gives Alexander the 'clue' to the relationship between Space and Time – that Time is in exactly the same

---

[1] For general information on Alexander see Emmet, D. 'Foreword to the 1966 reprint edition' of Alexander, S. *Space, Time and Deity* (New York: Dover Press 1966); Metz, R. *A Hundred Years of British Philosophy* (London: Allen and Unwin, 1938) pp 622 - 655 and Passmore, J. *A Hundred Years of Philosophy* (Harmondsworth: Penguin 1966) pp 265 - 76. For more detailed accounts see Brettschnieder, B. *The Philosophy of Samuel Alexander* (New York: Humanities Press, 1964); McCarthy, J.W. *The Naturalism of Samuel Alexander* New York: Kings Crown Press, 1948); Weinstein, M.A. *Unity and Variety in the Philosophy of Samuel Alexander* Indiana: Purdue University Press, 1983).

[2] Alexander *Space, Time and Deity* Vol 1 p 4. Care must be taken not to confuse Alexander's use of the word 'metaphysics' as the empirical study of the non-empirical with Anderson's rejection of 'metaphysics' as a rationalist construction of ideas. Although Anderson never used the word in Alexander's sense, his lectures on Alexander can be precisely defined as the empirical study of the non-empirical.

[3] *ibid* Vol. 1 p 11

[4] *ibid* Vol. 1 p 27. See also Vol. 2 p 75

relation to Space as mind is to the body. Time, he often said, is the mind of Space.

Alexander's examination of Space-Time was marked by a tension between a substantialist or materialist conception of Space-Time which is the origin of all things and a formal or logical view of Space-Time as the medium in which things exist. In his initial discussion of Space-Time, Alexander rejected physical, mental and mathematical conceptions of Space and Time, arguing for an empiricist or Absolute theory of Space-Time.[1] However he subsequently detailed a substantialist and evolutionary theory of Space-Time as the 'simplest being itself', the "..stuff of which all things, whether as substances or under any category, are made".[2] The movement of Time occurs in Space and at some point reaches a degree of complexity where matter is created. With the creation of matter and the subsequent creation of qualities, the process of 'emergence' begins, producing objects of increasing qualitative complexity, from the inorganic to the organic, from organism to animal and from animal to human, the latter of which is the highest point yet attained, although not the end, of this evolutionary process. For Alexander, Deity, is still to come.

However this evolutionary conception of Space-Time is at odds with Alexander's logical or absolute view of Space-Time. While elucidating his 'stuff' theory of Space-Time, Alexander also argued that Space-Time is an 'infinite given whole' where any thing or event is a point-instant, a differentiated complex "..within the one all-containing and all-encompassing system of motion".[3] This suggests that Alexander conceived of Space-Time as a medium in which things exist or are placed as point-instants and the logical or absolute nature of this view is well illustrated by his theory of the categories which he takes to be pervasive or universal features of things. Alexander identified seven distinct groupings of the categories - Identity, Diversity and Existence; Universal, Particular and Individual; Relation; Order; Substance, Causality and Reciprocity; Quantity and Intensity; Whole and

---

[1] *ibid* Vol. 1 p 180
[2] *ibid* Vol. 1 p 341
[3] *ibid* Vol. 1 p 183

Part, and Number – and while a detailed and critical exposition of these categories is a large part of the current work, it is important to note his statement that the categories have no origin.[1] If Alexander appears to vacillate on the question of whether Space-Time is a 'stuff' or a medium, his belief that the categories have no origin clearly implies that Space-Time itself cannot have an origin and hence cannot be a 'stuff' from which all things emerge. The tension in Alexander between a substantialist or emergent conception of Space-Time and an Absolute and empirical one is clear and it is perhaps not surprising to learn that Anderson only focussed on those books dealing with Space-Time and the categories, regarding the later work as nugatory.

Genesis of Anderson's lectures on Alexander.

One young student at Alexander's 1917 Gifford lectures was John Anderson. Himself a brilliant and talented student at Glasgow University, Anderson was at that time writing his M.A. thesis, having versed himself in the pre-Socratic philosophy of John Burnet, the traditional syllogistic logic of Robert Latta, the realism of Moore, Russell and the American New Realists, the Idealism of Henry Jones and the 'radical empiricism' of William James. As he attended these lectures, Anderson gradually became convinced by the perspicuity of Alexander's system, although he was too independent-minded to be a mere disciple and while he worked at the universities of Glasgow and Edinburgh over the next ten years, he began the slow process of reformulating and thinking through Alexander's philosophy.

By the time of his arrival at Sydney University in 1927, Anderson had worked through many of his objections and difficulties and in a series of articles over the next five years, presented his criticisms of Alexander's system.[2] Accepting the primacy of the Realist logic of external relations, Anderson criticised Alexander for departing from Realism with his theory of compresence, the

---

[1] *ibid* Vol 1 p 330
[2] See 'The Non Existence of Consciousness', 'The Knower and the Known' and 'Realism and some of its Critics' in *Studies* pp 60 – 67, 27 – 40 and 41 – 59 respectively.

corresponding error of mind as consciousness and its associated epistemological dualism, his theory of evolutionary levels of development, and his conception of Space-Time as a 'stuff'. Central to Anderson's criticisms of Alexander was his theory of the proposition. Anderson's understanding of the proposition was derived from his training in traditional logic and was a central feature of his philosophy. For Anderson the truth or falsity of a proposition is not determined by its context or its participation in the Absolute Idea, but by the simple fact of existence.[1] Any proposition must express something and will do so in the subject-predicate form. Any proposition will contain a predicate attached to a subject by the copula – is or is not – and will have the logical form 'S is P'.[2] Further, Anderson argued that any proposition will be either universal or particular[3] and hence concluded that there are only four logical forms of the proposition.[4] Although Anderson never published a full account of his logical theory of the proposition, his students knew it well through his lectures[5] and it formed the basis of his criticisms not only of Alexander, but of the pre-Socratics and modern philosophers such as Descartes, Hume and Hegel.[6]

After the last of these articles appeared in 1931, Anderson didn't publish or speak on Alexander or *Space, Time and Deity* again until 1939 and it was only in 1944 that he first lectured on Alexander's metaphysics in detail, a subject which he treated again in 1949. In both sets of lectures there is a common structure. Both begin with an Introduction which discusses the meaning of Realism and Empiricism and their relationship to Rationalism and Monism, in both there is a consideration of the

---

[1] See 'Propositions and Judgements' and 'The Truth of Propositions' in *Studies* pp 15 – 19 and 20 – 26 respectively.
[2] The 'is' in this sense being both affirmative and negative.
[3] Anderson rejected singular propositions as a special class of propositions.
[4] Universal affirmative (SaP), universal negative (SeP), particular affirmative (SiP) and particular negative (SoP). Anderson is clearly at odds here with the dominant tendency in twentieth century Anglo-Saxon logical theory which has emphasised a greater diversity of logical forms.
[5] There are several copies of Anderson's lectures on Logic in the John Anderson archives.
[6] See 'The *Cogito* of Descartes', 'Design' and 'The Place of Hegel in the History of Philosophy' in *Studies* pp 101 – 114, 88 – 100 and 79 – 87 respectively.

nature of Space and Time, including their interconnected nature as Space-Time, and finally in both there is a general theory of the categories and their classification into three separate groups: the logical categories, the mathematical categories and the physical categories. At this point however, the similarities diverge. In 1944 Anderson presented at least five different descriptions of the classification of the categories, whereas in 1949 there is only one such exposition. Significantly, the differences that occur in the description of the categories are differences of their relation to 'the proposition'. It is reasonable to conclude then, that the 1944 lectures were a 'work in progress' and that by 1949 he had come to a more definitive understanding of classification of the categories. This is not to say however that Anderson treated the categories equally, for while his discussion of categories such as causation and universality extends for several lectures, his discussion of categories such as substance or individuality don't even extend for an entire lecture. Another feature of these lectures which may puzzle many philosophically educated readers is Anderson's constant reference to the pre-Socratics, a reference that appears out of place in a discussion of Space-Time and the proposition. In fact, Alexander himself made frequent reference to John Burnet's work on early Greek philosophy and given Anderson's own appreciation of Burnet it is only natural that he would have continued and extended the use of him, especially with regard to Heraclitus.[1]

The 1944 Lectures on *Space, Time and Deity*

Introduction (Lectures 1 – 5)

Anderson begins these lectures with the statement that Realism will be assumed throughout the course, although he does not simply mean Realism in its narrow, epistemological sense, but also in its wider sense as a doctrine of independence or external

---

[1] For Anderson's fullest account of Heraclitus and the pre-Socratics see the 1928 Lectures on Greek Philosophy at the John Anderson web site.

relations.[1] In this sense, he argues, Realism is indistinguishable from Empiricism understood as a theory of things in general. Anderson then considers Alexander's definition of metaphysics as the 'empirical study of the non empirical' in terms of the possibility of proof in logic[2] which brings him to one of the most fundamental problems of philosophy: how can we say a philosophical position is self-contradictory or self-refuting? 'Refutation by self-contradiction' is a method which is particularly evident in Moore's 'refutation of Idealism' and while it is not clear the extent of the intellectual debt Anderson owed to Moore's 'refutation', he did consider one important question raised in that refutation – what meaning is there to the notion of the self-contradictory? Overlooking the obvious tension in saying that a position is *false* because self-contradictory, Anderson argued that it is impossible to assert that a philosophical position is self-contradictory, for if the contradictory of the false is true, then the 'self-contradictory' precludes the very possibility of truth.[3] However for Anderson the more intelligible meaning to the conception of the 'self-contradictory' is the 'self-refuting', for to say the something is self-refuting is to say that it is refuted or disproved by its incompatibility with the conditions of discourse. For example, to assert that 'There is no truth' is to make an assertion which is either true or false. If the statement is said to be false then there is no reason to believe it, while if it is said to be true then it refutes or is logically incompatible with the content of the statement itself.

---

[1] The epistemological meaning of Realism can be stated as the object of knowledge is independent of the subject of knowledge and the relation of knowing and has the logical form s/R/o. The ontological or logical meaning of Realism is that in any relationship a/R/b, 'a' and 'b' are independent from each other and the relation between them.

[2] Anderson does not mean here logical proof in the formal sense of consistency. He is referring to proof in metaphysics or ontology and specifically the question of how we can speak about things without assuming our own position to begin with.

[3] Anderson had previously discussed the nature of philosophical proof in 'Causality and Logic' in *Studies* p 123f and the problem of contradiction in 'Marxist Philosophy' in *Studies* p 306ff.

Anderson recognised as one of the major difficulties of any theory of the categories that terms like 'conditions of existence' must be used to define 'category', but that the term 'condition' must either be used in an unambiguous empirical sense in which case there is no 'thing' which is such a condition, or it must have a special, non-empirical sense in which case we cannot say what this special sense is. To avoid this difficulty, he suggests that the term 'category' might mean 'characters of existence' but even this presents its own problems. As a point of logic, any term in a proposition must have a significant opposite, but the categories have no significant opposite and therefore no category cannot be a term in the proposition.[1] Indeed the problems raised here generates for Anderson the fundamental problem of talking about the categories – 'how is logic possible?' How can we, in other words, speak of 'the proposition' as if it were a subject of discourse like 'man'? This brings Anderson to his most fundamental criticism of Alexander – his neglect of the 'proposition'. Anderson argued that Alexander's substantialist discussion of Space-Time as a 'stuff of which all things are made' could have been avoided if he had begun with a consideration of the proposition. For Anderson, the form of the proposition exhibits the spatio-temporal character of things, with the subject function indicating location, the predicate function indicating activity and the copula indicating occurrence or non-occurrence.[2]

Space-Time (Lectures 6 – 13)

Having established the basis of his philosophical and logical position, Anderson discusses Alexander's conception of Space-Time and begins by criticising the conception of materialism or substantialism. Physical Space-Time, he argues, postulates "..a primitive or original form of Space where all is connection and

---

[1] This is the problem of 'the unspeakability of the categories'. See Baker, A.J. *Australian Realism* (Cambridge: Cambridge University Press, 1986) pp 106 - 107.
[2] In a slightly different formulation he asserted: "Predicates give structure to subject and subject gives continuity to predicates, as Time gives structure to Space (breaks up its mere bulk) and Space gives continuity to Time)." Lecture 7

there is no distinction, and a primitive form of Time where all is distinction and there is no connection."[1] Any theory which proposes such a primitive Time and Space must explain how things with qualities could ever arise from pure Space-Time and while Alexander's contribution to this debate is largely in support of absolute Space-Time, he slips into confusion by trying to reconcile Newtonian Absolutism with Einstein's Relativity theory, resulting in a substantialist conception of Space-Time. Anderson argued that Alexander's approach is quite 'unpropositional' and it is only by treating things as both spatio-temporal and propositional, that his confusions could be resolved. "The propositional treatment of things is a treatment of them as connected and distinct, subject and predicate having to be together in the proposition and yet having to be distinguished from one another if any intelligible assertion is to be made, while the spatio-temporal theory of things is the theory of the togetherness and distinctness which can be found between any two processes and indeed within any single process."[2] Alexander's substantialist theory of Space-time must therefore be rejected and replaced with the view that Space-Time is a medium in which things occur. But Anderson recognises that even this conception has its problems for if Space and Time constitute a medium in which things exist, how can we even say this without implying that this medium itself occurs. Anderson then begins an extended discussion of the inter-relatedness of Space and Time, and in particular of the essential connection between the three dimensions of Space and the three characters of Time: successiveness, transitiveness and irreversibility in Time and one, two and three dimensions in Space. Having established these connections, Anderson turns to the problem of a situational logic, the logic of situations occurring in Space-Time. He argued that it is not merely that a situational logic is a spatio-temporal logic, but that a situational logic shows that we must understand Space and Time not as a kind of total receptacle in which situations occur, but rather as that which is involved in any situation at all. It is clear, he says, that nothing *less* can be understood by Space and Time than infinite divisibility and infinite extensibility.

---

[1] Lecture 7
[2] Lecture 7

Transition to the Categories (Lectures 16 – 17)

In moving to his discussion of the categories, Anderson criticises Alexander for conceiving of Space-Time as an 'infinite given whole' and argues that this difficulty arises because of Alexander's failure to treat infinite Space-Time in terms of the proposition.[1] This raises the issue of the distinction between the subject and predicate of the proposition and even though he concedes that the subject-predicate formulation leads to certain difficulties or 'paradoxes',[2] he concludes that it is only by this formulation that the confusions Alexander falls into can be resolved. In particular, Anderson argued that if the categories indicate what is involved in being, existence or occurrence, then they also indicate what is involved in being propositional. Hence Alexander's attempt to treat the categories as only being expressed as predicates, leads him to a substantialist view of Space-Time and the only way to resolve this difficulty is to recognise that they must also occur in the subject of the proposition. However the treatment of the categories as subjects raises the problem that categories have no obverse – that if we say that a category is X, we cannot say that it is not X – and Anderson suggests that the way around this difficulty is to treat the categories as forms of relation. This would mean that as relations, the categories could still be regarded as all-pervasive and yet have real issues raised about them. Having outlined the general nature of his spatio-temporal and propositional theory, Anderson now goes on to discuss the three groups of categories: the logical categories, the mathematical categories and the physical categories.

---

[1] "What I am suggesting is that to say that things exist in Space and Time is to say that they exist in the propositional form." Lecture 16

[2] For example, "...we recognise things by the places where they are located and at the same time recognise locations (places) by the things that are in and around them --- or, sticking to the subject-predicate question, that we recognise subjects by the predicates they have and predicates by the subjects they belong to". Lecture 16

a) The Logical Categories (Lectures 18 – 28)

Anderson considers firstly what he describes as the five categories of the proposition – Identity, Diversity, Existence, Relation and Universality – and articulates his general position as being that "..the distinction of the forms of the proposition is the best way of drawing attention to characters of the proposition as such, i.e., to what should be dealt with in a theory of the categories or in a theory of Space-Time."[1] In considering the category of identity, Anderson accepts Alexander's view that identity is the occupation of Space-Time and he identifies this with his own doctrine of location as the function of the subject of the proposition, concluding that identity can be described as 'being the subject of a proposition'.[2] However while it might be natural to conclude that difference is 'being the predicate', Anderson argued that difference is 'embodied' by identity and hence is also located in the subject location. The real distinction from the subject of the proposition is not the predicate, but the copula of existence. Anderson's discussion of the category of existence is brief, for he had already discussed the general features of the spatio-temporal nature of existence in some detail earlier, although in keeping with his identification of a spatio-temporal logic with a propositional logic, he did emphasise the identification of actual existence with the truth of the proposition. However the question of the completion of the proposition is not now simply resolved by adding the predicate, for the subject and copula must be in a relation to the predicate and Anderson now enters into an extended discussion on the nature of relation. Like existence, relation is a fundamental category which, apart from his discussion of relational arguments, he does not consider in detail. The key question for Anderson is whether predication is a relation or not and his rather ambiguous answer is that it is *not* a relation, although it *involves* relation.[3] Finally Anderson considers the category of universality which he understands as 'kind' or 'type' and is indicated by the predicate of the proposition. Universality occupies an important place in

---

[1] Lecture 19
[2] Lecture 19
[3] Lecture 22

Anderson's ordering of the categories, for he argued that while it can be understood in its logical sense, it can also be understood in a mathematical sense – as the 'all' in the universal proposition – and hence serve as a transitional category to the mathematical categories.

b) The Mathematical Categories (Lectures 29 – 36)

Having established the five categories of the proposition, Anderson turns next to a consideration of the mathematical categories: Universality, Particularity, Number, Order and Quantity. As already indicated, universality in its mathematical sense is indicated by the universal quantifier and this is contrasted with particularity or the particular quantifier – the 'some' of the particular proposition. Like many philosophers since Plato, Anderson insists that a universal is not a thing, although surprisingly he also asserts that a particular is not a thing either, even though he admits to having spoken that way in the past.[1] This discussion of universality and particularity as mathematical categories raises the question of the category of number and it was a distinctive feature of Anderson's view of mathematics that he believed it to be an empirical science and not a 'rational' science based on axioms. A logical theory of number, he concluded, can only be a theory of empirically observable whole numbers. From this theory of number, Anderson develops his theory of ordinal numbers into a general theory of the category of order. Anderson's discussion of order is again very brief and he moves on to a discussion of the category of quantity. He argues that from the mathematical point of view, quantity is the same as real number which exhibits a continuity not found in rational number. Anderson's discussion of the category of quantity is again brief although he emphasises that like the category of universality, it has two senses – as a mathematical category and a physical category.

---

[1] Lecture 26

c) The Physical Categories (Lectures 37 – 46)

Anderson now moves on to a discussion of the physical categories: Quantity, Intensity, Substance, Causality and Individuality. From the physical point of view he argues that quantity can be regarded as solidity or 'space-filling', although he rejects any materialism which claims that 'matter' is anything more than simple space-filling. He then discusses the category of intensity or degree and argues that in distinction to the category of order where there is no reference to quality, in intensity there is a correlation with quality, as in the difference of pitch. He next considers the category of substance which he characterises in terms of constitution or composition and argues that this is analogous to the conception of harmony which is found in Heraclitus. This leads Anderson on to an extended discussion of the category of causation and he criticises Alexander for not distinguishing properly between causality and change and for neglecting the conception of a causal field.[1] Anderson concludes with the category of individuality or 'thinghood' which he characterises as concrete identity which brings him to a contrast with the abstract identity he had begun with.

The Classification of the Categories

This completes the discussion of the categories, although what has been passed over in this discussion is the recurring discussion of the classification of the categories which occupies a large part of the latter part of the lectures. In his first 'preliminary and tentative' grouping of the categories in lectures 32-3, Anderson groups the categories in terms of Quality, Quantity and Physics but does not discuss their nature in any detail. In lecture 37 he describes the categories of quality as categories of pure logic or the proposition, the categories of quantity as mathematical categories which are concerned with the subject of the proposition, while the physical categories emphasise the logic of process. Three lectures later, he makes a

---

[1] For Anderson 's own discussion of the causal field see 'The Problem of Causality' in *Studies* p 129ff

further specification of the categories. The categories of quality are related to the four forms of the proposition, the categories of quantity indicate the region within which something goes on, while the physical categories are the categories of action or process. In his next lecture, he slightly modifies this description and describes the categories of quantity as extensional categories, while the physical categories are the intensional categories. In lecture 43 he varies his language yet again and now describes the first set of categories as propositional, situational or logical categories or what is common to Space and Time, the second set of categories are the categories of extension or quantity or what occupies Space and Time while the third set are the categories of intension or quality. In the next lecture he provides another description of the categories. In the first group there are "..ways in we give an account of things as in Space and Time, as located or in situations (Situational or Propositional Categories)", while in the second group there are "..ways in which we give an account of things *as* spatio-temporal, as having spatio-temporal characters or even, if you like, as spaces and times" and in the third group there are "..ways in which we give an account of things as *distinct* from Space and Time - in other words, as qualitative". As argued previously, these various formulations of the grouping of the categories suggests that Anderson was working through his ideas during 1944, a tentativeness which he had resolved by 1949.[1]

---

[1] In contrast to these varying classifications, in his 1949 lectures Anderson gives just one grouping of the categories. He argued that "the categories of first group are necessary for or are ways in which we can give an account of things *as in Space and Time or as in situations*, the categories of the second group are ways in which we can give an account of things *as spatio-temporal or even as spaces and times*... and the categories of the third group are ways in which we give an account of things *as distinct from Space and Time as qualitative*..." (Personal typed copy of the 1949 lectures on Alexander p 76, his emphasis. This copy was obtained from Dr. Brian Birchall, formerly of the University of New England, who attributed them to Mr. Bill Doniela. Mr. Doniela has in turn attributed them to Professor David Armstrong who believes they are notes taken by Mr. Eric Dowling.)

Conclusion

In summary, Anderson argued that spatio-temporal occurrences or situations can only be understood in propositional terms: something must be asserted and something must be denied and this implies a subject-copula-predicate structure. From this structure, Anderson deduced five categories of the proposition. Identity and difference are to be found in the subject location, spatio-temporal existence is indicated by the copula of the proposition, and relation and universality are to be found in the predicate. This last category gives us the transition to the five mathematical categories which are the categories of the subject of the proposition. These are not related directly to the proposition and are categories of location and extension. Universality is a transitional category and is contrasted with particularity, both of which taken together raise the category of number. With the consideration of number we have questions of order being raised and finally there is a general examination of quantity. This category provides the transition to the five physical categories or categories of process and the physical meaning of quantity as space-filling leads to the category of intensity or degree. From intensity, the question of substance or structure is raised which leads to an examination of the category of causation. After causation, he concludes with the category of individuality.

What conclusions then, can be drawn from Anderson's critical examination of Alexander's *Space, Time and Deity*? Firstly, from his criticisms of Alexander's 'stuff' theory of Space-Time, it can be seen that any physicalist or substantialist theory of Space-Time must be rejected in favour of a theory of Space-Time as a medium in which things exist. Since the basis of this criticism was Alexander's 'neglect of the proposition', then it follows that Anderson's derivation of the categories from the forms of the proposition is fundamentally correct. However it can be recognised that there is a lack of detailed analysis of some of the categories under consideration and his classification and description of the categories varies markedly throughout the lectures. The second of these difficulties is resolved by 1949 as the first issue may also be, although if not, that task belongs to a fuller critical analysis and development of these lectures. It can also be noted that the transitional categories of universality and quantity (and perhaps identity) have a double meaning depending upon which category heading they appear under. This means that we cannot ask 'What is universality?' without resorting to the question 'What context does it occur in?'. This conclusion would appear to contradict Anderson's rejection of the context of the proposition as significant in the determination of the truth or falsity of a proposition.

Secondly, and independently of the first point, Anderson must provide some theoretical account of categorial discourse. Even if we accept Anderson's explanation that the absence of the obverse of the categories implies that they must be relations, they must still be explicated in terms of the forms of the proposition and hence cannot be part of the content of the proposition. Anderson recognised this difficulty but provided no solution to it in these lectures. The first step in formulating this solution is to postulate *another* type of proposition where categories can be terms but are not existing things. However if Anderson takes this step, then we must then wonder how these categorical propositions which have no obverse are to be distinguished from the propositions in Hegel's method of dialectic which Anderson took so much time to refute. Also Anderson might have to face the question of how we can be said to know the categories? Is it, as in phenomenology, a question of 'intuition' or is it, as seems more likely, that the categories cannot be 'experienced' at all and our beliefs about them are conclusions drawn from the rejection of certain 'self-refuting' propositions? While this latter view would appear to be the one most obviously drawn from Anderson's logical writings, it is worthwhile noting that in his 1942 Lectures on Ethics and Aesthetics he appears to advocate the view that science and art are two different ways of appreciating or understanding the structure of a thing. If so, then it may be that the artistic appreciation of the categories is indeed a matter of 'intuition'.

John Anderson thought Alexander's *Space, Time and Deity* a 'mighty fragment' and he is the only critic of Alexander who has attempted a logical reconstruction of his metaphysics from an empiricist basis. Anderson's arguments in the 1944 lectures on Alexander are logical, acute and on the whole thorough-going, although ultimately, in terms of their philosophic enterprise, they remain unfinished. His criticisms raise questions to which he sketches solutions, but which in turn raise their own questions, some of which he recognised and some of which he didn't. This is, of course, no more than the working of the philosophic tradition itself and perhaps no better judgement of this work could be made than to say it is, like Alexander's work, a 'mighty fragment' in the tradition of philosophy, but a fragment nonetheless.

Lecture 1: Reading list and introduction: Plato and Kant the great guides to the categories; Hegel's multiplication of the categories 'reactionary'; Alexander as a 'realistic Kantian'

Read "The Non-Existence of Consciousness" (*A.J.P.P.*, March 1929)[1] --- but logical (ontological) questions [Space, Time and the Categories] will be dealt with more than epistemological questions.

Realism:

> Moore: "Refutation of Idealism" (in *Philosophical Studies*)[2]
> *The New Realism* (esp Marvin and Perry)[3]
> Russell: *Philosophical Essays*
> Russell: *Problems of Philosophy* (less realistic than earlier work)
> Russell: *Philosophy of Leibniz* (perhaps most important for this course)
> Russell: *Principles of Mathematics* (earlier part for general theory: later part for theory of Space and Time)
> Russell: *Our Knowledge of the External World* (discussion of logical problems and reference to Zeno's paradoxes)

Space:

---

[1] EN: this refers to "The Non-Existence of Consciousness: *Space, Time and Deity* by Samuel Alexander", (review article), *AJPP*, 7, March 1929, pp. 68-73. ENMW: "The Non-Existence of Consciousness" reprinted in Anderson, J. *Studies in Empirical Philosophy* (hereafter *Studies*) (Sydney: Angus and Robinson 1962), pp. 60 – 67.
[2] EN: this refers to G.E. Moore, "The Refutation of Idealism", in *Philosophical Studies*, (London: Routledge & Kegan Paul Ltd, 1922), pp.1-30.
[3] EN: this refers to "The emancipation of metaphysics from epistemology", by W. T. Marvin; and "A realistic theory of independence", by R. B. Perry; both in E. B. Holt, W.T. Marvin, W.P. Montague, R.B. Perry, W.B. Pitkin, E.G. Spaulding, *The New Realism: Cooperative Studies In Philosophy* (New York: Macmillan, 1912).

Kant: *Critique of Pure Reason* (possible linking of discussion of Space and Time with Zeno and with Kant's *Dialectic*: but Kant also important on Categories and their connection with forms of judgement).

Hume: *Treatise*, Bk I, Part II (Comparison of Hume and Kant on the question of continuity and discontinuity)

Leibniz : *Letters*, etc. (See Russell for Leibniz's views on Space. Leibniz is the typical rationalist: exemplified in *relativist* view of Space).

Spinoza on Extension (Cf. Alexander's *Spinoza and Time*, J. Caird's *Spinoza* and Joachim's *Study of the Ethics of Spinoza*).[1]

Categories:

Plato: *Theaetetus* (cf. Burnet[2]), *Sophist*, *Philebus* (the One and the Indeterminate Dyad), *Timaeus* (on Space)
Aristotle, Kant, Hegel. (Relation of the categories to the forms of judgment)

---

[1] EN: the reference here is to (1) Samuel Alexander, "Spinoza And Time" (The Fourth Arthur Davis Memorial Lecture, delivered before the Jewish Historical Society at University College, May 1, 1921), in *Philosophical And Literary Pieces*, (London: Macmillan & Co. Limited, 1939), pp.349-385; (2) John Caird, *Spinoza*, (Edinburgh: W. Blackwood, 1901); and (3) H.H. Joachim, *A Study of the Ethics of Spinoza*, (Oxford: Clarendon Press 1901).

[2] EN: this refers to John Burnet, *Greek Philosophy, Thales to Plato*, (London: Macmillan & Co. Ltd, 1914), Chapter XIII especially pp. 193-206.

Alexander[1] says that Plato and to a lesser[2] extent Kant are the great guides on the Categories. He neglects Hegel. There is some ground for this – in Hegel's *multiplication* of categories: there seems to be no reason on his view why there should be any limit to the number of categories. Hegel is in many ways reactionary as compared with Kant e.g. in abolishing the distinction between Categories (forms of understanding) and Space and Time (forms of sense) --- one of the most important distinctions in Kant, even if we can't retain it precisely in the form Kant gave to it.[3]

Alexander takes the categories as *derived* from Space and Time. If we treat Kant's "phenomena" as things themselves, we have substantially Alexander's position --- a "realistic Kantianism." (Allowing for general criticisms that apply to Hegel, we can say he is a more consistent thinker than Kant --- avoiding some of the deep Kantian cleavages --- even if consistency is gained at the expense of realism. Hegel more of a *logician* than Kant, though lacking some of Kant's philosophical insight. **[2]**

---

[1] MN: (S.A.). — EN: from this point onwards the text refers to the author of *Space, Time and Deity* as "SA". "Alexander" has been substituted for "SA" throughout.

[2] EN: the text here reads "less".

[3] MN: "The Place of Hegel in the History of Philosophy", June 1932. — EN: this refers to John Anderson, "The Place of Hegel in the History of Philosophy", *AJPP*, 10, June 1932, pp.81-91. ENMW: "The Place of Hegel in the History of Philosophy" reprinted in *Studies* pp 79 – 87.

Lecture 2: Realism assumed in this course but empiricism the theme: connection between empiricism and realism; the problem of proof in logic and the doctrine of the 'self-refuting'; the problem of 'conditions of existence' - categories have no significant opposite; how, then, is a situational logic possible?; Alexander doesn't begin with a propositional approach - his theory of predication; the problem articulated and the solution proposed.

Realist view taken for granted in this course: possible reference to theory of levels of knowledge and to the conational view of mind.[1] But question of knowledge only incidental here to consideration of Space-Time & Categories --- Empiricism, rather than Realism, as the theme.[2]

James's main contention is that the mind does not contribute relations (connectedness) to things any more than it makes them distinct (contributes distinctness); that relations are as much part of the given as things (terms). Close connection between Realism and Empiricism: Cf. Perry's essay on *independence* (*The New Realism*) --- realism treated as a doctrine of independence.[3] If this view is taken, realism becomes almost indistinguishable from empiricism --- i.e. becomes a theory of things in general, not only of knowledge. (The question of relation and distinction is not particularly a question of knowledge).

---

[1] NT: Cf. "Conational Psychology", Br. J. Psy., Dec 1911, "Mind as Feeling", AJPP, June 1934. — EN: the reference here is to (1) Samuel Alexander, "Foundations And Sketch Plan Of A Conational Psychology", in *The British Journal of Psychology*, 4, December 1911, pp.239-267; and (2) John Anderson, "Mind as Feeling", *AJPP*, 12, June 1934, pp.81-94. ENMW: "Mind as Feeling" reprinted in *Studies* pp 68 – 78.
[2] NT: Cf. "Empiricism", AJPP, December 1927, and {William} James, *Essays in Radical Empiricism*. — EN: the first part of this note refers to John Anderson, "Empiricism", *AJPP*, 4, December 1927, pp.241-254. ENMW: "Empiricism" reprinted in *Studies* pp 3 –14.
[3] NT: Cf. "Realism and Some of Its Critics", AJPP, June 1930. — EN: this refers to John Anderson, "Realism and Some of Its Critics", *AJPP*, 8, June 1930, pp.113-134. ENMW: "Realism and Some of its Critics" reprinted in *Studies* pp 41 – 59.

In introducing his discussion as the empirical study of the non-empirical ("non-empirical" to be taken as a technical expression here --- not to be understood as *not empirical*, or *unempirical*) Alexander speaks of his method as a method of hypothesis, insisting that he is not trying to *prove* this theory but only to work it out or expound it. There are difficulties affecting proof in Logic[1]; you tend to get a circular argument, proving a thing by itself. The approach to such discussions is mainly through the consideration of the conditions of discussion; supporting a view (without formally proving it) by showing that those who deny it are, *in their very denial*, assuming it (as they must do if it is inherent in the very nature of discourse). Thus it is argued against the doctrine of simple ideas (Locke, Berkeley and Hume), that those who uphold it have to present it *propositionally* i.e. in a way which wouldn't be possible on their assumptions, but only if we take a propositional view of things, and thus their argument "cuts its own throat."

Cf. the conception of doctrines as "self-refuting" (e.g. in Spaulding's contribution --- greatly influenced by Russell --- to *The New Realism*).[2] Actually it is not that a doctrine disproves itself but it is refuted by (is incompatible with) the characters of *discourse* --- in which it is presented, and for the possibility of which it commonly professes to account. In "The *Cogito* of Descartes"[3], objection is taken to any theory being described as self-contradictory on the ground that if you take a proposition to be false because it is self-contradictory (i.e., is its own contradictory) you are taking its contradictory to be false and therefore can't say what is true --- the falsity of a proposition normally being equivalent to the truth of its contradictory. If the contradictory of the false is the true, the self-contradictory precludes the possibility of truth. But if a proposition **[3]** is

---

[1] NT: Cf. "Causality and Logic", *AJPP*, Dec 1936. — EN: this refers to John Anderson, "Causality and Logic", (discussion), *AJPP*, 14, Dec. 1936, pp.309-313.) ENMW: "Causality and Logic" reprinted in *Studies* pp 122 – 125. For Anderson's discussion of 'indirect proof' see especially p 123.

[2] EN: this refers to E. G. Spaulding, "A defense of analysis" in Holt et al., *op.cit.*

[3] NT: March, 1936. — EN: this refers to John Anderson, "The *Cogito* of Descartes", *AJPP*, 14, March 1936, pp.48-68. ENMW: "The *Cogito* of Descartes" reprinted in *Studies* pp 101 – 114.

opposed to the conditions of discourse, we can roughly say that it is "self-contradictory" or "self-refuting".

It is argued in "Causality and Logic" that *conditions of discourse* is only a cover for *conditions of existence*; that the question is of showing that causality, e.g., is involved not so much (not merely) in what people say as in *things*.[1] But the best we could do in a particular case might be to show that the person who contests this (causality as condition of existence) or some similar point implies, in the statements he makes, the very views he is contesting.[2] In general, it is very difficult to expound a theory of the conditions of existence or of discourse; there is always the tendency to assume what we are professing to prove; and we might (frequently, at least) be forced back to Alexander's position that exposition, not proof, is the best we can offer: the position of *exhibiting* what we have in mind.

There is also the difficulty that any expression we employ in this connection is open to criticism: *conditions* in "conditions of existence" would have to be used in a very special way. When we say "X is a condition of the existence *of human beings*," we can make our meaning definite: if no X, no human beings, or wherever there are human beings, there is X (and wherever there is not X, there are no human beings) — where X might be *water*. But when we speak of the conditions of existence in general --- unless there were X, there wouldn't be *anything* --- it can be questioned whether the issue is properly stated, whether we can give any positive content to it. We cannot say that there is something that conditions or is a *sine qua non* of existence in general (as we *can* say there is of *human* existence),[3] because we can't see *existence coming into existence* under certain conditions as we can see, e.g. *houses* coming into existence under certain conditions; we can see a house coming to exist where there

---

[1] MN: What things *are*.
[2] NT: Cf. discussions with Miller and Boyce Gibson: AJPP, 1939. — EN: the reference here is to three discussion notes by John Anderson, "Logic and Ethics", *AJPP*, 17, May 1939, pp.55-65; "The Status of Logic", *AJPP*, 17, Aug. 1939, pp.164-169; "Logic and Experience", *AJPP*, 17, Dec. 1939, pp.257-272.
[3] MN: We can't postulate possibility of complete non-existence.

wasn't a house before, but we can't see *existence* coming to be where there wasn't existence before; we can't say that where there is existence, there is, e.g., causality, and *where* there isn't causality, there isn't existence; we can't postulate non-existence as occurring (existing) under certain conditions. It would appear then that when we speak of conditions of existence we are not using "conditions" in the ordinary sense; even that we are mixing empirical or non-empirical conceptions; or using an empirical conception to give an appearance of intelligibility **[4]** to something we intend in a different ("indefinable") sense. Cf. the criticism of the Socratic conception of "participation" because it is not to be understood in the empirical sense (having a part of) and yet the difference of its "logical" sense from the empirical sense cannot be definitely stated, so that the empirical sense does duty for (gives an apparent content to) the special sense. And there is the further criticism that the sense required must be *an* empirical sense or it would be nothing at all. Is the position the same with "conditions of existence" — that it depends for its acceptance on the empirical sense of "condition" (*sine qua non*) but has to be taken as having "not exactly" the empirical meaning — with no explanation of what the difference is? This is one of the major difficulties of any theory of Categories.

Alternatively, might we speak of categories as *characters* of existence (existents; of all existing things)? The question of presence and absence still creates a difficulty. Argued, as a point of logic, that any significant term must have a significant opposite; but the categories have no significant opposite — to call causality a category implies that we cannot contrast the causal and the non-causal. Alexander does not avoid this difficulty; he contrasts "pervasive" (belonging to all) with variable (belonging only to some) characters; but if there are no things *not* of a certain character, how can we *distinguish* that character?

There is the connected problem of the use of logical terms; e.g., "term" itself. The word *term* appears to be (grammatically is) on the same footing as the word *man* (having instances and conveying something as to these instances), but if it means only *thing* (not a particular thing, but "being of a certain sort" in general — "man" is a term = man is a sort of thing), the difficulty is to see how we could come to use the word or how we could take it to *convey* anything: we can't contrast *being of some sort* with *being of no sort*. We may have to argue that what is involved is a question of discourse, of our *attitudes to* and *ways of dealing with* things; that the meaning is not something independent of us but has this relational content ("man" is a term = man is an object of some interest of ours). But even if that would serve in this case, it certainly doesn't give us a solution of *all* our difficulties; we can't take the Kantian view that the categories in general are not independent of us, that they are our ways of dealing with or organising **[5]** the material presented to us; they must have an objective content, they are as much a part of what is presented to us as the "material." But, even if they have, there is still the difficulty of giving them content, of seeing how we can speak of "causality" or "the proposition" as if they were subjects of discourse like "man" (and how, at the same time, they can be distinguished from such subjects of discourse). Cf. the assertion "The least that can be and that can be known is a proposition"; what objectivity is there in that? What can be meant by upholding a situational or propositional logic (a) if we can't contrast a situation with a non-situation, (b) if we can? If "non-situational" doesn't mean anything, what does "situational" mean? This is testament to raising the fundamental question --- how is logic possible?[1] And the question is (as against Alexander's proposal to *present* without *demonstrating*) whether we can even begin to present such a theory without argument; whether, without some preliminary treatment of such difficulties, we can understand what Alexander is doing — whether, again, his "expository" line isn't a dodging of the difficulties, an assumption that they are settled in a particular way, with no indication of how objections would be met (or of how — by what criterion, on what basis — we could decide between different views, opposing "logics").

One line of criticism of Alexander — that he doesn't adopt a *propositional* standpoint at the outset. He starts off by speaking

---

[1] NT: Cf. reply to Boyce Gibson: AJPP, Dec. 1939. — EN: this refers to "Logic and Experience", see footnote 2 above.

of "Space-Time" and of "events." In fact, his "realism" might be said to be that which believes in *res* (things: i.e. as "fundamental"). He uses language much more appropriate to substantialism than to realism (in its *empiricist* sense) in a good deal of his exposition — particularly in the doctrine of Space-Time as "the *stuff* of which all *things* are made" --- and, while this accounts for many of his difficulties and has been rightly criticised (while, indeed, it leads to *insuperable* difficulties), it has led to some of his other views being too lightly brushed aside, to an underestimation of the general force of his work. If, instead of saying that things *are* Space-Time, he had said that things are *in* Space and Time, he would have had a better and more coherent position.

Generalising on the above — whatever way we may discover of dealing independently with logical problems, the main part of logical criticism must be in terms of discourse — must show that the person who rejects a certain view is not only assuming it elsewhere but *can't help* assuming it if he is to present a coherent theory at all.

[6] *Theory of Predication*. The part of Alexander's work which is most important for the relation of his theory to the theory of predication (propositional logic) is at the beginning of 2nd volume (beginning of Bk III) --- under the heading "The Clue to Quality." Here he comes nearest to a propositional view though he never gets round to formulating it. The point would be that the propositional form exhibits or typifies the spatio-temporal character of things: subject as location (region in which some occurrence takes place), predicate as activity, ways in which subject is *going on* — this being the *temporal* reference.[1] Alexander's point in The Clue to Quality ("Time is the Mind of Space," *corresponding to* Mind is the Time of Body) could be expressed by saying that the subject is the space of the qualities (as *body* is the region in which mentality goes on) and the qualities are the time (or indicate the temporal character) of the subject. (Qualities as *phases*?) Predicates give structure to subject

---

[1] NT: Cf. the *Sophist*.

and subject gives continuity to predicates, as Time gives structure to Space (breaks up its mere bulk) and Space gives continuity to Time (connects the fleeting instants; holds them together; prevents their mere separateness).

The theory can also be expressed in terms of James's view that the connections of things are just as independent as the differences of things – as against the "vicious intellectualism" which can't take in connection and distinction at the same time.[1] In those terms Alexander's problem can be formulated as that of *the connection and distinction of connection and distinction*; and the solution is found in the propositional form of things. It is in the proposition that we see the (connected and distinguished) connection and distinction of things. This is not opposed to Alexander's view that it is in *Space-Time* that we see this (see things at once connected and distinguished) but it is an elucidation of that view, and indicates the way out of many of Alexander's difficulties.

---

[1] NT: Cf. Hume's two principles in the Appendix to Bk I of the *Treatise*.

Lecture 3 Connection and Distinction: Alexander - Space as the form of togetherness and Time as the form of distinctness; these come together in Space-Time; Hume's 'rationalism'; rationalism and monism; Rationalism defined; Empiricism defined; James and 'vicious intellectualism'; Kant as the answer to Hume; Alexander as the answer to Kant.

The theory of distinction and connection and the relation and opposition (connection and distinction) between the two comes out in Alexander as the doctrine that Space is the form of togetherness and Time the form of distinctness (and that these two functions come together in Space-Time).

The difference between the rationalist and the empiricist treatments of connection and distinction may be brought out by reference to Hume's two principles which he cannot reconcile but neither of which can he give up, viz. all our distinct perceptions are distinct existences *and* the mind never perceives any real connection among distinct existences. Of course Hume formulates the problem in connection [7] with personal identity, the coherence of a body of perceptions to form "a mind." But in view of his use of "perceptions" so as to *combine* subject and object (perceiving and perceived), confusing something on the side of the cogniser with something on the side of the cognised, we can quite fairly treat Hume's problem as that of existence, of how things can hang together to make "the world" and not just "the mind."

There are two points on which we can base the charge that Hume is rationalistic. (1) One is the conception of a distinct existence (what appears in later theory as the atomic fact), of the elements or units out of which complex reality or experience has to be built up. And from that point of view the second principle is perfectly correct, viz. if you start with absolute elements, unitary simple beings, then they never *could* be connected together so as to form a coherent system, to form connected experience or any kind of connected existence. But of course the error there is in upholding the doctrine of elements --- a rationalistic error. If we don't believe in such elements then the problem of finding relations among them does not arise; if we don't believe in such elements then our distinct perceptions are *not* "distinct existences" in that sense, i.e., they are not isolated units which in the nature of the case could not be connected. They are merely different things, and there is no real difficulty in finding relations among different things; if there are relations at all, they must hold between different things. Now (2) if we don't take that rationalist view of distinctness, if we take the first principle merely to mean that our various perceptions (leaving aside the question of the sense of "perceptions") are different things, then the opposition between the two principles arises from a rationalistic interpretation of the second, from a rationalist view of *connection* viz, as identity. But to say that the mind never perceives identity between different things (i.e., between things which are *not* identical) would certainly not lead to the conclusion that a connected body of knowledge is impossible.

Still the rationalist does treat connections as forms of identity,[1] and that again illustrates the point that rationalism proceeds from ultimate units of which only an internal characterisation, if any, is possible: i.e., it proceeds from a view which debars us from finding connections, and that is why we get the recurrent tendency of rationalism to develop into monism, as in the Eleatic demonstration that the Pythagorean units cannot in the end be distinguished from one another, that they must coalesce into one, or, to put it in another way, that if we do recognise a single unit or a single ultimate, then that has to be everything, has to be "the world," because as soon as we recognise [8] other things, we recognise situations in which the first thing exists, ie. we are forced to abandon its unitary or ultimate character.

Rationalism is a doctrine of identities in that it puts forward certain entities as *the* explanations of things, and these entities

---

[1] NT: Cf. "The Knower and the Known". — EN: this refers to John Anderson, "The Knower and the Known", *Proceedings of the Aristotelian Society*, 27, 1926-27, pp.61-84. ENMW: "The Knower and the Known" is reprinted in *Studies* pp 27 – 40.

have to be taken as self-explanatory, which means as pure identities: and that means again that they are indistinguishable. Empiricism on the other hand rejects the notion of identities and in general of *explanations* as distinguished from facts or as something above the facts; empiricism is concerned all the time with complex situations and thus rejects Hume's conception of a distinct existence and equally of a connection (i.e., of a "rational" bond, mutual *inherence*); and as far as it (empiricism) is concerned, not only is there no *opposition* between connection and distinction, but the two are bound up together --- i.e., to recognise a *situation* is to recognise connection and distinction occurring together without any antagonism. And when there is taken to be an antagonism between the two, it is only through the concerning of one or both in a rationalistic manner.

James's doctrine of vicious intellectualism comes in here. Vicious intellectualism is a form of (or a way of describing) rationalism, James's point being that the rationalist proceeds from the fact that saying A and B are distinct is *not the same* as saying they are connected to the conclusion that these two assertions are opposed. Of course this way of putting the matter might be questioned; it might be maintained that when we say two things are connected we *are* saying that they are distinct or at least our statement is unintelligible unless we *think* they are distinct; and similarly the statement that they are distinct would be unintelligible unless we thought that they are connected --- though of course there are many different ways in which they may be[1] connected. (Doctrine of vicious intellectualism in *A Pluralistic Universe*: James's exposition of the opposition between empiricism and rationalism is not thorough, but he gets on to some important points. He claims that he is more radically empiricist than Hume because he says that connectedness is just as real; just as much a part of things, as distinctness, i.e., that what we are confronted with are not isolated things but complex situations, and there is no question of building up the complex out of the simple.)

---

[1] EN: the text here reads "may be", with "(are)" written above it.

The philosophy of Kant could be represented as an answer to Hume's problem: i.e., Kant is setting forth forms of connection, connections which do hold among our various perceptions, viz. the forms of sense and the forms of understanding --- Space, Time and the Categories. Our perceptions are connected in the one Space and the one Time and under such categories as causality. (By *perceptions* here **[9]** would be meant *objects* of perception, things perceived.) Unfortunately Kant does not arrive at the complete solution; he could still be said to adhere to Hume's *second* principle in so far as the connections which the mind perceives among its objects, are not real connections but phenomenal connections, they are not connections independent of our modes of cognition; and this phenomenalism of[1] Kant is a sign of the persistence of a rationalist strain in his thinking, of the continuance of a belief in an original distinctness (distinction) among the materials of our knowledge, a distinctness which has to be overcome by (our) principles of cognition. He is certainly unable to maintain that position consistently; he can't really account for, or give any reason for believing in, the original distinctness, and he would logically be driven to abandon that conception, thus arriving at real empiricism --- at the position that what he calls phenomena are things themselves, are actually things[2], and, connected with this, that what he calls forms of cognition are forms of existence.

Putting the matter broadly we can say that that is the step taken by Alexander; viz the treatment of Kant's phenomena as actual things, the rejection of the notion of things themselves as some kind of distinct existences or essences lying behind the objects with which we are acquainted; and to that extent[3] Alexander's theory may be said to derive from Kant's, one point of special importance in both theories being the different status given to Space and Time on the one hand and the Categories on the other. Of course, Alexander takes a different view of the relation between the two; for him they don't have different source [sic]

---

[1] EN: the text here reads "of", with "in" written above it.
[2] EN: the text here reads "are actually things", suggested alternative formulation, written above it, "or actual things".
[3] MN: In that sense?.

but Space-Time is the source of the categories --- the categories are simply the features things have as spatio-temporal. But it may fairly be said, granted that some of Kant's difficulties arise from his not seeing this point or making this connection, that a similar doctrine is at least adumbrated in Kant, that the suggestion for it is there, for instance, in the doctrine of the Schematism of the Categories.

Lecture 4 Rationalism treats relations as identities; Idealism as monism; objective and subjective Idealism; the problem of unity and diversity; the problem of causality; predication.

We were speaking of distinction and connection, and of the interpretation of distinction so that it excludes connection, making it amount to severance, and of connection so that it excludes distinction, making it amount to identity.[1] It is characteristic of *rationalism* to treat relations as identities. This is especially so in the theory of knowledge where we have the identification of subject and object, the treatment of them as at least *aspects* of the same thing. This is commonly called idealism but it is really rationalism. [10] It seems better to keep the term Idealism for monistic doctrine, a doctrine of the *ideal* or totality of things, as in Hegel. Of course Hegel combines his monism or totalism with the treatment of reality as mental or spiritual, and it is possible that in all monistic theories we might find some emphasis on mind, so that there might be a case for the conception of Idealism as "mentalism." But some theorists (e.g., Berkeley) make mind fundamental without asserting a totality (without, at least, being *explicitly* totalistic) and it is thus that we have the distinction between "subjective idealism" and "objective idealism". It seems better to reserve *Idealism* for an objective idealism like Hegel's, and to treat the subjective variety as just *a rationalistic account of knowledge* (calling it, perhaps, subjectivism).

The insistence on mind (or tendency towards that insistence in monists generally) might come in in this way --- that monists are not going to present mere blank identity as their reality; they want it to have some sort of content, some sort of diversification, and so they introduce diversity *into* their unity and you have the various conceptions of "unity in difference," most explicitly in Hegel. Even Parmenides,[2] so far from asserting a blank unity

---

[1] MN: "Knower and Known"; "Realism and Some of its Critics".
[2] MN: Who comes nearest to blank unity: unity without difference --- who wants to deny difference.

which would be indistinguishable from nonentity, attaches various predicates to his One, though we might say he couldn't consistently do so. That is the problem --- of giving some consistency to the conception of *unity in variety* or *variety in unity*, of giving some force to Leibniz's notion of an "intensive unity," of a thing remaining *one* throughout the multiplicity of its aspects; and of course Leibniz solves the problem of how these different aspects can mean no real or substantial difference in the thing, how they can all represent the thing, how the real meaning of each of them can be neither more nor less than the substance of which they are aspects, by identifying predicates with *perceptions* i.e. the various characters of a thing are various perceptions of the thing or are the thing from different points of view: (Not *external* points of view: they are different *powers* of the thing or the thing raised to different powers.) He applies this not merely to the monads (substances) but even to *formal* theory, to the theory of the predicates of *any* monad or substance, to Logic and Mathematics: so that in Geometry, e.g., any proposition or theorem is a particular representation of geometry or is geometry from a certain starting-point, the suggestion being that you could take any proposition in geometry, work back from it by analysis to the axioms and other original identities, and then work forward from these to all the propositions of geometry --- so that the whole of geometry could be *unfolded* from any single [11] geometrical proposition. Thus it is wrapped up in each of them in a particular way (for each). Actually it is false that any geometrical proposition can be reduced to or unfolded from identities, but the common rationalist view of geometry supports Leibniz 's way of thinking and allows him to carry over these conceptions to his treatment of actual substances and to say that if you knew one of the perceptions of any substance you could pass to all other perceptions (of it). If it is argued that this cannot be done in practice, Leibniz replies that it can be done by the Infinite Mind.

The point is that even there you get an unexplained diversity viz. how it is possible that these should be those various points of view; and of course you get a confusion in the treatment of predicates as perceptions i.e., in the same old[1] amalgamation of a qualitative and a relational treatment of things. But again this is the kind of view that is very commonly held, especially in regard to mind, and it is that which gives plausibility to the doctrine of intensive unity, because the mind, being at once identified with and distinguished from its "contents" (what the realist would call *the objects of its knowledge*), can be regarded as expanding to take in anything in the world or contracting so as to be distinguished from anything in the world, and so we get a unity which can embody endless variety --- the point (of criticism) being that that unity, that pure subject, simply does not exist. But by taking it now in a qualitative and now in a relational way, by maintaining the doctrine of "consciousness" (as Alexander also does in spite of his realism), these thinkers are able to combine unity with diversity and, with the aid of this logically peculiar but nevertheless quite common view of the mind, to make their monism plausible. (Cf. Bosanquet's assertion that there is nothing in our experience which we cannot take as self and nothing which we cannot take as not-self.) That is an indication of how useful mentalism is to upholders of a monistic view and how it comes about that what is idealist in my sense is also idealist (in the more common sense) in emphasising mind.

Another example of the rationalist treatment of relations as identities is found in the case of causality, and it was Hume's great contribution to philosophy that he attacked and uprooted the rationalist view of causality. For we can see that if the effect is simply the cause or is just something embodied in the cause, then nothing has really happened and we have no occasion to talk about anything really[2] being caused. The essential point here is that the rationalists are trying to, but can't intelligibly, get over temporal differences (cf. description of this kind of thinking, "mysticism," as an attempt to stop or turn back time). But of course Hume cannot **[12]** make the issues thoroughly clear because he himself holds a rationalist view of time, considers it, i.e., as made up of individual units, and it is left to Kant to give the time theory of the continuity of time, though even then with a

---

[1] EN: "(same old!)" is written as MN, with an insertion mark in the text.
[2] EN: "(really)" is written as MN, with an insertion mark in the text.

rationalist colouring because he treats continuous time as applying only to phenomena and he has the notion of underlying or ultimate forces which condition the phenomenal would without belonging to it. (In Kant there is a Leibnizian as well as a Humean strain. It is interesting to see where the two strains diverge and where they are entangled. Kemp Smith leans to Humean interpretation of Kant; James Ward to Leibnizian.)

Allowing then that Hume doesn't thoroughly settle the matter, at least he strikes a powerful blow against rationalism and helps on the recognition of the importance of time, involving, as it is commonly put, the distinction between the relation of cause and effect and relation of ground and consequent. In Descartes you get a mingling of different views but mainly the view of the effect as bound up or comprehended in the cause, and it is that view of causality, that kind of rationalism, that is being specifically attacked by Hume. Two views of causality (1) comprehension, (2) creation. In the creation view you have not *the effect* in the cause but *the power to create the effect* lies within the cause and the effect can be regarded as something quite different from the cause. But this too is rationalistic and cannot in the end be separated from the comprehension view, for to say that A has in it *the power to produce B* either is meaningless or, as Hume shows, means that we can know B by knowing A, and that brings us back to the point that B is somehow comprehended in A. Notice that Berkeley who upholds the creation view, who takes agents, viz. minds, as of a quite different character from things produced, viz. ideas, nevertheless regards the ideas as *in* the minds, i.e., as somehow comprehended by them; and that is another example of the way in which the confused view of mind helps out rationalists, viz. by concealing the inconsistencies in their doctrines.

It is important to see that, even if we distinguish cause and effect from ground and consequent, or causality from implication, in that the former involves temporal order, still we have to guard also against a rationalist view of implication; we have to see that it is not a form of identity but, if it exists at all, is a real relation among distinct things.[1] And similarly with predication --- even if it is in predicative terms that we explain the meaning of identity, even if we explained it e.g. as coextension and thus presented it in the form of **[13]** two A propositions, still we have to distinguish a proposition from an identity, have to distinguish *A is B* from *A is A*, have to realise that A & B are in some sense *different things* or else the proposition would be meaningless. And that is another way in which the Idealists have made their position plausible, viz. by amalgamation of the relation of subject and object with that of subject and predicate.

---

[1] MN: Implication as category? *Substance? Order?*

Lecture 5 The 'necessity' of mathematical truths; Leibnizian theory of analysis; predication as a form of identity; clarity and vagueness; empiricism – the proposition is not derived from anything - problem of 'essences'; Alexander on the mental and the neural; his evolutionism.

Suggested topics for final paper;

1. The realist theory of knowledge. Alexander, Marvin, Perry, Moore, Russell
2. The nature of aesthetic science. Croce, Carritt, Richards, Anderson
3. Nominalism
4. The science of history. Cf. last year's question on "the subject of history" (reference to Croce's doctrine of *liberty* as subject of history[1]; cf also Hegel). with present title more emphasis could be put on question of *method* --- has historical study methods other than those of other studies? According to Croce (?) history deals not with particulars but with universals. See H.D. Oakeley (Aristotelian papers, and books) on nature of history; perhaps not very profound but may suggest a point or two.[2]
5. Pragmatism
6. Existential import of proposition. Keynes[3] --- esp. doctrine that a universal proposition doesn't imply the existence of its subject, while a particular does.

---

[1] EN: this refers to Benedetto Croce, *History As The Story Of Liberty*, (trans. Sylvia Sprigge), (London: George Allen and Unwin Limited, 1941).
[2] EN: the reference here is to (1) H.D. Oakeley, "The World As Memory and As History", *Proceedings of the Aristotelian Society*, NS27, 1926-27, pp.291-316; (2) H.D. Oakeley, "The Status of the Past", *Proceedings of the Aristotelian Society*, NS32, 1931-32, pp.227-250; (3) H.D. Oakeley, "Perception and Historicity", *Proceedings of the Aristotelian Society*, NS38, 1937-38, pp.21-46; and (4) Hilda D.Oakeley, *History And The Self*, (London: Williams & Norgate Ltd, 1934).
[3] EN: this refers to John Neville Keynes, *Studies And Exercises In Formal Logic*, 4th ed., (London: Macmillan, 1906).

7. Personal identity. Hume, Butler, modern psychological theories (multiple personality, layers or strata of mentality). Question of the sort of plurality compatible with personal identity --- leading on to question of identity in general. Various doctrines of self or selves. In Idealist doctrine a person or mind has self or identity in a higher sense than any other reality has. cf. expanding and contracting mind --- this capacity would give peculiar character to the identity *of a person*. Realists would say mind is no more a "self" than anything else. Whole doctrine of *self* worth looking into.
8. Method of analysis. Logical positivists and the Cambridge school. (Articles by Passmore)[1]. Also so-called "mathematical analysis" --- from conclusion to premises or data --- started by Plato (see *Republic*). Leibniz and analysis. [14]
9. Logic as Inquiry. See Dewey, Logic, for a final exposition of his logical views. (Connected with topic 5.)[2]
10. Meaning. Connected with nominalism. Cf. *The Meaning of Meaning* (Ogden and Richards) and a good deal of the work of the positivists.[3]
11. The Nature of Mathematical Science.

View that mathematical truths have a peculiar *necessity*; cf. Leibniz, truths of reason versus truths of fact; doctrine of analytic proposition. Even if we deny necessary truths, it is important to see what justification people thought they had for believing in them: e.g., Hume, who is less empirical than Berkeley in his attitude to mathematics. As opposed to Hume's doctrine of "relations of ideas," Berkeley argued that the truths of

---

[1] EN: the reference here is to John A. Passmore, "Logical Positivism (I)", *AJPP,* 21, 1943, pp.65-92; John A. Passmore, "Logical Positivism (II)", *AJPP,* 22, 1944, pp.129-153; and possibly also to John A. Passmore, "Philosophy and Science", *AJPP,* 17, 1939, pp.193-207.
[2] EN: this refers to John Dewey, *Logic, The Theory of Inquiry,* (New York: Henry Holt & Company, 1939).
[3] EN: this refers to C.K. Ogden and I.A.Richards, *The Meaning of Meaning, A Study of the Influence of Language upon Thought and of the Science of Symbolism,* (London: Kegan Paul, Trench, Trubner & Co. Ltd, 1923).

mathematics have to be found out by observation. But no amount of empiricist criticism has affected the prevailing of the rationalist view of mathematics.

Connected with this is the Leibnizian theory of *analysis*, of the reduction of the truths of rational science to certain primitive or primary proposition or ideas --- in the end, their reduction to one single idea, identity itself or the pure notion of subject. For Leibniz necessary truths or necessary predicates are those which belong to subject as such or as he puts it those which are characteristic of any possible subject, as contrasted with those which belong specially to some actual subject.

This is connected with treatment of predication as a form of identity --- really with [the][1] view that ideas or essences, individual natures or "notions"(Leibniz), are prior to propositions, that a proposition or set of propositions is just the unfolding of a certain notion, the predicates thus unfolded not really adding anything to the original notion itself but merely bringing out its character more clearly. The suggestion would be in fact that the more clearly you brought out the multiple aspects of a subject, the more clearly you would be grasping *its identity*.

Of course, apart from other difficulties (from the whole difficulty of multiplicity and[2] unity, or of a predicate which added nothing to the subject so that the proposition would seem to be unnecessary and the subject sufficient), there is the difficulty of the notion of "clarity," a notion found in Descartes as well as Leibniz though perhaps not quite in the same sense. At any rate, this notion of clarity which you find in the Continental Rationalists is very closely connected with the whole conception of *rational science*; and the Cartesian influence or French thought generally is seen in the way the French pride themselves on the clarity of their thought and even of their language --- not just in Maths but in any subject: cf. ethics and moral theory in France, which insists on clear and definite ideas but is a **[15]** rigid and

---

[1] EN: text here reads "with view".
[2] EN: the text here reads "and", with "in?" written above it.

artificial sort of thing, not doing as much justice to moral facts as vaguer ideas could do.

Clarity can often mean that we are trying to cover a whole range of facts by a limited number of (conceptions), whereas vagueness may mean that we are trying to get hold of facts (to form a *notion* of them) not yet made precise, and so it (vagueness) would be characteristic of a growing body of knowledge, and thus, in my view, of any knowledge at all --- i.e., on the view that knowing is always *learning*, the alternative being the view of knowledge as the *possession* or *property* of the mind. And so you find James, who is interested in these processes and not just in a finished system, pleading for "the rehabilitation of the vague," in "Stream of Consciousness" chapter,[1] where he talks about the "fringe" of ideas surrounding any given idea which is in the focus of consciousness; i.e., (taking "idea" as *thing thought about*) we think of anything as having various connections and against a certain background, as in a situation and as having characters[2] and relations of which we are only vaguely (nascently) aware and of which we should become *definitely* aware only by turning our attention on them, only as[3] some difficulty arose, some apparent *contradiction* which we had to try to get over.

There is also here the question of words. We tend to suppose that knowledge is not definite unless we can definitely formulate it; but if we look into the matter we find that all the time we are making discriminations and following out paths of connection, where sometimes we could not, even if we tried, put our criterion[4] into words and where, at any rate, as far as our experience goes on, we *don't* find words, perhaps don't even find *definiteness* for our criterion.[5] (Cf. our seeing someone and saying 'That's an American soldier' though we haven't any definite knowledge of what criterion we employ, what we *judge by*.) There is a question whether "vagueness" is the right word to

---

[1] MN: *Principles of Psychology*.
[2] EN: the text here reads "which has", with "and as having" written above it.
[3] EN: the text here reads "as", with "if" written above it.
[4] MN: Criteria.
[5] MN: Criteria.

use for all this; but at least if we try to remove all that isn't clear and distinct, we'll be removing most of our cognitions.

James's *Principles of Psychology* is important for its philosophical content, even apart from the very important last chapter and Chapter IX (Stream of Consciousness). James was not a realist but has[1] done work of value to the realist movement in his treatment of relations as external (against Bradley) and it was he who gave the main urge to the thinking of the New Realists (Marvin, Perry) (though none of them stuck to their realism). James also influenced Alexander. It is *Kant's* theory of Space and Time that has influenced Alexander most, but he has also been influenced by James especially on spatial relations (cf. the chapters on Space and Time in the *Principles*).

The whole attempt to take notions or essences as[2] primary in Reality and propositions as secondary is unsound. The empirical view is that the proposition is not derived from anything. If we did start from notions, we could never unfold **[16]** any propositions from them, and if we gave an account of identity it would have to be in propositional terms. In discussing "The Clue to Quality," in considering that the mental process and the neural process *are the same thing*, Alexander nevertheless gives a different status to the two; the neural process is treated as subject and the mental process as predicate of that subject, whereas a thoroughly empirical view would just as readily take the mental as subject and the neural as predicate (otherwise we would have the doctrine of *things* and *qualities*, capable of standing apart from the proposition). Alexander's position here is connected with his evolutionism, his doctrine of higher and higher levels of reality; and in so far as he holds that view and treats the mental as essentially a predicate of the neural or physiological, and that in turn as a predicate of the material and that again as a predicate of pure Space and Time, he is falling back into a rationalism similar to that of Leibniz, he is supporting a doctrine of absolute subject

---

[1] EN: the text here reads "James has", there is a MN "was not a realist but", and an insertion mark between "James" and "has".

[2] EN: the text here reads "notions as", there is a MN "or essences", and an insertion mark between "notions" and "as".

or substance, with which his spatio-temporal theory of a *logic of events* (to be real = to occur) is not really compatible.

Lecture 6 Question of mental quality: Alexander's evolutionism – the doctrine of levels; Space-Time as a 'stuff' – Alexander's substantialism or materialism; criticism of materialism - how could qualitative things ever arise from pure Space-Time?; – Spencer – criticism of substantiality – mind not 'higher' than body.

Question of quality: Alexander treats mentality as a quality of organic, physiological or cerebral processes but wouldn't say that neural is a quality of the mental. Connected with hierarchical theory of reality, doctrine of development of reality to higher and higher levels. Evolutionism runs through Alexander's theories and weakens them. It has led to his description of mind as having a neural basis. Doctrine of a *basis* is different from that of *placing*: it implies that the neural is more substantial than the mental --- which is its *attribute*; this is in line with the doctrine of essence or doctrines in which substance and attribute are of different levels or orders.

The doctrine of levels is not a solution of the problem of quality. You couldn't put all qualities in hierarchical order; even on Alexander's showing there are many qualities on the *same* level. Also, if you took mental processes as a *species* of neural processes and so on a higher level, you would have to admit the possibility of intermediate species, *species of the neural* of which the mental is in turn a species, so that you would have any number of levels --- whereas it is quite clear that Alexander really postulates only a limited number of levels and takes mental as coming next after organic. In fact, his whole doctrine of levels is based on a distinction among sciences which might well have a social rather than a logical basis. You have mathematical science and pure kinematics (theory of motion), which would be concerned with the categorical --- with what is on the lowest [17] level of all; pure Space-Time. Then you have the level of matter, with the corresponding science of physics. Then you have a suggested level (Alexander is doubtful here) of *chemism*, in the main that of the "secondary qualities" with which chemistry is concerned. Then you have the organic level, studied by the science of biology, and then the mental level, studied by psychology, and then the possibility of any number of higher levels if we only knew them. It is clear that that doctrine is largely arbitrary, clear also that (though Alexander doesn't *reduce* everything to pure Space-Time but asserts the reality of the "higher levels") the theory is largely of a substantialist kind, of the sort that has commonly been called *materialism*, in that pure Space-Time is the stuff of which things are made or the material which constitutes them (from which they have been composed).

Now from the *propositional* point of view (which, I suggested, is required to fill out the Space-Time theory, to make it both intelligible and defensible) any such doctrine of substance, and hence a doctrine of levels, cannot be accepted. It is just as natural to treat the neural as qualifying the mental, to *say all mental are neural* (as Alexander would *have* to say) as to say that some neural are mental or have the quality of mentality.

This whole discussion of course would have to be linked with the general criticism of materialism, of the doctrine of "matter" as the substance or real nature of things, for if it is said that any two things we like to take have materiality in common, that wouldn't be to say that this quality *constituted* them any more than their other qualities did. In fact, we might regard their materiality simply as their possession of mass, something involved in their occupation of space and so, for Alexander something categorical; but what we should in any concrete sense call their "substance" would be what is *peculiar* to them, and so would be anything rather than their materiality. Thus if the physicist can investigate the characters and behaviour of anything irrespective of the various chemical compositions which it might have, that is not the least to say that he is investigating something more fundamental than the chemist is, but rather that the chemist in dealing with a thing's peculiarities would be giving a more positive or substantial account of it.

And these considerations, which could be advanced in criticism of all materialism --- the consideration in particular that there is no ground for calling what is common to things their *substance* any more than what is peculiar to things (a criticism which would apply most strikingly to[1] the Milesians as well as to a great many subsequent thinkers) --- are connected with what has been recognised as perhaps the most serious difficulty in Alexander's system (similarly with Anaximander) --- the difficulty of explaining how from pure Space-Time, i.e., Space-Time without qualities, things having qualities (things of a concrete character) could ever arise. [18] The same difficulty applies to any doctrine of an original substance, even if it is not quite so abstractly conceived: (viz). that we can give no account of the arising of heterogeneity from homogeneity, i.e., of the same antecedent thing giving rise to many quite different consequent things.

This would apply to Herbert Spencer's theory of homogeneity and heterogeneity, of greater heterogeneity developing in a given system and consequently greater complexity. No exact meaning can be given to this terminology. If you take the organic as genus and the mental as species, then the mental has *greater intension* than the organic, but that is not to say that the mental is "more complex" than that part of the organic which is *outside* the mental. For that outside part will also have peculiarities so that it also will be more complex than the whole (the genus). There is nothing in the fact that men are a species of animals to show that men are more complex than *other* animals. That is the sort of logical doctrine that lies at the root of Alexander's theory of greater complexity. The extension --- intension rule applies only to the relation between species and genus, not to the relation between two different species of the same genus (i.e., it applies only to the relation of inclusion). No real conclusion can be drawn in the case of intersecting classes, where it would be a question of *enumerating* the members of a class and the qualities they have in common; so with exclusive classes. (This is an example of the looseness of thought in evolution theories; there is no reason for saying that men are more complex than horses in the fact that men are a species of animals and horses occur in another part of the genus.)

---

[1] EN: the text here reads "apply to", with MN "most strikingly", and insertion mark between "apply" and "to".

In the "Non-existence of Consciousness" I expressed the view that Alexander complicates his argument by treating mind as *consciousness*, taking consciousness as the *quality* of the mental; partly for that reason his refutation of the common theories of mind-brain relation is not very convincing. We can see that his way of treating mind works in with the doctrine of substantiality (or ordinary sense of substantiality). It is often said that a brain process is more substantial than a mental process, and this can more easily be said if the latter is identified with a conscious process --- because consciousness *is* a relation even if that hasn't been brought out explicitly. So if we rejected the relational theory of mind and found a mental *quality* (say, feeling or emotion), there would be much less ground for attributing less substantiality to the mental. Emotion is just as substantial as cerebration (cerebral process).

It is of course a very curious feature of Alexander's theory that he has to say that the mental process and the brain process are the very same thing and yet to treat mentality as something "higher" than the rest of the thing's constitution. But that sort of view is certainly contributed to by the relational theory and of course by the doctrine of *self*-relation that forms part of it (the doctrine of self-consciousness and the Cartesian *cogito*), because it is the self-related, in its particular formulation as the self-sustaining, that specially represents the notion **[19]** of a *higher* reality --- a thing is higher just because it is not dependent on other things and it is not dependent on other things just because it is *self*-dependent. I have argued (Design)[1] that the notion of self-dependence is never a stable one, that conflicting elements in it lead to insoluble problems. It is the conception of self-dependence as contrasted with other-dependence that gives plausibility to the conception of higher and lower being, and it is always by reference to mind that that sort of theory is filled out --- the relational doctrine of mental processes goes with the doctrine of self-relation. If a qualitative view is taken from the outset, more *difficulty* is encountered in giving the doctrine of

---

[1] EN: this refers to John Anderson, "Design", *A.J.P.P.*, 13, 1935, pp.215-222. ENMW: "Design" is reprinted in *Studies* p 88 – 100.

self-dependence a footing (if it is possible at all). The spring or motive of such views (of dependence and independence) is their social meaning --- higher and lower = on a higher and lower social grade. Here we have just the fact that relational views do help to maintain the distinction between higher and lower entities: or it might be best to say the two are bound up together so that whenever you find one you find the other.

Alexander's main contribution to theory is of an anti-relationist or absolutist kind. In particular by a doctrine of absolute Space and Time he would secure his empirical position, but he vacillates on the point, and tries to get a theory of Space and Time that will cover both absolutism (Newton) and relativism (Einstein), and in so doing he gets into confusion but is able to cover it up by the prevailing relational theories of *mind*. In particular he has a theory of "perspectives," or of the characters of things *from a place*, which only the persistence of relational and essentially anti-realist conceptions would permit of. The whole doctrine of ways of apprehending (Bk III) affects a good deal of his argument and would have to be abandoned by a consistent realist. And a realist would have to abandon the doctrine of Space and Time as *constituting* things and say that things are *in* Space and Time. At any rate it can be seen how substantialism affects Alexander's general view.

Lecture 7 Alexander's treatment of quality unempirical and unpropositional; propositional theory – the mental and neural occur in same place; identity of the spatio-temporal and the propositional; 'stuff' theory inconsistent with propositional theory; criticism of 'Time is the mind of Space' (mind is the Time of body); Space as togetherness or continuity - Time as distinctness or structure; criticism of physical Space-Time.

Alexander doesn't really give the clue to quality or handle the question in an empirical way. He introduces rationalistic conceptions of *levels* and of *stuff* which are quite unpropositional. It is only in terms of the proposition that his work could be thoroughly empirical, and this would conflict with the doctrine of higher and lower levels no matter what could be said about evolution. (i.e., even if minds had come out of the non-mental, this is no reason for calling them *higher* than the non-mental). Evolutionism and progress have affected the whole of Alexander's work, and for the worse.

If you took the propositional theory you could see without reference to levels just[1] in what way it could be said that mental process and neural process are *in the same place*, viz. that **[20]** the same process, the same *subject*, has two characters, neural and mental, neither being on a higher level than the other. And on the side of "stuff" we could say that what is common to things is not any kind of material, is not any term of a proposition as in the notion of "pervasive *characters*," but is what is conveyed in the *form* of the proposition, what I have called (with special reference to Heraclitus) *complex activity* with the subject in any proposition emphasising more the notion of complexity and the predicate that of activity. That view (which I associate with the *Sophist*) could be expressed by saying that any predicate could be put in the participial form, i.e. when we say *X is red*, we could (emphasising the activity point) say *X is redding* or *X is going on in the red way*, so that "way of going on" is the function of the

---
[1] EN: the text here reads "see just", "without reference to levels" is written in the margin, and an insertion mark between "see" and "just".

predicate or the sort of thing the predicate has to convey; and similarly place of going on (or conditions of going on) is what is conveyed by the subject; and finally the mere *fact* of going on is what the copula signifies.

That is, expressing the matter roughly, to treat things as spatio-temporal is the same as to treat them as propositional; and although Alexander doesn't come explicitly to that view, he at least constantly refers to the occurrence of qualities at places --- in other words, he *so far* (to that extent) develops a logic of events, in terms of which mentality is not something over and above certain physiological processes --- some kind of spirit of which they are the body --- but is a quality of these processes, something that occurs in them. And without going into Alexander's discussion of the various mind-body theories we can see that this conception, of the mental as really *in* the physiological, gets rid of the vague notion of parallelism or concomitance, since to say that a mental process and a bodily process occur at the same *time* is no reason for saying that they belong to one another or "correspond" in any peculiar way, but if they also occur in the same *place*, or even merely with a definite spatial relation to one another, then we can speak positively of their connection.

The propositional treatment of things is a treatment of them as connected and distinct, subject and predicate having to be together in the proposition and yet having to be distinguished from one another if any intelligible assertion is to be made, while the spatio-temporal theory of things is the theory of the togetherness and distinctness which can be found between any two processes and indeed within any single process. In fact the theory of Space and Time may be described as showing how this is possible, showing more exactly the nature of togetherness and distinctness, and thus showing more exactly the significance of the proposition. The point is, though it is at best *implicit* in what Alexander says about quality, that, things being together and distinct as spatio-temporal or as occurring in Space and Time, the *form* of this occurrence is the propositional form. Some connection here with Kant's theory of the categories, with the

Schematism and the Analogies. The Metaphysical Deduction connects the categories with the forms of judgment and the Schematism connects them with temporal (and really with spatial) presentation. [21] Now the doctrine of Stuff (which we might describe as an ultimate subject of which everything else is predicated) is really inconsistent with the propositional theory, but still the actual discussion of the relation between Space and Time within Space-Time is a discussion of the way in which connection and distinction imply one another, i.e. connection and distinction *among things*. It remains thus that consistent adherence to the *stuff* theory would make it impossible to account for distinction, that as in the case of Eleaticism the assertion of the common or fundamental reality would involve a denial of differences; and of course as in the case of the Pythagoreans Alexander's attempt to get out of this difficulty is merely an evasion --- the attempt, viz. in terms of *complexity*, mind and body being alike modifications or determinations of Space-Time but mind being *more complex* than body (cf. Pythagorean theory of arrangements). This ("more complex"), however, has no meaning in spatio-temporal terms, for we cannot really say that *Space and Time* are more complicated in a mental than in a non-mental process. Actually then we have to reject both the notion of *stuff* and the notion of *complexity* which, instead of giving the clue to quality, really reduce(s) quality to quantity. (Important, regarding reference to Eleaticism and Pythagoreanism, to be able to classify views into types; one main object of historical study of philosophy is to enable us to see the recurrent problems and the recurrent types of inadequate solution.)

At beginning of Bk III, Ch II, Alexander gives a "formula for Space-Time," viz. that *Time is the mind of Space*; i.e., that the relation between Space & Time within Space-Time is comparable to the relation between body and mind in the human being (or in any other being that exhibits mentality). I would suggest that we could understand this comparison better by taking it in the first instance in the other way i.e., instead of saying Time is the mind of Space, saying *mind is the Time of body*, because that is to be taken as equivalent to saying that mind *qualifies* body (or qualifies bodily processes) and of course, correspondingly, body *locates* mind. Coming back now to the original formulation (Time is the mind of Space)[1] we can take this to mean that Space gives Time location and that Time gives Space distinction or qualification, and while we can't really speak of Space and Time as *things* having such relations to one another, we can see that Alexander is essentially treating Space as the form of togetherness or connectedness and Time as the form of distinctness, i.e. (he is) saying that it is as spatial that things can have a place of occurrence and thus a continuous existence --- that it is as spatial, in other words, that things can be subjects --- and similarly it is as temporal that they can have peculiarity or distinction, can be predicates. Another way of putting it[2] is that Space gives continuity to Time and Time gives structure to Space, and that could be put more exactly by saying that Space gives continuity to *things* while Time gives them structure, just as body gives continuity to mind, gives it a place of existence, so that incidentally even if it has only intermittent existence we can **[22]** speak of *the same* mind on account of the continued existence of the body it is associated with; and on the other hand mind can be said to give diversification to body, to give a certain arrangement or plan to its activities.[3]

How far these expressions are metaphorical we needn't at present inquire, but one thing is clear --- that such considerations require a reference to spatio-temporal *things*, not to a mere abstract or "pure" Space-Time; and another point is that whatever reason we might have for associating connectedness especially with Space and distinctness especially with Time and whatever we might *mean* by doing so, empirically the two (connectedness and distinctness)[4] always go together, even in regard to Space and to Time, and so we can speak of spatial *distinctions* just as much as spatial connections and of temporal *connections* just as much as spatial connections --- in particular, of *temporal continuity* as much as of spatial continuity. Cf. point that subject and predicate as each sorts of things (having both universality and

---

[1] EN: the text here reads "(T. is the mind of Sp.)".
[2] NT: way in which Alexander puts it --- reference?.
[3] MN: labour, enterprise!
[4] EN: the text here reads "(c. and d.)".

particularity), though in a given proposition one has the function of locating (particularity) and the other of describing (universality): i.e. though *being a subject* is distinguished from *being a predicate* --- exemplified in distinction between combination of subjects (extensive combination or disjunctive term) and combination of predicates (intensive combination or conjunctive term).[1]

The doctrine of physical Space-Time (Bk I, Ch I) postulates a primitive or original form of Space where all is connection and there is no distinction, and a primitive form of Time where all is distinction and there is no connection. These forms are brought together (to form Space-Time) and it is assumed that there is no antithesis between distinction and connection in the whole that they form. But if, empirically, connection and distinction always go together, it appears that these "primitive forms" *are not empirical.*[2]

---

[1] EN: the last sentence of this paragraph is enclosed in square brackets.
[2] EN: the last sentence of this paragraph is enclosed in square brackets.

Lecture 8 Criticism of Alexander's substantialist view that Space-Time is a 'stuff'; rejection of levels of qualities and compresence – problem of theory of perspectives; general theory of Space-Time; Space as togetherness – Time as distinctness; how can we advance a theory of Space-Time?; things as spatio-temporal.

Implicit at least in Alexander's exposition of The Clue to Quality that not only are things together and distinct in that they occur in Space and Time but that the form of occurrence is the propositional form. No difference in kind between subjects and predicates, only a difference in function: anything in Space-Time can have either function, can place or be placed. Alexander's failure to *develop* a propositional theory may be connected with his treatment of Space-Time as the *stuff* of which things are made, i.e., as the ultimate subject (corresponding to *substance* doctrines of pre-Socratics and Spinoza). Any such theory leads to the attempt to treat qualities as quantities (or quantitatively) — as in Alexander's doctrine of *complexity*. If we reject this notion of substance we are free to recognise any difference of quality that may be presented to us, while at the same time rejecting Alexander's evolutionism, his doctrine of higher levels. We could recognise two things as having the relation of species to genus (e.g. All mental are bodily, some bodily are not mental) and we might have a technical usage, that "higher" meant (being) the species, but there would be other species in the genus (other things "higher" than the genus) and **[23]** there would be no question of a progression from the least to the most complex --- no question, i.e. of a single series or scale of qualities. Alexander of course has to select some special qualities as giving a higher level but can give no reason for the selection; it is not explained why we should not treat some particular species of men as "higher" (at a higher level) than man in general. All this is linked up with Alexander's doctrine of enjoyment and contemplation.[1] The other point (connected with use of expression "higher") is that, just as we recognise the mental as a species of the bodily, so we could recognise the development or origin of the mental from

---

[1] MN: cf. "Non-Existence Consciousness", *AJPP* 1929.

something *bodily and not mental*. This is in line with Alexander's evolutionary view but doesn't justify it --- in particular, doesn't justify the giving of an *ethical* significance to "higher."[1] If the technical meaning of "higher"[2] is extended to take in, as well as being a species, being "later" than the rest of the genus, it may still quite well be that what is later in time is lower in the *ethical scale of values* (assuming that there is such a thing).

If we reject substance, then, we can recognise differences of quality without any question of differences of level. But strictly on[3] the Space-Time theory (stuff of things) we cannot make qualitative distinctions --- everything being "substantially" the same --- and the problem faces Alexander in its sharpest form when he takes the *qualitative in general* as originating from the non-qualitative (*things* from pure Space-Time). And Alexander finds it just as difficult to make distinctions among *relations* as among qualities: e.g. when he speaks[4] of the relation between the knower and the known as *togetherness* or *compresence* --- which we might take as an assertion that the things *are* related and not an account of *how* they are related. Of course since Alexander treats things as *motions* (or events) we might say that the togetherness of two things is their presence in the same motion, implying continuous processes between the two as in the theory of sense-knowledge expounded in the *Theaetetus*; but even that does not seem sufficient to distinguish one relation from another --- in fact, the treatment of knowledge as togetherness would seem to imply that anything can know anything else and, in particular, that knowing is *symmetrical*, just as is implied in James's theory of "intersection."

Alexander of course tries to get out the difficulty by his theory of *perspectives*, according to which we are together only with some things viz. those which fall within our perspective or point of view, and not with all the things that fall within Space-Time. But

---

[1] MN: "Higher" misleading.
[2] EN: inverted commas added.
[3] EN: the text here reads "But on", "(strictly)" is written in the margin, and an insertion mark between "But" and "on".
[4] EN: the text here reads "we speaks".

this would seem to be opposed to realism --- to the view in particular, that things may be in our presence even if we do not know them at all. Alexander's difficulties here would seem to be connected not only with the *stuff* theory (perspectives being his way **[24]** of avoiding the *block universe* of the Eleatics) but with his treatment of consciousness not as a relation but as the distinguishing *quality* of mind. I myself distinguish in this connection between relations in the strict sense, viz. spatio-temporal relations, and relations in an extended sense (e.g. knowing) which involve a reference to qualities as well as to spatio-temporal relations; but this view of *strict* relations doesn't imply the reduction to them (strict relations) of relations in the wider sense; reducing knowing, e.g. to togetherness; since if we only had spatio-temporal relations (succession, proximity etc.) we shouldn't have the required relation of knowing.[1] The point would be that spatio-temporal relations are necessary but not sufficient for the relation of the knowing, that knower and known have to be together with and distinct from one another whatever else they may be.

Passing on, then, to the general theory of Space-Time, we seem to find the suggestion in Alexander that Space is the special form or ground of togetherness and Time the special form of ground of distinctness, that Space and Time have these distinct functions within Space-Time just as the subject and predicate, occurring together in the proposition, have distinct functions there. And here we are confronted with the difficulty, already touched on, of how we are able at all to put forward the Space-Time theory. If Space and Time constitute the medium in which things take place, how can we *say so without implying* that this medium takes place or occurs, so that it is itself in the medium --- how can we get over the paradox of Zeno that Space must be in Space (and similarly Time must be in Time) --- and *can't* be? Now Alexander's solution, as far as it goes, would be that Space is in Time and Time is in Space or, in his own terms, that Space is temporal and Time is spatial, though he still insists that Time is not Space and Space is not Time --- a very difficult view to

---

[1] MN: Anything could know anything.

maintain. At any rate, whether we use Alexander's conception of *stuff* or prefer the description of Space and Time as the *medium* of things, we have to give some account of the togetherness and distinctness of Space and Time in Space-Time or, as Alexander puts it, in Motion.

Now Alexander urges more defensibly that it is by reference to Space that we specify Time and by reference to Time that we specify Space, and so we can take the two together as conditions of the possibility of occurrences; and it is vital to this theory that, while we cannot conceive anything spatial which isn't temporal or anything temporal which isn't spatial, we can distinguish these two descriptions. We have noted that although it is Space-Time that accounts for the togetherness and distinctness of things and in which Space and Time are themselves together and distinct, Alexander takes Space particularly as the ground of togetherness and Time as the ground of distinctness. These would be what he calls "pure Space" and "pure Time" which he admits we can consider only by *abstraction*, since in Space [25] as we experience it we find both togetherness and distinctness (there is[1] spatial distinction as well as spatial connection) and similarly in Time as we experience we find both (temporal connection as well as temporal distinction) --- a position that would seem to be unavoidable if, as has been argued, togetherness and distinctness (or connection and distinction) are bound up together. It might be contended then that such abstraction is impossible and that *what Time contributes to Space* and *what Space contributes to Time* are meaningless questions. However, Alexander does profess to make these abstractions, to find pure Space in the form of mere *bulk*, i.e. undifferentiated extension, and pure Time in the form of the merely instantaneous, as mere disconnection; and if these abstractions have any point, it would be that the conceptions of bare Time and bare Space can be taken together as establishing Space-Time in its full complexity, that they are necessary and together sufficient for Space-Time as a medium (or stuff, as he puts it) of all things whatever.

---

[1] EN: "there is" is written as MN, with insertion mark between "(" and "spatial".

In this connection we can make use of the later formula that Time is the mind of Space, mind and body being distinguished as the active and the passive (a position similar to that which arises in the *Sophist*), the suggestion being, then, that it is by being in Time that things are capable of activity and by being in Space that they are capable of being acted on or of being a field of action. As we may put it, slightly varying the formula, Space or body gives continuity to Time or mind, Time or mind gives specification to Space or body; a position comparable to the relation of subject and predicate in the proposition. (This is connected with the doctrine of the Limit and the Unlimited in the *Philebus*. These unite to form things, the Limit corresponding to distinctness and the Unlimited to togetherness.[1] The theory in the *Sophist* is complicated by reactionary views, by the doctrine of highest kinds but something can be made of the account of activity and passivity without implying that one would agree with the Stranger's conclusions. Similar problems arise in the *Philebus*.)

We might argue then that in distinguishing the functions of Space and Time within Space-Time Alexander should not talk about *pure* Space and *pure* Time any more than one should talk about a pure subject and a pure predicate; but, allowing him that starting-point, we can take him to be saying that Space by itself is pure bulk of undifferentiated extension, and to break up this togetherness and introduce differentiation Time is required (Time breaks up spatial bulk --- allowing the metaphorical expression), and similarly that Time by itself is pure distinctness or instantaneousness, and to connect the instants together, to get what we call *duration*, Space is required (Space links together the fleeting instants of Time). And the point would be that we can and must distinguish and relate these two factors, that things can be accounted for only as spatio-temporal, not as merely spatial or merely temporal, but also that it is just because of this dual character that we can give any account of Space-Time itself, viz. by referring Space to Time and time to Space, or, as I should put

---

[1] NT: Cf. Burnet's discussion of the later dialogues. — EN: this refers to John Burnet, *op. cit.*, Chapter XVI, pp.260-270.

it, by treating Space as in Time and Time as in Space, just as we treat things as in both Time and Space. **[26]**

Lecture 9 The difficulty of speaking about Space and Time; lack of concreteness in Hegelian Idealism; Alexander's debt to Kant; the spatio-temporal as conveyed by the propositional form; the medium of things cannot be Space alone nor Time alone; the argument from repetition; the characters of Time and Space.

Waiving other difficulties for the present, we can consider at least the possibility of getting over the difficulty about Space and Time, (viz. how we can talk about them as if they were things and how we can talk about Space as in Space and Time as in Time) by specifying each of the two factors by reference to the other (giving an account of Space by reference to Time and of Time by reference to Space) and thus make specific the notion of Space-Time, instead of having to treat (the medium) as inexpressible.[1]

Whatever the difficulties of formulation may be, there is a concreteness about the conception of Space-Time that there isn't in the fundamental conceptions of Idealist philosophy. Cf. in Hegel, The Idea --- that which is expressed in anything. Hegel is merely stating and not solving the problem; in saying that everything is an expression of "the Idea," he is saying that everything is an expression of something we know not what. If we accept the theory of Space-Time, at least we have something concrete. Idealists want to get away from concreteness; they treat Time as one particular existent among others, not as a feature of things in general, because they want to turn back Time (to deny its irreversibility), to go from the concrete to the abstract (Idea). On the other hand, in so far as Hegel's *stuff* or *force* is to be taken as *mental* and not just as the general possibility of existence, you have Hegel treating *something particular as a condition of existence,* and so falling into the same sort of error as that of which he would accuse his opponents.[2] These thinkers take Space as not applying to everything, take mind as non-spatial;[3] and if we contrast the spatial with the non-spatial, we are treating Space

---
[1] MN: To avoid treating S. and T. as things, or as inexpressibles.
[2] MN: Something empirical as the "non-empirical".
[3] NT: cf. Alexander on Mental Space-Time.

as particular, as a limited thing, and reducing it to the empirical level.[1] [Treatment of Alexander's conditions of existence (Space and Time) as particular existing things, and of particular existing thing (mind) as condition of existence]. The sort of criticism Alexander would make of this (reduction of Space and Time to particulars) would be that, in doing so, we are implying the Space and Time we are professing to deny, that any theory of the non-spatial or non-temporal assumes in spite of itself that these things are spatial and temporal.[2]

Here we can see the importance of Alexander's debt to Kant; in Kant you get a clear distinction between the forms of sense (Space and Time) and the forms of understanding (categories). Alexander supplements[3] this by treating the forms of understanding as determinations of Space-Time, whereas in the Hegel position the distinction (of Space and Time from categories) is broken down; Space and Time are treated as particular conceptions, which is going back, in a manner, to the Cartesianism that Kant overthrew. These questions are connected with that of the concreteness of Space and Time as the medium of things (as that in which things are). This theory will have to be connected with the distinction between the form and the matter (or material) of the proposition, the suggestion being that spatio-temporal is conveyed by the propositional form and not by any particular term, though that still leaves the difficulty of how we can go on to speak of it (spatio-temporality), to use the apparent *terms* "Space" and "Time." **[27]**

From the position we have now reached we might treat the abstract conception of Space (conception of *bare* Space) as an attempt to treat Space alone as the medium of things, to think of things as simply being in Space, so that Time, if we could think (speak) of it at all, would be merely one empirical thing among others, one particular thing in Space. And Alexander may be taken as saying that to think in that way, i.e. in a supposedly

---

[1] MN: The Non-empirical empirical.
[2] MN: To discuss mind (even as non-spatial) necessarily involves treating it as spatial.
[3] MN: advances on.

purely spatial way, is to rule out the distinctions between things, leaving unbroken extension --- the "block universe" to which thinkers like Parmenides and Bradley (those, namely, who deny or explain away Time) are said to reduce things.[1] It might be said that Alexander's method of treating Space and Time without reference to the proposition leads him into a similar position, but, allowing for that, it might still be said that the above are the sort of views Alexander is looking for.

The argument would be, then --- suppose the medium of things to be simply Space, then things are not distinct from one another; but things *are* distinct from one another, therefore the medium is not simply Space. ("Medium" is another expression with which we would have difficulties. Ordinarily it expresses a relation between two concrete things, and the notion of a medium of things in general has a certain weakness. Cf. my criticism of "participation" as having a trans-empirical sense though it is only in empirical terms that we can understand what is meant.) In precisely the same way we could have the argument that things are connected (or together) and therefore the medium of things can't be simply Time. That, then, is the first part of Alexander's argument on Physical Space-Time --- a negative argument that the medium (or, as he would say, stuff) of things cannot be Space alone and cannot be Time alone, for in the one case there would be no distinctions and in the other case there would be no connections --- and it might be possible to link this part of the discussion with the Analogies (especially the second) in the *Critique*.

The second part of the argument will then be intended to show that Space and Time *can* be taken together as constituting a medium in which there would be both connection and distinction; and then the third part of the argument will show that they *must* be taken together in that way --- that each of them "demands" the other. Now in showing that Space and Time can together constitute a medium of things (that they can be together though distinct), Alexander founds this argument on *repetition*. As he

---

[1] NT: cf. Moore, on Bradley and Time in *Philosophical Studies*. — EN: this refers to "The Conception of Reality" in G.E. Moore, *op. cit.*, pp. 197-219.

puts it, Space can be repeated in Time and Time can be repeated in Space, or, as we might prefer to put it, things can be in different places at the same time and things can be in the same place at different times.[1] Thus Space and Time may be said to vary independently but together to define a situation. If we can have what we may call spatial and temporal coordinates such that neither determines what the other will be (such that you can't infer the spatial from the temporal or the temporal from the spatial), then Space and Time can be taken as together giving a formal **[28]** determination of things, as *formally* specifying a situation (apart i.e. from its *qualitative* peculiarities). That is, you would have a specification of the form "Here now X," where X is some particular quality (e.g. man). The spatio-temporal designation is formal, man (the quality) is material, and the two comprise the whole situation. (Some difficulties in passage from this formula to the propositional form --- discuss later.)[2]

Passing on to the third part of this fundamental argument (Vol. I, pp. 56-60?) we find Alexander contending that Space and Time *must* be thought of in relation to one another, and that it is by this togetherness of theirs (along with distinctness --- neither being reducible to the other) that we can find empirically both togetherness and distinctness in each of them (especially spatial distinction and temporal connection) though, abstractly considered, Space is pure togetherness and Time is pure distinctness. Alexander's argument is then: The characters that we attribute to empirical Time are such as can be understood only by taking Space along with Time, and similarly the characters we attribute to empirical Space require for their understanding the taking of Time along with Space; and still the two sets of characters are quite different from one another, Space having three dimensions and Time three fundamental characters (successiveness, irreversibility and transitiveness) which cannot be described as dimensions.

Now Alexander wants to show not merely that Time requires Space and Space requires Time but that there is an essential

---

[1] MN: Spaces and times (places and dates) of things vary independently.
[2] MN: S and T can be ? (not stuff).

connection between the three dimensions of Space and the three characters of Time --- in fact, he wants to establish a connection of mutual implication between:

> the successiveness of Time and one dimension of Space;
> the irreversibility of Time and a second dimension of Space;
> the transitiveness of Time and a third dimension of Space.

Putting it otherwise, the contention is that successiveness is necessary and sufficient for one dimension, irreversibility for two dimensions, and transitiveness for three dimensions. The difficulty however would seem to be that, on that showing, Time will *also* have to be three dimensional and Space will have to have the three fundamental characters, that Space and Time in fact could not be distinguished --- and that is a difficulty which I think Alexander doesn't get over. Also, some of his special arguments are not cogent --- he can be said to get the correlation wrong --- but still it is possible to *get* a correlation, whatever we may find to be the most exact way of expressing it, and to see, in particular, that it is *irreversibility* that should be correlated with three dimensions. [Position may be this (a) that there are such things as spatial transitiveness, spatial irreversibility (though these three are not characters *of Space*, in the same way as they are characters of Time), (b) that spatial successiveness is necessary and sufficient for one spatial dimension... spatial irreversibility for three spatial dimensions, but (c) that there is no logical connection but only an analogy between spatial irreversibility and temporal irreversibility.] **[29]**

Lecture 10 Alexander's contention that mind and body are genus and species - general characterisation of genus and species; the 'mutual necessitation' of Space and Time; importance of the proposition; successiveness and one-dimensionality; analogical character of the statement.

We have been discussing the questions raised in Bk I, Ch. I (pp. 56-60), where Alexander contends that Space and Time have to be taken together in order to account for the characters we empirically ascribe to them; e.g., empirical Time has connection as well as distinction, and empirical Space has distinction as well as connection, and there (in that fact) we have Space giving continuity to Time and Time giving structure to Space, just as, in the proposition, the subject may be said to *give continuity*[1] to the predicate and the predicate *structure*[2] to the subject, and just as, in Alexander's analogy ("Time is the mind of Space"), body gives continuity to mind and mind gives structure or particular determinations to body. Here however Alexander implies an *order* that we can't admit --- assumes that body is essentially subject and mind essentially predicate. It can be said that mentality (being mental) distinguishes[3] some bodily processes from others, whereas being bodily doesn't distinguish some mental processes from others, because all mental are bodily; in other words, the relation of mental to bodily can be expressed as that of species to genus. But Alexander has no right to speak of the genus as essentially subject and of the species (or its difference) as essentially predicate. In definition, you can distinguish in the defining complex the genus from the difference and can say that the genus is the subject of the "defining proposition" whereas the difference is its predicate --- e.g. in the definition of men as *rational animals*, "animals"[4] is shown by its substantive form to be the genus and "rational"[5] by its adjectival form to be the difference: i.e. the defining proposition would be

---

[1] EN: the text here reads "give continuity", with "locate" written above these words.
[2] EN: the text here reads "structure", with "intension" written above it.
[3] EN: the text here reads "distinguishes", with "differentiates" written above it.
[4] EN: inverted commas added.
[5] EN: inverted commas added.

Some animals are rational. But the distinction is only one of function, and the defining complex might as well be *animal rationals*[1] and the defining proposition Some rationals are animal. There is no absolute distinction between genus and difference --- any term could function in either way.

Returning to the question of the detailed relation between Space and Time, their "mutual necessitation", we can say that Alexander's argument is not cogent, some of the connections he seeks to establish don't exist, but there may also be real connections that he has overlooked (hasn't brought out).

First of all, there are difficulties as to the nature of Alexander's argument in general. If we take his thesis to be that it is only in Space-Time that Space and Time can have the characters we experience them as having, that would seem to imply that Space and Time are experienced as particular subjects (as *things*) having various predicates; and we might accordingly correct the statement and say that it is only because *things are at once in Space and in Time* that we can distinguish three dimensions and recognise the three connected characters of successiveness, irreversibility and transitiveness. But even then it might be argued that this is not intelligible, that we can intelligibly treat the one sort of thing as conditioning (or being necessary for) the other only if we can suppose **[30]** the possibility of the condition's *not* being fulfilled, only if we can suppose that there are not Space and Time (or there is not Space-Time) --- which, however, on Alexander's view would be a meaningless supposition.[2]

Now whether this is a complete way of escape or not, it would still seem that it is the *complex* nature of the medium that is important --- just as it is the complex nature of the *proposition* that is important in dealing with terms; the fact that we cannot take predicates apart from subjects or subjects apart from predicates --- it is just because there is that distinction, because the proposition has two distinct terms, subject and predicate, that

---

[1] EN: emphasis added.
[2] MN: Nature of Knowing --- propositional. Being not a subject or a predicate, and therefore not a stuff.

it is possible, even if mistaken, to suppose a term prior to or independent of proposition. In the same way, then, (it can be argued), it is *because there is in Space-Time a distinction between Space and Time* that we can understand, though we do not agree with, a proposal to take them separately, to think of a pure Space or of a pure Time. And, on the positive side, just as we can describe a thing by the characters it has, or refer to a character by the things it belongs to, without departing from the propositional standpoint, so, it may be said, we can determine Space and Time in relation to one another without departing from the Space-Time theory. This may sound metaphysical -- (metaphorical?) -- and may be inexact, but it suggests a way of getting over the initial impasse.

Assuming then (on the lines suggested) that Alexander's argument is intelligible, we may take it as beginning with the contention that there cannot be successiveness in Time unless there is a distinct dimension, a possible direction, in Space and similarly that there cannot be a direction in Space unless there is successiveness in Time; or that, within Space-Time, one-dimensionality and successiveness are bound up together. This is not to say they are identical, for then we should lose the distinction between Space and Time within Space-Time; but it might be said that in thinking of successiveness we are bound to think of one dimension, and vice versa, that in specifying the one we are at the same time specifying the other --- though in this particular case (successiveness and one dimension) it might be contended that there *is* identity, that what is one dimensional is successive and what is successive is one dimensional, so that Time actually is one dimension. In fact this is a point that is quite commonly made, though we should have to distinguish much as ever between the temporal dimension and one spatial dimension, and actually it might be better to keep the term *dimension* for Space, and simply to say that the sort of successiveness we find in Time [31] or rather the sort of relation we find among successive *instants* in Time or the sort of relation we find among successive terms in temporal series is the same as the sort of relation we find among terms arranged in a single spatial dimension.

However, if we formulate the matter in this way we have only an analogy, that is, we should be finding a certain resemblance between a temporal arrangement and a spatial arrangement of things without having found any reason for saying that Time is necessary for Space or Space for Time. And if we complete the argument and say that *as in Time* (qua temporal) things are in transitive, irreversible succession and as in three-dimensional Space things also exhibit transitive, irreversible succession (or, if succession is taken as a temporal term, some spatial correlate),[1] if in that way we can complete the analogy, still we have no ground for arguing that the two are necessary for one another, for arguing that there could not be spatial irreversibility unless there were temporal irreversibility, and vice versa. The only ground would be if we could really think of the non-temporal and discover that it had to be non-spatial as well (or similarly in the other direction), which by definition we cannot do.

It seems to me then that Alexander should say that merely as a matter of fact, without any question of necessity, things exist in a medium at once spatial and temporal; though he might argue that it is because of its spatiality *that we can describe* its temporality and vice versa --- for clearly such *descriptions* could be absent even if the conditions themselves could not be. And in the same way a possible way of supporting a doctrine of categories as pervasive characters of things would be to say that while, e.g., a thing cannot *be* without being caused, we can think of it without *thinking* of it as caused, and so the knowledge that it is caused can come as a real discovery. (This is thrown out as a suggestion but I doubt whether in this or any other way we can save the doctrine of "pervasive characters.")

We cannot simply say that the three dimensions, on the one hand, and the three characters on the other are necessary and sufficient for one another, because then Space would be Time and Time would be Space; we have to maintain, e.g., that although Time has the three characters, it is not three-dimensional but one-

---

[1] MN: Continuity?.

dimensional. What we shall have to say is that we can distinguish between spatial characters and arrangements of things and temporal characters and arrangements of things, and that the one casts light on the other; and further we can say that the two go together in *this* sense that if things are events or "motions" (to use Alexander's term) then any set of things we like to take will exhibit both kinds of arrangement, the spatial and the temporal.[1]
[32]

Over and above the general conditions and criticisms that apply to Alexander's argument, there are special criticisms to be applied to his attempt to set up a connection between irreversibility and a second spatial dimension and between transitiveness and a third spatial dimension.[2]

---

[1] MN:?.
[2] EN: this paragraph is enclosed in brackets.

Lecture 11 Motions: the problem of definition of a straight line; empirical grounds for geometry; irreversibility and transitiveness; criticism of 'point-instants'.

As regards correlation of the three characters of Time and the three dimensions of Space (a) if it is a case of analogy (the same *sort* of relations discoverable in Space as in Time), there is no ground for saying that the one is necessary for the other, (b) if the one *is* necessary for the other, we may be taken as identifying Space and Time, not distinguishing them.

Alexander may say, however, that we are dealing not with separate units of Space and Time but with *motions*, and that the recognition of successiveness as characteristic of a motion is necessary and sufficient for the recognition of the motion as of one dimension (one-dimensional). That is a fairly important point --- that experience of Time may be necessary for the recognition of direction. It is connected with the Euclidean problem of the definition of a straight line. Russell, e.g., criticises the common definition of it as the *shortest distance* between two points on the ground that nothing has been said to show that there is one distance shorter than all others between two points, so that the definition is question–begging; and what, it might be argued, Alexander is trying to bring out is just that the assurance of the uniqueness of that relation (i.e. of a unique straightness or a unique *direction* between any two given points) is bound up with the assurance of the uniqueness of Time, that Time is, if you like, the *model* of the straightness which we recognise as one particular feature of a spatial situation; at any rate, that the shortest distance is *coordinated* with the shortest temporal interval, though that "coordination" might call for further analysis which it would be rather difficult to give.[1] Putting it in terms of motion, the suggestion is that it is precisely because a motion is temporal (occupies time) that it can be found to have direction. In reply to the contention, then, that there is no *proof* that there is

---

[1] NT: Something in Kant somewhere about Time as the prototype of the straight line or of direction?

only one shortest distance, we might be able to say that we have the notion of direction and in that notion we have already the notion of uniqueness or straightness (in its distinction from all other directions), so that it is not a question of proof but of observation (direct experience).

The appeal to direct experience (empirical grounds) is opposed to the attempt to base geometry on *purely logical* grounds.[1] [33] A case in point is the "axiom of parallels" (Euclid's fifth postulate): the question how you could *prove* that two intersecting straight lines cannot both be parallel to a third straight line. And again the point is that you *see* it, and that your seeing it is bound up with your recognition of *direction* and *difference of direction*, i.e. that ability to recognise the direction (including straightness) of a line carries with [it][2] the ability to recognise *the same* direction and *a different* direction in other cases, which means that we can recognise parallels and also things intersecting, and therefore we can see that to deny the "axiom" is to say that two directions are at once the same and different; and even if we could prove it, that proof would still have to rest on something we simply *find* to be the case --- which would not in the least mean that there were alternative geometries in which that was *not* the case, the point being that anything we could call a geometry is a set of proposition which someone or other affirms to be true, and while we can consider what would follow from the supposition that some geometrical proposition is false, the important question is whether it actually is true or false.[3]

Discussion would be along the same lines in the case of the straight line --- straightness would be a matter of experience, and knowledge of it might be bound up with the uniqueness of *temporal* direction. The phrase "bound up" covers up some difficulties here; making it, for example, a question of our experience (our finding certain things together or "associating" them), whereas the real question is of being (whether they are

---

[1] NT cf. criticism of Russell in my "Empiricism".
[2] EN: the text reads "with the", "it??" is written in the margin, with a question mark between "with" and "the".
[3] NT cf. "Empiricism" again.

together). It may be replied however that the reason why we have to think of them in that way is that they are in that way --- that knowledge is of motions, because motions are what is --- that our procedure is determined by *the logic of events*. But this consideration would lead us to oppose the doctrine of starting with abstract Space and abstract Time and bringing them together to generate the complex Space-Time system. The point would be that we *cannot* think of something which is outside the complex Space-Time, that in thinking of something we call "pure Space" we are *already* thinking of it as within the Space-Time system and couldn't derive the latter from it. These considerations (with rejection of abstraction) bring us nearer understanding what can be done (empirically) along the lines of Alexander's argument and where an empirical argument would diverge from his. It would be in similar terms (logic of events; what is involved in the knowing and *in the being* of motions) that we would approach (interpret) Alexander's arguments concerning the second and the third dimensions; but we would have to make a vital alteration in the correlation as he presents it. **[34]**

Alexander fails to establish the other connections and in particular he fails to argue to a three-dimensional system, for he has to show not merely that to recognise that a succession is irreversible is to introduce an additional dimension and that this is also done by recognising that a succession is transitive but that the dimensions additionally introduced are distinct from one another, i.e. not simply[1] that each character implies a second dimension but that the two together constitute a second and a third. Now his only argument to show that the dimensions implied by irreversibility and transitiveness respectively are independent of one another is that irreversibility and transitiveness (or betweenness) have been proved to be distinct and therefore the dimensions they imply must also be distinct. But in the first place his proof that these two conditions as he defines them are distinct is not a sound one; and in the second place even if it had been, he should not have treated each of them as adding a dimension to a one-dimensional system but, having

---

[1] EN: the text here reads "imply".

treated one of them in that way, he should have exhibited the other as adding a dimension to a *two*-dimensional system.

One source of difficulty is Alexander's whole argument here is that he carries it out in terms of what he calls "point-instants." Now it might be said, first of all, that the use of this hyphenated term implies acceptance of that intimate relationship between Space and Time which it is supposed to be the object of *this whole argument (Bk I, Ch I)* to establish. And another objection is that it is assumed in this usage that the point is the unit or ultimate constituent of an extension and the instant of a duration — as against the view that all the constituents of an extension are extensions and all constituents of a duration are durations, and that there is no such elementary unit as the point, the instant or the point-instant.

However, the conception of point-instants is useful to Alexander in his argument because it enables him to treat the units or elements of a motion sometimes as spatial and sometimes as temporal and thus by ambiguity to arrive at conclusions which strict logic would not support. Thus in his argument regarding "betweenness" (pp. 54-55) he uses the illustration of pendular motion to show that transitiveness and irreversibility are independent: in particular, he is making out pendular motion to be an example of irreversibility without transitiveness. Now the series he is here characterising as irreversible but not transitive cannot be the series of instants in the motion in question, i.e., cannot be merely *the temporal series*,[1] because then there would be no point in the illustration, and the series, on his own showing, would be transitive as well as irreversible. It must then be either the series of points in the path of the pendulum or the series of point-instants **[35]** (i.e., the correlation of the points which the motion passes through with the times at which it does so --- each point-instant requiring both a spatial and a temporal coordinate to identify it). Now if we take the points, then transitiveness *as Alexander understands it* does not hold, but equally irreversibility does not hold. The point is that Alexander has really defined

---

[1] EN: the text here reads "*the temporal series*", with "(Time)" written above it.

transitiveness so as [to]¹ *include* irreversibility, the formula being not merely "If A is before B and B is before C, then *A is before C*" but also "*C is not before A*." And if the series of points does not exhibit transitiveness in this sense, it is simply because it does not exhibit irreversibility --- and so Alexander has not got his illustration of irreversibility without transitiveness. But, having proved the absence of transitiveness, as he conceives it, by reference to the points, he shifts his ground and proves the presence of irreversibility by reference to the *instants* (or to the temporal character of the point-instants) where, in fact, if we take this view, if we introduce the temporal coordinate, we have a series which is not merely irreversible but also transitive, even in Alexander's sense.

To sum up, then: Alexander relies on the instants to *assert the irreversibility* of the series, and he relies on the points to deny its transitiveness in the special sense of asymmetrical or irreversible transitiveness, which really amounts to *denying the irreversibility* of the series; and we can say that it is by confusedly including irreversibility in transitiveness that Alexander makes the latter appear the more advanced or complicated character whereas if we take transitiveness in the natural way, meaning merely that if A has the relation to B and B has it to C then A has it to C, without any implication as to whether C has it to A or not, then pendular motion gives, with respect to the points (which *recur*), an illustration not of a series which is irreversible without being transitive but of a series which is transitive without being irreversible: (and with respect [to]² the instants, or to the point-instants on account of their time-component, a series which is both irreversible and transitive --- but these features come in either case from the time-series, and pendulum illustration is of no real relevance.) This is in line with the view I am going to put forward --- that it is transitiveness that should be correlated with a second dimension and irreversibility with a third, that Alexander has taken them in the wrong order.

---

[1] EN: the text here reads "as *include*"
[2] EN: the text here reads "respect of the instants".

Lecture 12 Alexander's confusion of transitiveness and irreversibility; discussion of pendular motion; difference of direction fundamental to transitiveness in Time and two dimensionality in Space; absolute difference of direction fundamental to irreversibility in Time and three dimensionality in Space.

This lecture supplementary to last, in which I criticised Alexander's distinction between transitiveness and irreversibility as illustrated in pendular motion, and pointed out that instead of its being shown that there can be irreversibility without transitiveness it is shown that a series can be transitive without being irreversible. Suggestion of a correlation *different* from Alexander's between characters of Time and dimensions of Space. [36]

In Alexander's argument there are two defects (1) that when he is rejecting transitiveness (as being involved in pendular motion) *he mixes* up transitiveness and irreversibility, making the latter a part of the former; (2) that, having made this confusion, he rejects transitiveness, really by reference to *the points* which do not show irreversibility, and asserts

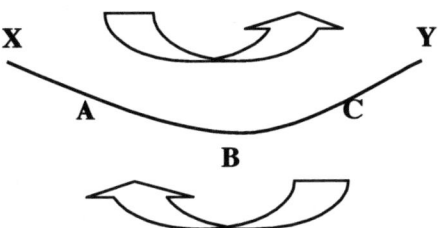

irreversibility by reference to *the instants* (which also show transitiveness), and so by shifting his ground he arrives at the conclusion he desires (requires).

The illustration is of pendular motion from X to Y and back again. Alexander argues that if A is before B and B is before C, then C may be before A, viz on the back swing (from Y to X).

But this is no argument at all against the ascription of transitiveness to the series, viz. to the series of points, because all we require of transitiveness is that if A is before B and B is before C, A is before C (A r B, B r C, therefore A r C) and there is nothing in that argument to tell us that C couldn't also be before A. It is quite possible, as far as transitiveness is concerned, that the relation should be reversible and thus C could be before A on the back swing (in which, incidentally, C is before B and B is before A) without any effect on the transitiveness of the series.[1] (Where r = is an ancestor of, ArB and BrC imply ArC and imply Anot-rC, but this relation is irreversible --- ArC itself implies Cnot-rA]. It is only because Alexander unwarrantably imports irreversibility into transitiveness (imports *C can't be before A*) that transitiveness can be denied in this particular instance. Many relations are transitive and reversible (e.g. equality).

You can, then, have the transitive relation with or without irreversibility, and the fact that the series of points is not irreversible doesn't show that it is not transitive. And now, in arguing that the series *is* irreversible, Alexander must take it as a series not of points but of point-instants or (essentially) instants; at least its irreversibility *depends* on temporal irreversibility (the irreversibility of Time). We should thus have A_1, before Y on the[2] right hand swing, but then Y would be before not A_1, but A_2

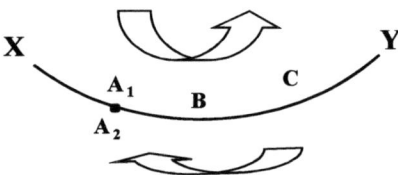

on the leftward swing, A_1, being distinguished from A_2 simply because we are now taking the temporal coordinate into account.

---

[1] MN: (A = B = C = B = A).
[2] ENMW: Diagram below occurs at this point.

If we were concerned with irreversibility, with a relation such that if A has it to B then B doesn't have it to A (A*r*B ∴ Bnot-*r*A), the example of the pendulum would be quite beside the point. (The reason why the successive positions of the pendulum in Time constituted an irreversible series would just be that it is a series in Time, a series, then, which **[37]** exhibits all three temporal characters and thus, as I say, is of no particular advantage to us as an illustration --- we are illustrating the characters of Time by the characters of Time!) If the illustration has any force, it is only because we are concerned with the series of points and in that case, contrary to what Alexander says, we have transitiveness without irreversibility, i.e. having gone over the points in a certain direction we go over them again in the reverse direction so that we come back to any point that we originally had. Alexander's relation here is "comes earlier in the series than"; and this is transitive but not irreversible because whatever point on the arc comes earlier in the series of positions of the pendulum than a given point also comes later in the series than it.[1] As Alexander takes the characters in this argument, irreversibility is a part of transitiveness, and this is an additional weakness in his attempt to show that by reference to three independent characters we can build up a system of three independent dimensions.

Turning now to the argument as he should have presented it, and allowing as before that there are difficulties in the way of its exact formulation but that it is a question of connected characters of any motion, we can say that just as successiveness corresponds to one dimension (the notion of a *series* to that of a *direction*: though the former might be said to emphasise the diversity of the terms, the latter their continuity, the two expressions thus indicating the functions Alexander ascribes to Time and Space respectively in Space-Time), so *transitiveness*, with its recognition of difference of relation, as in the case of B which is before C and *is after A* (or has A before it), can be expressed by saying that there is a *difference of direction* from B, or can be "correlated" (leaving aside the difficulties that might be raised as

---

[1] EN: this sentence is enclosed in square brackets.

to that expression) with difference of direction; and, on the spatial side, to speak of different directions from a point is to speak of an *angle*, and angle is the mark of a two dimensional system or is necessary and sufficient for two dimensions. The notion of difference of direction, then, is fundamental alike to the transitiveness of Time and to what we may call the two-dimensionality of Space.

Where you have A*r*B and B*r*C, then B has two relations --- the relation *r* to C and what Russell calls "the relation converse to *r*" to A. In the case of Time, these relations are *before* and *after*,[1] and of course are irreversible. But leaving aside that question and considering the case where *r* is reversible, it is one thing to say that B has the relation *r* to C and a different thing to say that C has the relation *r* to B; or, more generally, it is one thing to speak of "what B has the relation *r* to" and another thing to speak of "what has the relation *r* to B" even if these two classes coincide. [38]

There is difference of direction in a series indicated by transitiveness,[2] and, spatially speaking, expressed by an angle which is the mark of a two-dimensional system. Whether it is only an analogy is a further question. To show that it is more, we shall have to be able to show that two-dimensionality (or difference of spatial direction) is "bound up" with transitiveness just as one dimension (a direction) is bound up with successiveness. We might have to use the formula previously used; just as we said that to be able to show successiveness is to be able to know one dimension, we may have to say that to be able to know transitiveness is to be able to know two dimensions. (Or just as we said that it is because a motion has temporal successiveness that it can be found to have direction, so we might say that it is because a motion has temporal transitiveness that it can be found to have difference of direction --- to exhibit

---

[1] EN: the text here reads "these relations are before and after".

[2] NT: "call it B*r*C and B $\overset{\cup}{r}$ A, = A*r*B". EN: — the symbol " $\overset{\cup}{r}$ " is repeated in the margin. As Anderson explains in Lecture 25, " $\overset{\cup}{r}$ " is a symbol for what Russell called "converse relation".

divergence). It is to be noted that recognition of difference of direction does not mean recognition of departure *from the straight* on the part of the motion or series we are considering: in that case, temporal difference of direction might be questioned. But, even if we take the two types of relation possessed by a point B in a straight line, in order to know that the relation of B to A is different from the relation of B to C we have to bring in the notion of turning --- of a "straight angle" or angle of 180 degree.

And, since there is no actual turning in Time, this might be held to support Alexander's view that, in order to understand difference of directions in Time (the difference between having predecessors and having successors), we have to be acquainted with Space, in which actual turning is possible. (It might also be said, on the side of Space, that we couldn't grasp the meaning of a "straight angle" if we weren't acquainted with angles or turnings of *less* than 180 degree --- with crossings or plain divergences.)

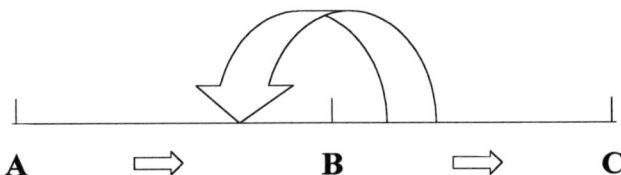

Having arrived at the two-dimensional system, having two dimensions defined by an angle or turning, we can go on, on that basis, to establish a *third* dimension correlated with irreversibility. Irreversibility comes in in the notion not simply of a difference of direction or turning but of an *absolute* difference of direction --- the sort of difference we recognise in Time between *before* and *after*. As far as transitiveness is concerned, we could indifferently have used before and after; we could say If A is *after* B and B is after C, then A is after C; i.e., logically the position is the same whichever of the two relations we select. [39] But of course in our temporal knowledge, in our theory of time, we cannot always substitute one of these relations for the other. We have to recognise that, in whatever respects *before* resembles *after*, there is still an absolute difference between them, that it is one thing to say that A is before B and a totally different thing to say that A is after B, that the statements are not merely distinct but incompatible.

In recognising, then, this absolute difference of temporal direction we are brought to the notion of an absolute difference between one turning and another, between a positive and a negative turning, and the recognition of this difference geometrically or spatially speaking, is necessary and sufficient for three dimensions. As we may put it, after is the negative of before just as turning clockwise is the negative of turning counter-clockwise; but to make that distinction absolute we require three dimensions, for in saying that B is the clockwise turning and A is the counter-clockwise turning, we have to say that the figure is considered or looked at from this side, for of course if we looked at it from the other side A would be the clockwise turning and B would be the counter-clockwise turning.

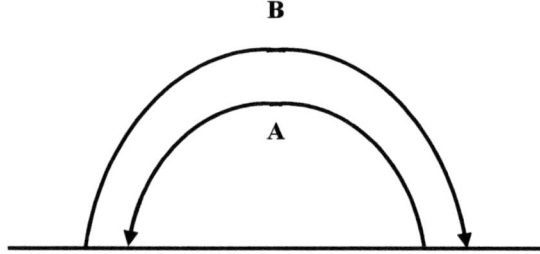

In making, then, this absolute distinction we are considering the situation three-dimensionally, and the three-dimensional relation involved is referred to by some mathematicians as a "screw," because it is illustrated in the use of a screw, the point being that when we turn to the right (clockwise) the screw, if it is a right-handed one, goes in and when we turn the other way (counterclockwise) it comes out; and of course we could have a left-handed screw of which the opposite would be the case; and the difference between a right-handed and a left-handed screw is something that can be grasped only three-dimensionally and something, again, which illustrates the negative relation of one temporal direction to the other.

Mathematically the position is presented as a relation between three positive directions. If we have the positive directions of the X and Y axes, then we'll have one type of solid angle if the positive direction of the Z axis is inward (down through the paper) and another type of solid angle if the positive direction of the Z axis is outward (up off the paper).

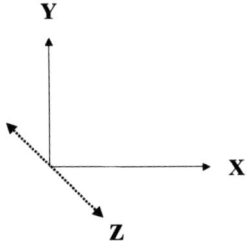

You get the same sort of relation in the human body: a set of three "positive" directions whose relation is constant, so that if you change one of them you change one of the others but not both; thus, if you turn around, putting your front in the position your back was in and vice versa, you also exchange the positions of your right and your left, your up and down remains unaltered.[1]
[40]

The interrelation makes it possible to alter (from the point of view of a spectator) any two of the directions but impossible to alter only one or all three. Cf. Kant's reference[2] to the relationship of the hands; the fact that by no sort of translation can the left hand come to occupy the precise space that has been occupied by the right hand (to occupy a "mirror" space). Cf. also Wells's "Plattner story" where the reversal (left to right) of a man's viscera was taken to imply that he had been "beyond" three dimensions.

---

[1] MN: e.g., Right, front and up (head) have a spatial relation, differing from that of right, front and down, etc.
[2] NT: in one of the early works, or in the *Prolegomena*?

This "screw," then, is the spatial irreversibility which corresponds to temporal irreversibility --- The case of the hands can be expressed by saying that you cannot transpose two *similar* solids with a different *screw*; whereas, in the case of gloves, such transposition can be made because (neglecting thickness) it is a question of surfaces. In the same way, we can suppose a triangle to be transposed, and turned round in the process, so as to be exactly superimposed on another, because there is a third dimension, there is space *off* the plane, in which the turning round can be imagined to take place.[1]

Thus the spatial irreversibility connected with three-dimensionality is an argument against the recognition of *more* than three dimensions of Space (there couldn't then if there were more than 3 dimensions, be irreversible screws). And it is noteworthy that modern (mathematical) doctrines of more than three dimensions of Space are coordinated with the conception of reversible Time; that spatial and temporal irreversibility are taken to fall together. As against this, Alexander's view (and I should say the empirical view) is that they stand together.

---

[1] EN: in the text this sentence is enclosed in round brackets.

Lecture 13 Successiveness, transitiveness and irreversibility in Time and one, two and three dimensionality in Space; problem of abstraction; the intractability of qualities.

It had to be shown that a succession implies and is implied by one dimension, a transitive succession ... two dimensions, and an irreversible transitive succession ... three dimensions. But it is important to remember that Space and Time vary independently, (that it isn't Space and Time themselves that are coextensive --- otherwise, Alexander would be giving up all ground for using the expression Space-Time); and thus it may be said that the mutual implication is among the characters of *Space* and that what Alexander's argument should show (what the corrected argument does show) is the way in which Space and Time *work together* --- the way in which through the successiveness of Time [*not* its continuity] we can be aware of direction in Space, through **[41]** transitiveness in Time of turning or *difference of direction* in Space, through irreversibility in Time of *absolute* difference of direction (absolute direction of turning) in Space. Or, putting it in objective terms (not in terms of our awareness), that it is as being successive in Time that a motion can *have* direction in Space, as having transitiveness in Time that a motion can have direction in Space (or that *motions* can have different directions), as having irreversibility in Time that it can have absolute difference of direction (or be three-dimensional) in Space --- or can occur in three-dimensional Space. This still brings up the problem of *abstraction* --- the question how we can say that something is enabled by its temporal successiveness to have some other character, unless we can consider things which don't have temporal successiveness, which by hypothesis we cannot do. Solution may be connected with distinction between instants and durations --- hence between position and motion --- because we can without abstraction explain what is meant by an instant viz. as the point of division between two successive phases of an event or parts of a duration. Even so, we don't see an instant *becoming* a duration.[1]

A question that can be raised in regard to irreversibility is whether to speak of "spatial irreversibility" on the one hand and "temporal irreversibility" on the other, means more than to speak of quality (in the sense of suchness, being such and such --- *quale*) i.e., whether spatial irreversibility doesn't just mean the character of *spatiality*, and temporal irreversibility *temporality* --- what is special or unique about being spatial and being temporal respectively.

This might be compared with Kemp Smith's reference[2] to the *intractability* of qualities --- particularly of what he calls "secondary qualities" --- this intractability meaning simply that they cannot be reduced to anything else or transformed into one another or shown to be built up or "constituted" in such and such a way --- that they cannot be "rationalised." (So spatial irreversibility is spatial intractability, is the *limit* to the transformations which a thing *qua* spatial can undergo; and similarly with a thing *qua* temporal.) The point is that the physicists have attempted to give a rational equivalent (or reduction), e.g., of colour, saying that colours are just vibrations at such and such a rate (that this vibration is the *reality* of colour); and then the doctrine of intractability amounts to this, that such a quantitative account of things (with universal transformability or exchangeability of equal quantities) is inadequate, that in whatever way we can correlate red, e.g., with a particular rate of vibration we have not *reduced* red to that "primary" or quantitative character --- the quality red still remains in all its peculiarity. [42] In the same way, physicists have attempted to "rationalise" Space and Time, to make them simply quantitative and thus, incidentally, *reversible*; and Alexander's argument, as

---

[1] EN: in the text the last two sentences of this paragraph are enclosed in round brackets.
[2] NT: (in Prolegomena to an Idealist Theory of Knowledge). — EN: this refers to Norman Kemp Smith, *Prolegomena to an Idealist Theory of Knowledge*, (London: Macmillan and Co. Limited, 1924). Anderson, who was Kemp Smith's colleague at the University of Edinburgh, had read the proofs of the book and made some comments that were acknowledged in the preface.

an attempt to pass directly from one to the other, to make Time *formally imply* Space and Space *formally imply* Time, may be said to compromise with, or give an opening to, rationalistic physics --- in which connection Alexander's weak treatment of spatial irreversibility, with no hint of the real point, the "screw," is significant.[1]

We might suggest then that what emerges from the discussion of spatial and temporal irreversibility is that there is a similar intractability of Space and Time or of "primary qualities," that they also, whatever common features they may have, are not reducible to one another. This is connected with (our previous discussion of) the empiricist rejection of the "rationality" of mathematical science,[2] with the view that true mathematical propositions are just as "synthetic" as any other propositions, have to be learned as matters of fact ("brute fact"), as against the notion of their being *truths of reason*; and thus if we say that there could be a certain transference or passage between one spatial dimension or direction and another, but that such transformation is impossible, that we have irreversibility or non-transformability, in a certain type of three-dimensional relation, the suggestion would be that here we are simply recognising *what is peculiar to Space* viz. that it is as a matter of fact a three-dimensional system, and, whatever parallels we may find, this can certainly not be transformed or translated into *what is peculiar to Time* --- and vice versa; our recognition of the difference between *before* and *after* contains something that cannot be expressed spatially.[3]

And thus, for example, when physicists use a spatial direction to illustrate temporal order or a temporal series, that will never be more than an illustration; it will be defective precisely in that, while *spatially* we could take the items in the opposite direction, *temporally* we could not. [This is not quite accurate: we can consider a series of events from later to earlier as well as from

---

[1] MN: Empiricism the philosophy of intractability. — EN: in the text the last sentence of this paragraph is enclosed in round brackets.
[2] NT: cf criticism of Leibniz in "Empiricism".
[3] MN: This irreversibility emphasises *difference*, not similarity between T. and S.

earlier to later: and a spatial direction (say from left to right on this paper) can be absolutely fixed if we can determine which side is up and which side is *top* (the latter might be difficult). But the point is there could never be any *reason* for correlating left with earlier rather than with later.] Hence, such an illustration should not be used, as it seems to have been, as actually helping to establish the reversibility of Time.[1] **[43]**

---

[1] MN: Rationalism concerned to "save hypotheses" and remove facts (i.e., remove intractabilities.) Suggestion that in pure mathematics we can get beyond these "intractabilities": can have multi-dimensional systems, imaginary numbers etc. But these are based simply on *analogies*, which can break down. If the entities were merely inclusive, we couldn't have any mathematics of them: we could as easily deny as assert any given "proposition." .

Lecture 14 Bradley on a) qualities and relations b) Space and Time; the problem of ultimate 'units'; rationalism of Leibniz and Russell; the problem of absolute terms; situational logic and spatio-temporal logic; Heraclitus and his all inclusive system – rejection of the 'universe' or 'cosmos'; belief in ultimates and the desire for security.

Bradley on (a) qualities and relations, (b) Space and Time.

Bradley treats *Space and Time* as relations between terms, and there are special problems here. But the general problem is that of establishing any coherent view of terms and relations, any view that doesn't lead into antinomies --- to the impossibility of bringing terms and relations together or the impossibility of keeping them apart. The fact (as he takes it to be) that we cannot speak without falling into these difficulties leads Bradley to his theory of the unsatisfactoriness of appearance. For Green, on the other hand, only the related (i.e., appearance) is real, and since it is mind that relates things or makes them real, mind cannot be just one thing among others but must be in a supreme position, must *transcend* reality. In this way, Green is more of a Kantian than a Hegelian. Bradley who is more Hegelian considers that the relational way of thinking is defective and that the Absolute is supra-relational. [Wouldn't Green have to say this about mind? Or is mind realised in the system which *it* organises?] Empiricism would say that the supposed supra-relational itself involved relations and would be subject to the same difficulties as "appearance".

Now on Space and Time Bradley brings up the old question of the unit, the fact that when we take a given space to consist of a number of smaller spaces we can do this indefinitely and never arrive at the unit. The unit, then, is nothing, and therefore the totality is nothing. The question of constituents (and ultimate constituents) is of course a familiar one; it is involved in all rationalist theories; it lies behind the Pythagorean theory of units and Atomism. The suggestion is that unless there is something absolutely solid, there could never be anything at all. It is this which gives rise to Zeno's paradoxes, which are unsound because they assume at once that there is no end to division and that there is an end to division (and Bradley is simply following this unsound line.) It is one thing to say that you never arrive at a least and another thing to say that you do arrive at a least which is nothing. Zeno's paradoxes fail because they depend at once on empirical facts and on the rationalist doctrines which are being attacked.

The same sort of rationalist view is found in Leibniz and Russell --- in the doctrine that the complex implies the simple. Empiricists say that there are no ultimate units, no constituents which do not themselves have constituents, in fact, no ultimates of any kind; but we should still understand that what the rationalists are looking for are ultimates or units, in the sense of something which is just a unit, which is uniquely numbered one and couldn't possibly be numbered in any other way --- the view I take to be rejected **[44]** in the Heraclitean fragment regarding *couples*. I take Heraclitus to be saying that something could just as intelligibly be numbered one as numbered two, and there is nothing which has a unique number, which is one and nothing but one, two and nothing but two, etc., and indeed there would be no such thing as mathematics if there were such absolute units --- we could never speak of any number higher than one unless, to take the simplest example, there could be such a thing as *a* couple: something which is in some sense one and in some sense two.[1]

In the same way, then, Bradley in dealing with relations is postulating absolute terms, that which is a term and nothing but a term, that within which there could be no relation or differentiation, and it is the postulation of such terms, of what I should call essences or natures, of *pure* beings of one kind or another (that whose *whole* nature it is to be X), which is characteristic of rationalism, and it is that which inevitably

---

[1] EN: the reference here is to fragment 59 in Burnet's list, viz. "Couples are things whole and things not whole. What is drawn together and what is drawn asunder, the harmonious and the discordant. The one is made up of all things, and all things issue from the one." John Burnet, *Early Greek Philosophy*, 4th ed., (London: Adam & Charles Black, 1930), p.137.

involves us in antinomies: or putting it in logical terms, it is the doctrine which makes the term fundamental and the proposition derivative, instead of taking the proposition (or, in spatio-temporal terms, the situation) as fundamental. (The point is that in speaking of a term (thing) as something which can enter a relation we are already speaking of a situation, something which has within it distinguished and related things, and having *terms in relation* as involved in it we are not faced with any problem of how *it* can enter into a relation --- how, being a term, it can also be related.) The doctrine that the least there can be is a complex situation is the only way of escaping the antinomies which Bradley works out.

At the same time we should notice that these antinomies arise logically from common notions, particularly from the notion of the *thing* which may have various *characters*, from the antithesis of substance and attribute, the whole point of propositional theory of things being not that it sets up a distinction between substance and attribute but rather that it indicates that there is no such logical distinction, that whatever can characterise can be characterised and vice versa. That is how I have commonly criticised Locke, Berkeley and Hume. They take their point of departure from *natures*, or simple entities and try to derive complex situations or propositions from them; and they can't do it. But they cannot avoid using propositions even if their fundamental position does not allow them to. There is no such thing as an absolute *term* (that which can *have* relations) but every term has inner relations and inner differentiations.[1] **[45]**

Now that is where the empirical theory is linked up with the spatio-temporal theory, the point being not just that a situational logic is a spatio-temporal logic, but that the situational approach shows us how we are to understand Space and Time, not, viz., as something additional to situations, e.g., as a kind of total receptacle in which situations are --- since that at best would turn Space and Time themselves into one particular situation --- nor again as relations, as something holding between situations, the

---

[1] NT: i.e. 1. Locke, Berkeley and Hume can't indicate a passage from the simple to the complex; 2. Anything they present as simple is really complex.

relational view of Space and Time being that of spatial and temporal relations between units which would not themselves be spatio-temporal, but rather as something involved in situations, as something the recognition of which is part of the recognition of any situation at all.

If we take the sort of view[1] which I have attributed to Heraclitus (in fact, taken to be the main feature of his logic) viz. that there is no such thing as an absolute unit and, in the same way, no such thing as an absolute totality, that anything we like to consider is both a system of constituents and a constituent of other systems, then we should say that he fell into inconsistency with that principle in so far as he recognises an all-inclusive system or universe (and certain of the fragments seem to imply that he did) --- a cosmos to which, on his own admission, nothing could happen, which would be absolutely static because it would have no environment with which it could interact, nothing with which it could, in his terms, *have exchanges*. And in exactly the same way, we should not regard Space and Time as all-inclusive, as a receptacle of particular events of whatever extent; we should rather regard them as part of what is meant by saying that there is *no* all-inclusive totality, nothing which contains everything else, but that every container is itself contained.

No doubt there are many difficulties about any attempted formulation of this view. If, e.g., we say that Space and Time are *conditions* of the infinite divisibility and corresponding infinite extensibility of things, we seem to be treating them (Space and Time) as particular things, but at least it should be clear that nothing *less* can be understood by Space and Time than the existence of this infinite divisibility and infinite extensibility. Even if it is only a negative description we can still, I think, find some significance in the statement that in knowing any situation we are knowing it as having no ultimate constituents and against a background, or in an environment, which has no ultimate limits.

---

[1] EN: the text here reads "of which", with "view?" written in the margin, and a question mark between "of" and "which".

This doesn't explain how people come to believe in ultimates. Explanation would involve psychological and sociological issues that would not elucidate the logical position. We would associate such doctrines with the desire for security or safety --- the "ultimate" being that which can't be taken away or destroyed – **[46]** and even that might have an empirical counterpart in the conception of that which is essential if not to the continued existence of *things* at least to the continued existence of society. But, allowing for all that, I would say that the rejection of simple natures is bound up with the sort of recognition of infinite divisibility and simple extensibility I have spoken of and that these are essential features, at least, of what is to be understood by *the spatio-temporality of things*.[1]

---

[1] EN: in the text this last paragraph is enclosed in round brackets.

Lecture 15 Situational logic recognises externality everywhere; cf Leibniz and the Pythagoreans; internality in Leibniz, Berkeley and Kant; empiricism and mind.

The situational logic recognises *externality* everywhere, different parts of everything. The logic of *internality* is not content with accidental relations; it wants to find an original unity or fundamental nature from which attributes or specifications arise, though they are still subordinate to the original or central unity. Cf. Leibniz's doctrine of the monad or *intensive* unit (or atom); it is to this that Hegel refers in saying that Leibniz made the step from substance to subject, from substance as *divisible* to subject as *self-sustaining* or founded on itself (from external to internal). And naturally any thinker who is dominated by this conception ("subject"), who wants to reject externality or treat it as subordinate or not having the same claim on reality as internality, would be in difficulties about Space.

Cf. Pythagoreans and the question of intervals between units. Space is a [the?] form of externality; it is necessary and yet impossible to treat the units as spatial. Hence you get incommensurability between units and intervals --- and so, more generally (on *internality* or *identity* theory), between inner natures and outer relations. And there, although Alexander can hardly be said to depreciate space, although he takes Space and Time as philosophically fundamental, he still shows how much he is tied to the standpoint of internality when he tries to spin history --- the evolution or development of things --- out of Space-Time; attributing to Space-Time, then, the sort of internality or essence which Leibniz attributes to his monads, the history of any monad being the unfolding of its inner nature. (This notion, of course, is nonsense; why should an essence "unfold"?)[1] Since Alexander also has this unfolding notion, reality being something that Space-Time spins out of its inner resources, it is not surprising that he links his view with a peculiar kind of *theology*.

---

[1] ENMW: Cf. Anderson's 1942 lectures on Aesthetics where he speaks positively of 'unfolding'.

Where, then, internality is the dominant feature of a philosophy, it is particularly difficult to give an account of Space. Thus Leibniz has to treat Space as the object of a confused way of thinking (i.e., really as *appearance*), a view which would make reality a bare uncharacterisable identity. On the relativist view of Space, you immediately strike insoluble problems: e.g., that of the plurality of substances --how can this be if they are not externally (and objectively) related? Leibniz assumes a universal monad (having some of the characteristics of the theological "Creator") which harmonises the finite monads ("in" which they are related) but he cannot show the relation between this supreme monad and the finite monads; he would have to treat them as its predicates and so come back to the single substance of Spinoza.[1]
[47]

Berkeley is in a somewhat similar position in his reduction of Space to a multitude of particular ideas of extension, in the minds of various substances (subjects); the problem of the relation of finite minds to the Infinite Mind in his theory is of the same character as Leibniz's problem of the universal monad, and Berkeley could similarly be forced to say that "finite minds" are only ideas in the Infinite Mind.[2]

Kant's position is more complicated, treating Space as a form *of phenomena*. It is not here (as with Leibniz) a question of confused thinking but of the only way of cognising something that is not absolute reality. One difficulty is how the phenomenal is to be related to a reality which is presumably non-spatial, and

---

[1] NT: cf. Dawes Hicks: "The Monads of Leibniz and the Modes of Spinoza", *P.A.S.*; also Critical Realism. — EN: the reference here is to (1) G. Dawes Hicks, "The 'Modes' of Spinoza and the 'Monads' of Leibniz", *Proceedings of the Aristotelian Society*, 18, 1917-18, pp.329-362; and (2) G. Dawes Hicks, *Critical Realism: Studies In The Philosophy Of Mind And Nature*, (London: Macmillan & Co. Limited, 1938).

[2] NT: cf. Aristotelian symposium on whether finite beings have substantive or adjectival existence. — EN: this refers to the symposium, "Do Finite Individuals Possess A Substantive Or An Adjectival Mode Of Being?", with symposiasts Bernard Bosanquet, A.S. Pringle-Pattison, G.F. Stout, and Lord Haldane, *Proceedings of the Aristotelian Society*, 18, 1917-18, pp.479-581.

another is how the phenomenal and spatial is to be related to the phenomenal and non-spatial, as for Kant *mental* phenomena are presumed to be (also, how anything phenomenal can be taken as non-spatial at all). The bulk of modern philosophers take the view that mind is not spatial and hence take its relations as "internal", take it as the supreme unit. With this denial of externality go mystical theories of identification ("members of one another") which Russell[1] says ought to have been Berkeley's line.

The empirical counterpart to this view is that of relations between minds as belonging to the same movement, which passes through them; though minds are spatially external to one another they participate in common movements. The (idealist) theory (of) mind is an extreme example of the attempt at a theory of internality, the attempt to find individual units. You couldn't uphold multiplicity at all on a theory of internality. It is in the interests of some sort of *security* that such doctrines of mind as "self-sustaining" etc., are put forward. Cf. The question of Time and Eternity (see McTaggart),[2] where temporal reality is treated as a "manifestation" of eternity, and the question of the *destruction* of mind as a unity (annihilation of substance). On the sort of view (internality) we have been considering, Time as well as Space would have to be treated as illusion or appearance. The doctrine of eternity is typical of idealist thinking.

---

[1] NT: Problems of Philosophy?
[2] EN: the reference here is to J.M.E. McTaggart, "The Relation of Time and Eternity", *Mind*, 18 (71), 1919, pp.342-362; and possibly also to J.M.E. McTaggart, "The Unreality of Time", *Mind*, 17(68), 1908, pp.45-74, and the related Chapter 33 on 'Time', in J.M.E. McTaggart, *The Nature of Existence*, Volume II, (Cambridge U.K.: Cambridge UP, 1927), pp.9-31.

Lecture 16 Transition to the categories: Alexander treats Space-Time as an infinite whole; his failure to treat the question in terms of the proposition; Space and Time and the propositional form; subject and predicate of the proposition; 'paradoxes' of the situational logic.

Book II, Ch. I on the Nature of the Categories.

Summing up (previous discussion) Alexander says that Space-Time is an infinite given whole --- a formula which he goes back upon in Ch. X (The One and the Many). In any case we can reject the formula as it stands, arguing that just because Space and Time are infinite they are not wholes and do not together constitute a whole. The position (recognition of infinity) could roughly be expressed by saying that *all wholes are parts*, and whether Alexander calls Space-Time a whole or not **[48]** his treatment of it does involve him in some of the difficulties that I said would apply to Heraclitus if he really believed in an all-inclusive system, though it is the Heraclitean logic that enables us to bring some of the objections to the notion in question.

The difficulty for Alexander arises partly from his failure to treat the question in terms of the proposition, to see, i.e., that existence in infinite Space and Time is what is conveyed by the copula, granted that we may find it hard to explain how such amplification is possible. We have the special problems of how we are able to use expressions like *proposition* and *copula* themselves as if they were logical terms. It is clear, nevertheless, that Alexander, in not treating the matter propositionally, in not making the distinction between the *material* (i.e. particular terms) and the *form* of the proposition, comes up against insoluble problems, is forced to treat Space and Time as things (which he really cannot consistently do), the taking of *the thing* as *primary* being, as I've indicated, at least closely akin to the doctrines of Idealists such as Bradley, and Alexander having no real answer to Bradley so long as he doesn't insist upon a propositional logic. And of course it is when Space and Time are treated as things or as collections of things that the categories appear as qualities, or at least as predicates, of these things and that their nature cannot be clearly set forth.

What I am suggesting is that to say that things exist in Space and Time is to say that they exist in the propositional form, and one of the important things to notice there (again one of the matters on which Idealism is confused) is the difference between subject and predicate --- a point touched on in "Universals and Occurrences" (June, 1929) and again in my review of Campbell's "Scepticism and Construction"[1]: cf. Bosanquet's logic in which *symmetry* is a mark of the ultimate real, a position which makes the starting-point of any problem (viz. Non-symmetrical relations) unintelligible. So when I contend that the subject *locates* the predicate, I am saying that a reference to Space is required to make the distinction intelligible, i.e. that unless there is absolute Space we cannot, as we must, distinguish subject and predicate. But (I also say) that although a subject locates, it is not an absolute or ultimate location, that it in its turn can be located, can be a predicate of another subject; and in that connection we get the paradox that we recognise things by the places where they are located and at the same time recognise locations (places) by the things that are in and around them --- or, sticking to the subject-predicate question, that we recognise subjects by the predicates they have and predicates by the subjects they belong to. These "paradoxes" should be taken as really signifying ways in which we develop or expand our knowledge (we go to subjects to get a better grasp of predicates, etc)[2]; they will be misleading only if we forget that knowledge is of propositions from the outset. (i.e., not of subjects without predicates or of predicates without subjects) and thus that from the outset we distinguish what locates from what is located so that even although we can never specify an absolute location, *location or spatiality* is an ingredient in all that we know, i.e., in all that we take *to be,* **[49]**

---

[1] EN: the reference here is to (1) John Anderson, "'Universals' And Occurrences" (discussion note), *AJPP*, 7, 1929, pp.138-145; and (2) John Anderson, "*Scepticism and Construction* by C. A. Campbell" (review), *AJPP*, 13, 1935, pp.151-156. ENMW: "'Universals' and Occurrences" is reprinted in *Studies* pp 155 – 121.

[2] EN: the remark in brackets is written as a MN and marked for insertion in the text.

and that is what is meant by referring to the *absoluteness* of Space. And we could argue in a similar way about Time.

Now these considerations, whether they are defensible or not, at least indicate something of what is meant by a theory founded upon or concerning itself with the form of the proposition, the emphasis here being on *the distinction between subject and predicate* as part of that form, and my suggestion as to the amplified significance of the copula would lie along the same line of thought. If the categories, then, indicate what is involved in *being*, what I am saying is that they indicate what is involved in being propositional, apart from the peculiarities of any given proposition, so that it will be improper to treat them as predicates, even as a special class of predicates (what Alexander calls *pervasive* as against *variable* characters of things), since as predicates they would belong to the material, and not to the form, of the proposition.

Alexander's confusions here are aided by his substantialist view of Space and Time, by his treating empirical qualities just as characteristic (characters) of certain spatio-temporal complexes, these space-times being themselves the primary existents apart from all special qualities, and of course his treating the qualities themselves as complications of, as *made of*, Space and Time. Such a view does not account for empirical qualities at all,[1] for the existence of such a thing as red or sweet, and when, in spite of the doctrine of Space-Time as the stuff of things, empirical qualities are recognised, they then appear as *hovering over* or *standing above* what they are supposed to qualify, much in the same way the forms stand over particulars.

This substantialist treatment of Space and Time, then, shows how the categories come to be regarded as predicates, but also indicates the reason why no satisfactory solution of the difficulties can be arrived at.

---

[1] MN: intractability.

Lecture 17 Problem of the 'historical'; Alexander's treatment of the categories as predicates - categories must also be subjects; categories as relations; categories have no obverse

In the *Sophist* we find the same weakness in Plato's position, the doctrine of the *highest kinds* being a treatment of the categories as *pervasive characters* (incomplete emancipation from theory of forms) (from the unhistorical).

Question what is meant by history (historical). In saying that things are historical, we are assuming certain fundamentals. In order to treat things historically, we have to have some notion of what history itself is --- this itself not having a history (cf. Heraclitus on the *eternity* of the "word"[1]).

It isn't a question of *being supported by a certain set of experiences* in the belief that things have causes; it is something which belongs to experience as such and doesn't derive support from particular experiences. Unless there is a causal principle (that things occur when and only when certain conditions are given) the conjunctions that occur in particular experiences are not evidence at all. Only if there is a causal principle has the presence of X when Y occurs any force (any evidential value). What the experience could confirm is that X is the cause of Y, if Y has a cause; *not* that Y has a cause. If causality has to be argued for, it has to be argued for as involved in the nature of existence --- and the "experimental evidence" of scientists is quite inadequate (quite beside the point). [50] The notion of the categorial is involved in even the particular researches of scientists --- they are assuming a view of the *nature of existence*. Philosophers have to tackle the question directly (*reduce*

---

[1] EN: this is an apparent reference to fragment 2 in Burnet: "Though this Word is true evermore, yet men are as unable to understand it when they hear it for the first time as before they have heard it at all." Burnet renders the Greek ςςςςς (logos) as "Word", it can also mean law, rule, or principle, as well as the discourse that is the statement of the law. See John Burnet, *Early Greek Philosophy*, p. 133.

assumptions) and they do so by reference to *logical form*. It is thus that we see the weakness of the doctrine of highest kinds, particularly of *being as the highest kind* --- this would have to be expressed by saying that "All things are", which is not a proposition, having neither a predicate nor, strictly speaking, a subject --- "things" not being a logical term.

Taking the question of categories in general and Alexander's treatment of them as predicates, the position I have supported in logic would involve us in saying that in that case they must also be subjects, that if you are going to be able to attribute (e.g.) particularity to all things, then *the particular* must itself be a thing of which we could speak, and again if we are going to treat all things as different (difference as a character of all things) then *the different* would also be a class that could intelligibly be spoken of --- which I don't think is the case and which I don't think Alexander would allow: and in that case (certain things being treated as predicates but not subjects) there is a metaphysical difference of level, to which real empiricism is opposed; and this is connected with Alexander's ignoring of the proposition, his discussion of these matters simply by setting forth a number of terms. ("Categories *belong* to all existents" --- treats them as predicates, sets up an absolute order or hierarchy which we shouldn't have.)

The connection of this with his substantialism is indicated by the sentence immediately following (p. 189): viz. "if that hypothesis be sound (that existents are differentiations of Space-Time) we should expect to find that pervasive features of things in the characters of their ultimate foundation" --- i.e. of Space-Time, which is the fundamental substance or subject, with which its predicates would have to be contrasted but which in that case, like the One of Parmenides, the substance set above its attributes, becomes simply indescribable and in fact nothing at all. Cf. Argument in "The Meaning of Good",[1] that where you do get a term represented as a pure predicate and as unable to function as

---

[1] EN: this refers to John Anderson, "The Meaning of Good", *AJPP*, 20, 1942, pp.111-140. ENMW: "The Meaning of Good" is reprinted in *Studies* pp 248 – 267.

subject, you will have some kind of relativism, i.e., the notion of the so-called predicate will be ambiguous, covering both a qualitative and a relational meaning. Moore, I have argued, cannot treat good as a subject because it does not really belong to the subjects of which it is predicated, it is attached to them in a quite peculiar way after the attribution of their ordinary qualities, though again there is a partially qualitative sense which keeps it from being recognised as a pure and simple relation. That is, you can say such and such things are *wanted by me* and then formally use it as a subject, can speak of *commodities (things) wanted by me*: but that would be a subject of a rather different kind from what I should call a strictly logical subject like red things --- something to which you can go [51] and see whether it has this or that predicate: you cannot simply go to wanted things or things wanted by me --- that does not give you a *straightforward location*[1] --- you can get it only by going to the situations, "X wants this," "I want that" etc.; i.e., you have the whole complicated situation to take into account in the first instance (from the outset).

Ordinarily then, the treatment of things as being predicates but not subjects would conceal some sort of relational usage, and the question could then be raised how far the *categories* are relational predicates, how far understanding of them involves the introduction of relational material. And that is one view that is taken of Alexander's categories (or any categories) --- that they are really types of relation, as it is quite apparent that some of them are, e.g., causality, and that might be connected with a point that could be made, in terms of my logic, against the treatment of the categories as universal predicates, characters of everything: viz. that a proposition attributing a category to a thing would have no obverse, that when you say X is C_1, (the first category whatever it might be) you cannot equate that to X is not-C_1, because there is no such thing as "not-C_1": i.e. there is no real issue settled by the attribution of a category to a thing and therefore no real information conveyed by doing so.[2] That difficulty would be diminished, at least, if we treated the

---

[1] MN: a starting point.
[2] MN: C_1 – 1st category, C_2 – 2nd etc.

categories as forms of relation, because we would then still regard them as all-pervasive and yet be able to raise real issues *concerning them* (in which they are involved). We should say that there is no real issue as to whether X is or is not caused but there is a real issue as to whether it is or is not caused by Y. Similarly, if we took particularity as a category, we could say that there is no real issue as to whether A is or is not particularised but there is a real issue as to whether A is or is not particularised in B [Similarly, as to whether it is *a particular C*]. Now if that is the position, if we can only get a real issue by further specification, by going beyond the category to another term, we can still on this view account for the *apparent* issue regarding the category itself: e.g. if we can significantly say that X is not caused by Y [and perhaps by any of a group of agents we are interested in], that would indicate how we could form the general notion of not being caused at all, how we could fancy there was a meaning in "X is not caused" even though we were wrong in doing so, and how then there could be an issue whether or not causality is a category (is categorial), even though causality (or being causal) is not a logical term, i.e. is not the sort of thing we recognise [or we recognise it is not the sort of thing] as locating or being located.
[52]

Lecture 18 Identity: as a relation; as coextension; the problem of coextension; the doctrine of unlimited intension.

Possibility of locating categories as relations, leading to getting over some of the difficulties of treating them as terms (whether A is cause of B a real question even if Whether A is cause is not) and thence to explanation of how there can appear to be issue of latter type, issue as to whether *X is a category* --- on which there are in fact divergent views: cf. – as opposition between view that *everything is causal* and epiphenomenalism, view that some things have no causal force, and between view that everything is caused and belief in "freedom", belief that some things are not brought into being by anything else. (i.e., beliefs, respectively, that some things have not initiating force of their own and that some things don't require an initiating force from outside). Similarly, belief that *there are* universals implies that particularity (being particular) is not a category --- though this doctrine (similarly with the causal ones) would be held with some confusion.

Bk II, Ch. II. Identity, Diversity and Existence.

There is a difficulty about treating identity as a relation, on the realist view that a relation holds between two different things, but popularly at least we do raise the question of identity in the same sort of way as we raise the question of causality --- agreeing, i.e., that *Is X identical or not*? is not a real question, we seem to attach some meaning to the question "Is X identical *with Y* or not?" Is it or is it not possible to identify this and that? (e.g., we should be said to *identify* the author(s) of the Ern Malley poems as McAuley and Stewart[1]). However, there are still difficulties even if we take, as seems quite reasonable, identity to be at least co-extension: i.e., if we identify X and Y only when XaY and YaX,

---

[1] ENMW: This is a reference to the Ern Malley hoax discussed by Anderson in Cullum, G. and Lycos, K. (Ed.) *Art and Reality* (Sydney: Hale and Ironmonger, 1982) pp 78 - 79.

then that would not seem to cover the entire usage because we should say that, although X and Y are coextensive terms, they are not *the same* term, and we shouldn't say that X is coextensive with X: that, like the ordinary identity A is A, would be considered to convey no information at all.[1]

What emerges here is that there is a broad sense of identifying in which we identify different things, different terms as in the case of X and Y, and there is a narrower sense of identity in which we say that being different means *not* being identical. Now it may be that the narrower sense cannot be made good, that we can assign no precise meaning to "the same", in the sense in which different things cannot be *the same*, but at least it would be vitally important in considering Alexander's or any other theory of identity to decide which of these two senses was the one we were concerned with.

Now if for the sake of argument we took identity to mean coextension, we are faced with what may be called the problem of coextension, the question whether there ever are two coextensive terms; and here we are faced with a difficulty at the outset if we reject identical propositions, that even where XaY and YaX, X and Y are not coextensive in the sense of being predicable, i.e., significantly and truly predicable, [53] of precisely the same subjects, for, whereas Y is predicable of X, X is not predicable of X (XaX not being a proposition), so that, curious as it may seem, X belongs to the extension of Y but not to the extension of X. We might try to get out of the difficulty by saying that, when we say any term of which X is predicable is a term of which Y is predicable and vice versa, we really mean any term other than X and Y themselves, though it would certainly seem curious to accept A as part of Y's extension on the strength of the syllogism XaY, AaX, therefore AaY, and yet not to accept X as part of Y's extension though Y is predicable of X in exactly the same way as it is predicable of A. [A solution other than the

---

[1] ENMW: In much of the discussion that follows, Anderson utilises traditional syllogistic logic. Although Anderson's own work on logic is as yet unpublished, he follows the conventions and expressions contained in Latta, R. and MacBeath, A. *The Elements of Logic* (London: Macmillan and Co. 1953).

acceptance of "identical propositions" is to say that *X and Y are coextensive* means neither more nor less than *XaY, YaX.*]

What would commonly keep this problem from being recognised is just the fact that the ordinary logician would mean by the extension of a term the various *individuals* to which the term as a general description would apply; but that resort is not possible to a logic which *attacks* the distinction between the purely particular and the purely general, which considers that any term, even a so-called individual, must have generality, must be a sort of thing. And similarly the formulation in terms of *place*, the assertion that the extension of Y is the various places where Y occurs, would not seem to get over the difficulty if it is argued, as I have done earlier, that we cannot specify places except in terms of or by reference to qualities. Here of course there is the possibility of saying that, although we cannot know a place, cannot "identify" it, except in terms of qualities, still those qualities are not what is meant by its being a place, and that we can say quite significantly that *wherever X occurs, Y occurs* (taking that as the spatio-temporal interpretation of XaY) even though we could never specify those places of occurrence except in other terms, qualitative terms; and similarly YaX will mean that in the places where Y occurs, X occurs (that the places where Y occurs are places where X occurs), and hence the two propositions XaY and YaX would be a statement of coextension [of *coincidence* of places.]

It might be contended that two "coextensive terms" are not really different terms, that if X and Y are inseparable in reality then what we really have is two *words* for the same sort of thing, not two different sorts of thing that accompany one another – and in that case we should have only one term, just as in the case where we have words in different languages standing for the same sort of thing; taking Moore's example, *good* and *bon* and *gut* are three words standing for a single term or sort of thing. And then the question might be raised whether this objection, assuming it to be sound, would apply equally to complex terms, whether, as in the formal theory of definition

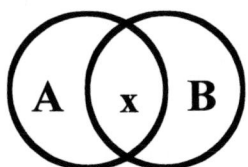

where X is the common part of two intersecting classes A and B, the terms X and AB cannot be regarded as different though coextensive terms; whether the complex term is not arrived at in a different way --- by cutting off, so to speak, the outlying parts of A and B, and whether then it [the part of A cut off by B or the part of B cut off by A] couldn't be said to have what certain theorists call a different *intent* from X **[54]** or what is sometimes called a different primary meaning even if X and AB as descriptions are applicable to precisely the same things.[1] One question would be whether "primary meaning" can have anything but a subjective sense, i.e. one relating to the knowledge and interests of some particular person, but having no relevance to the question of the characters of the sorts of things referred to, which would be what logic was concerned with;[2] [i.e. there might be no *objective* primariness (primary meaning)].

Now another question here would be whether the doctrine of unlimited intension, the doctrine of the "infinite complexity" of things, wouldn't affect the issue --- the position being that any predicate carries with it any number of other predicates, and the question being whether, in view of that complexity, it isn't quite possible that X and Y always occur in precisely the same places even though they are different qualities.[3] Now the fact that two terms have a different intension might not be enough to show that each of them, being complex, has some other term coextensive with it, in the sense of something quite peculiar to it. There might, taking two terms P and Q supposed not to be coextensive, be some special combination of terms RST which occurred

---

[1] NT: cf. Stout, Manual of Psychology — EN: this refers to George Frederick Stout, *A Manual of Psychology*, 4th ed. (revised by C.A. Mace), (London: University Tutorial Press, 1929).
[2] EN: in the text this sentence is enclosed in round brackets.
[3] MN: Qn how cd we know which is which — answer that, when 2 qualities go together *in fact*, we can still know one without knowing the other. (But how, if we knew *both*, could we tell to which of them *another person* was referring?)

neither in Q nor in anything else except P, even though R occurred in many other places and similarly with S and similarly with T. This, however, involves a certain misunderstanding of what is meant by a complex term; it would suggest the very doctrine of (certain) ultimate and indescribable qualities which, on the theory of infinite complexity, is being denied. Indeed, on the complexity view,[1] even in knowing the conjunction RST, we are in that very fact knowing something quite peculiar and not just knowing the putting together of a number of intellectually separate entities; and equally, in knowing P, we are already knowing something complex even if we only use one word for it, something with a varied content even if we haven't tried to set out that content in a number of different descriptions. And not only so, but on this view, apart from the complications that we recognise but do not name or recognise vaguely but not *distinctly*, there will be qualities of the sort of thing in question which we do not recognise at all though they are just as much *there* as those we do recognise.

We may encounter some of these problems again in discussion of Alexander's theory of substance, but what I am suggesting here is that the doctrine that two "simple" terms, in the sense that each is referred to by a single word, cannot be coextensive in the sense that they cannot be distinct qualities or distinct sorts of things which nonetheless always do occur together, (that doctrine) may quite well be based on a doctrine of simple terms in another sense, a doctrine of simple or ultimate or unanalysable qualities (the *elements of description*, as we may put it) --- a doctrine that empiricism is *bound to reject*. **[55]**

---

[1] EN: the text here reads "on complexity view", "the" added between "on" and "complexity".

Lecture 19 Identity: in a narrower sense; Alexander's debt to Hegel; Kant: the categories and the forms of the proposition; categories as involved with the form of the proposition; identity as being a subject.

On the whole I would say that it is possible for two terms to be coextensive --- for X to be different from Y and yet to be, in the broad sense, "the same thing". This still leaves us with the question of the *narrower* sense of identity in which there would be no question of one thing being identical with *another*. Here I would say that Alexander doesn't really argue thoroughly the question of specific categories --- his discussion is incomplete (fragmentary) and there are many possible views that he doesn't consider (some of his chapters are particularly weak: others better: but no *systematic* discussion). It may be said that on the whole, even if his view of the categories should be correct (even if he should give a sound list of categories), his explanation of them might often be quite wrong; that he often takes a hasty view, as here on *identity*, even if he were right in holding that it means occupation of a space-time.

Though Alexander refers to the later Platonic dialogues and to Kant as sources of his doctrine of the categories, it also, I would say, owes a great deal (unacknowledged) to Hegel; when he takes existence or determinate being to be the unity of (to unite) identity and diversity (difference),[1] he is simply following the first part of the Hegelian exposition of the categories, where Hegel takes being and not being as synthetised in determinate being or something. (He also uses *becoming* to designate the synthesis of being and not-being). Generally speaking the categories are not very clear-cut in the Hegelian logic, which is perhaps inevitable when he proposes to develop one out of another, to treat them as successive stages in the self-unfolding of the Idea; and that is exemplified in the extraordinary profusion of categories in Hegel and in the recurrence of practically the same conceptions at what he supposes to be three different levels --- the levels of being, essence and the notion. The supposition is

---

[1] MN: when he says it is the *union* of identity and difference (*Sophist*? Kant?)

that we start with the most abstract (form of the Idea), bare being, and work up to the most concrete, the notion or the Idea itself, but the difficulty is to know why logic, or the doctrine of the forms of the Idea, shouldn't on that view cover everything, embrace all science, why there should be any such thing as historical or particularised reality and not just a procession of conceptions --- but we might argue that in some sense Hegel does take logic as embracing all science and does take any historical particularisation, any *concrete* (historical or particular) situation, as a stage in the unfolding of the Idea; whereas Alexander draws a definite line between the categories and empirical conceptions, particular descriptions of things, a line which it is especially hard for him to draw since he thinks that all things are specifications of Space-Time itself, that Space-Time and nothing else is that of which things are composed. The admission that there are empirical qualities (red, etc.) is an admission that things are not composed of pure Space-Time.

However, if we are going to have a theory of the categories which [56] is not arbitrary, if we are going to be able precisely to determine what are categories and what is to be understood by them, we must like Kant in his Metaphysical Deduction of the Categories connect them with the proposition, though perhaps not so much with the different forms of proposition referred to by Kant as with the form of the proposition, with what is common to all propositions. Of course without accepting Kant's classification of propositions we might still say that what we are really doing in distinguishing types of propositions is to bring out more clearly what is involved in the proposition as such. Let us say for the sake of argument that in distinguishing the affirmative and the negative propositions (making the distinction of *quality*) what we are really doing --- or what is of importance to logic in what we are doing --- is to indicate that every proposition has at once an affirmative and a negative character [affirms something and denies something, whether it is formally affirmative or negative] --- and it might be possible to take a similar line in regard to the distinction of *quantity*; the general position being that the distinction of the forms of the proposition is the best way of drawing attention to characters of the proposition as such, i.e., to what should be dealt with in a theory of the categories or in a theory of Space-Time.

[*Quality*. Bringing out the negative character of affirmative propositions and the affirmative character of negative ones; might be said to be what is done in obversion. *Quantity* --- possibility of bringing out the universal character of (or the universality in) particular propositions, and conversely? Bosanquet etc., viewing particular as really universal, or as not really a proposition until universal is brought out. XiY: *what* X are Y? AXaY, etc. In any case, to say X is Y is to recognise that some specific X are Y and thus to recognise the possibility of a syllogism AaY, AaX, therefore XiY, even if it is not *solely* as the conclusion of such a syllogism that a particular proposition is grasped. As to "the particular in the universal"[1], we have (a) subalternation, (b) recognition of the possibility of syllogisms in which our proposition (XaY) is the major premise; thus recognition of pairs of propositions AaX therefore AaY; thus recognition of possibility of arguing AaY, AaX therefore XiY --- thus back to subaltern.][2]

So, in terms of Alexander's description of identity as occupation of a Space-Time and of my own doctrine of *location* as the function of the subject in a proposition, it may be possible to take as the meaning of identity *being a subject*[3] and thus to recognise it as something that is involved in any proposition whatever, to recognise it as belonging to *the form of the proposition*. Thus when we "identify" a thing in the sense of locating it, we can be said to be finding out what *subject* it is. [Or, in finding its identity, are we finding *its* subject? When we try to *identify* the perpetrator of [57] a crime, we are looking for an X of which we can say "X is the perpetrator". This form would suggest *coextension* --- we want to be able to say that X and X alone did it. But here we have the assumption of individuals --- even if X is

---

[1] MN: This is the "particular in the universal". — EN: 'This' in the MN refers to the whole of the previous sentence, beginning with "In any case...".
[2] MN: A term's identity comes out in its being a subject: like its kind in being a predicate.
[3] MN: *having* place? (every situation has place).

coextensive with the perpetrator (and of course it is not impossible that there were many perpetrators) we think of him as especially the subject[1]: i.e. perpetrating the crime is *one* of the activities of a continuing existent: thus we are seeking to know of *what* continuous history the criminal action forms a part. Also "the perpetrator" could be regarded as short for "the subject (whatever it may be) of which perpetrating the crime can be truly predicated", i.e., as stating a problem or question --- *of whom* is it true that he *did this*? Thus seeking an identity (seeking to identify) is seeking a subject --- or place.] That is not of course to say that we are not at the same time describing or characterising it; as already argued, we never have a pure subject but always a descriptive term, a term which may also be a predicate; we never have a simple subject but always something complex, something which will involve diversity, even though *identity* and *diversity* (or difference) can still be said to have different meanings; and this necessary complexity of *the subject or the identity* forces us again to criticise Alexander's doctrine of point-instants as the elements [identities] of Space-Time, as the things to which ultimately the categories apply, because a point-instant [no extension; hence nothing?] could have no qualities and could not then be any sort of subject.

Now if we say identity means being a subject, we might be tempted by way of symmetry to say that diversity means being a predicate, or that it is the predicate which in the proposition conveys diversity. And without going into that question for the moment, we can at least see that the diversity of subject and predicate, the fact of the two being different terms, is necessary for the significance of the proposition, necessary so that we may have a real assertion, a real issue and not just a form of words. And we should observe that just as the subject can also be a predicate the predicate can also be a subject, so the predicate also has in it the element of identity --- though we need not take this as the generic identity or universality which Alexander distinguishes from bare or numerical identity. Rather it would be just that same bare identity, the point being that when we say that

---

[1] MN: We want to identify the *perpetrator* or *perpetrators*.

certain things are of *the same* kind, we are not using "same" in the precise sense in which we speak about *the same thing* or, as I have put it, in which we refer to a thing's being a subject.[1,2] **[58]**

---

[1] NT: See Hegel's *Logic*, trans. Wallace -- early part on the categories.
[2] NT: Alexander, though weak on many of the categories, has solid discussion of causality — EN: this second note occurs immediately below the one noted in previous footnote.

Lecture 20 Difference or diversity: as being a predicate; involved with the subject; identity embodies difference; identity embodies all other categories; the copula as occurrence – existence and truth the same; the category of existence; the copula as a relation; positive and negative copula; existence involves relation; the five categories of the proposition

"Generic identity" would come under another category --- not that of identity but that of universality.

When we approach the second category, the category of difference (or diversity, as Alexander calls it) we have the problems, what is its relation to identity, and, again, what does it mean in terms of the proposition: and we might be tempted to maintain that if we considered identity as *being a subject*, difference would mean *being a predicate*, though actually being a predicate could be taken as Alexander's generic identity, as exemplifying the category of kind or universality --- for though, as we have seen, all terms are general, it is as predicates that they *exercise* their generality, that they function descriptively. From that point of view difference would not be the same as being a predicate, though there is the interesting question whether we do not know, or get to know, qualities as *differences*, as distinguishing marks between one thing and another, as solutions of problems. [Whether we don't *come to know* (learn) things *by the want of them.*][1]

Another line of approach might be by saying that having treated identity as *being a subject* we are then faced with the fact that a subject is not a whole proposition, that differentiation or distinction is required even for the subject to be a subject, that it is required in other words, in order that the location may locate; and we might even say that identity in some way *embodies* difference, that to have identity is to have distinction; and here we might, without subscribing to Hegelianism, see something in Hegel's view of the unfolding of categories from one another, of

---

[1] MN: and the satisfaction of the want ? (Ah! *That* is it!).

all the subsequent categories being somehow involved in the first one, identity --- in this sense, that a subject or thing is not a thing in itself, is not a self-subsistent or simple entity, is actually propositional or situational --- that propositions or situations are not made up by taking things and adding relations, that the thing is not prior to the proposition but that what we call a thing already embodies relations, has within the various distinctions which are explicitly set out in the proposition or (perhaps more accurately) in a group of propositions.

It is, then, in the sense that the subject or thing is already a proposition or situation that the category *identity* could be said to embody all other categories. But even so, even if we could work out or expound a set of propositions that could be said to be embodied in a subject, the subject as such is not a proposition; it, so to speak, calls for propositional completion; and it is the recognition of this incompleteness or *pointing beyond itself* of the subject that would lead us to say that in recognising identity we at the same time have to recognise difference. The point is not just the one already made that even if the subject and predicate were coextensive the two would have to be recognised as different terms --- the distinction here is not specially between the subject and the predicate but between the subject and the rest of the proposition. Of course **[59]** it could be said that any such line of argument is of a forced character, that there is no such necessary order of categories, that what has to be recognised is just that in any situation we find identity and we find difference and we find a number of other such features; but without going into the question of the order of the categories at this stage, we can, I think, see some force in the contention that the subject comes first,[1] this being what gives colour to, even if it does not justify, philosophies which take the thing or term as prior to the proposition, the simple as prior to the complex --- in a word, philosophies of *essence*.[2]

The next element in the proposition, the next thing with reference to which we can distinguish a category, is the *copula*. It is, of

---

[1] MN: *where* before *what*.
[2] EN: the last sentence of this paragraph is enclosed in round brackets.

course, recognised even in theories which don't admit the universality of the subject-predicate form (don't admit, i.e., that all affirmations are of the form *S is P*) that a *verb* is required in an assertion, that this verb conveys the actuality of whatever is being asserted, and that gives us the category of existence[1], gives us the notion of actual occurrence over and above the notion of location. Now without going into some of the more difficult cases, we can see that the ordinary verb has two functions, a formal one and a material one, that it conveys something specific, some special character of what occurs or is actual, over and above the mere fact of occurrence which is conveyed in any proposition; and it is this *formal* feature, this fact of occurrence, that is conveyed peculiarly by the copula, the verb other than the verb to be having the functions at once of copula and of predicate, a fact which is partially indicated in some grammatical forms. --- If you say *X grows*, that amounts to *X grow is* where the grow is material, the *is* is formal: which we normally indicate by putting the copula (formal) next the subject and saying *X is grow(ing)*.[2]

The category of existence conveys the function of the copula in the proposition, and I have suggested as alternative expressions "actuality" or "occurrence" or "actual occurrence"[3], and of course, since I hold that (actual) occurrence is what is meant by truth, that means that for me the notions of truth and existence are the same. But of course whenever you raise the question of truth you also raise the question of falsity, just as in raising the question of identity you also raise the question of difference, and the point can be connected with the previous one in this way --- that just as the subject isn't the proposition or *isn't by itself*, so the subject with the copula isn't by itself; it raises the question of ways in which this combination of location and occurrence can be completed, a point which is implied in the very use of the expression *copula*, signifying something which has to *couple* or relate things, and at the same time it raises the question of different ways of coupling, the distinction between the positive

---

[1] NT: cf. Alexander, Bk.II, Ch.II.
[2] MN: Willis. ENMW: The intelligibility of this sentence is improved by inserting 'to' between 'subject' and 'the'.
[3] MN: also continuity. — EN: inverted commas added in this line.

(affirmative) and the negative copula **[60]** --- and these considerations bring us to the category of relation, the point being that existence involves relation in the same way as identity involves difference. And of course the relation is completed by the introduction of the other term, the predicate, the introduction of *what* the subject is related to in one or the other way, of what it is that occurs at that location and what does not occur at that location; and this brings us to the function of description, to the category of quality or universality or kind (the *generic* Alexander was speaking of.)

A first consideration of the form of the proposition gives us those five categories of Identity, Difference, Existence, Relation and Universality. We could say again that existence and relation are features of any situation, the one having regard to the fact that it is a situation, that it takes place, the other to the fact that it is complex, has constituents; and the point of the category of universality is that it is a situation of a certain kind or description, the indication of this being pre-eminently the function of the predicate.

Lecture 21 The five categories of the proposition (cont.) - Relation: possible distinction between predication and relation; the function of the predicate - the qualitative predicate and Time - the predicate as activity.

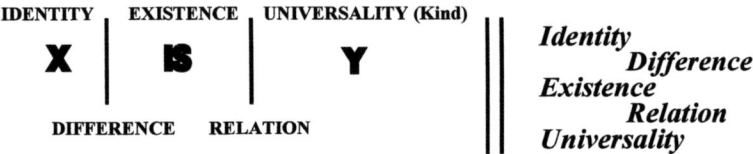

Just as identity (because it is a *limited* identity) expands into difference (or *other*), so, in thinking of existence, you have something limited --- you have to think of difference of existence, *other existence* --- and so you have to bring in relation. (Take suggestions so far, in Alexander's manner, as hypotheses.)

We have now to consider the very important question of the distinction (if any) between predication and relation; whether predication is a *type* of relation; whether relation is something *distinct from* (over and above) predication. We regularly make a distinction between qualities and relations in that a relation holds between two things, whereas a quality does not raise the question of a second thing.

It seems clear that there is quite a definite distinction between predication and other relations, and yet it also seems clear that predication is some sort of relation (is a relation in some sense), because just as we say a relation has two terms, so a proposition (predication) has two terms, and we have important considerations of whether the terms can be interchanged similar to the question what relations are reversible or symmetrical.[1] We

---

[1] ENMW: This sentence is reproduced as it appears in the manuscript. The meaning becomes a little clearer if 'which is' is inserted after 'interchanged' and 'of' after 'question'.

have different types of what we may call the predicative relation, i.e., we have the four forms, just as we have different types of *spatial* relation, etc. We could still of course distinguish between a relation in which the two terms were external to one another, in which the second term lay outside **[61]** the region indicated by the first, and the case in which the second term did not lie outside but fell within that region (as we should take to be the case in predication); but that would not be enough to distinguish between what I've hitherto referred to as *relations in the strict sense* and the attribution of a quality to a subject; for if we take the relation of *containing* (A contains B), then the second term here falls within the region referred to by the first and yet it is certainly what we call an *external relation* in the sense that there can be no general argument from the characters of one term to those of the other, that, roughly speaking, anything can be inside anything else [chalk in my hand], so that the criterion would not seem to be an adequate one (viz. falling inside v(ersus) falling outside); and then again there is the difficult case of whole and part, i.e., the case where B is not merely inside A but is what we call a part of A, as when we say that a person has as hand or a foot [finger in my hand]: this *having a part* would also have to be distinguished from having a predicate, even though in some sense the part is not a separate thing and even though its qualities may largely not be independent of the qualities of the whole and vice versa. This would imply that the conception of location is not an adequate account of the function of the subject, since a part is certainly located in the whole and yet the relation is not the same as when a quality is said to be located in the subject, i.e., when the subject is said to be *qualified* in a certain way.

Now the difficulty may be partially met by taking that account of the function of the predicate, i.e., the qualitative predicate, which associates it specially with Time (this question being obscurely linked with the discussion in the *Sophist*), the conception of the predicate, namely, as an *activity* of the subject or a way in which the subject is going on, from which point of view the statement that X is red would be more exactly expressed by saying that X is *redding* or going on in the red way. [And the subject wouldn't just *locate*, wouldn't just be the *place where* the activity is going on but would be *what* is going on in that way.] It is accidental that in some cases in English there is a ready transition from an adjectival to a substantive form and vice versa and from either form to the form of a verb; what we may call an *operational* form, whereas in other cases there is no such ready transition [no verb "to red"] and we have a conception which is peculiarly adjectival or peculiarly substantive or peculiarly operational in English usage.[1] Logically there is no distinction between the adjectival, the substantive and the operational --- these are just different ways in which[2] we can consider any material whatever.

Something more, then, is conveyed by saying that red, e.g., is an activity of a certain subject than by merely saying that red exists, or goes on, within a certain region; being red, in other words, is not the same as having something red inside or again as having a red part, though in both of these cases red is going on inside the subject in question --- to say that I have something red in me (e.g., blood) is not the same as saying that I am red. **[62]** Of course, any quality that I may have, e.g., humanity, is not all the qualities I have, and the suggestion is made[3] that any such quality occupies a particular part of me, not the whole; but it may be argued that that would amount to saying that a particular part of me is human and another part not --- which is certainly not what we mean when we say that I am human or that I am a man. In fact, that illustrates an important distinction, among the predicates of a given sort of thing, between those which are predicates of the whole subject but not of all parts of it and perhaps not of *any* parts of it, those which are predicates of the whole subject and of any parts of it, and those which are predicates of parts of it and perhaps of all parts of it but not of the whole. For example, it is true that I am a man and not true of any part of me that it is a man; on the other hand, it is true that I am organic and it is true of any part of me that it is organic. So that we seem to require the notion of a quality or activity of a whole subject with no question of marking off within that subject the location of the activity in question --- except perhaps in a temporal sense, taking the whole

---

[1] MN: so *adverbial* — "manner" — another *form* of the same material.

[2] NT: *categories* in which?.

[3] NT: cf. Alexander on substance.

subject to be the being throughout its history (a person throughout his life, e.g.,) and considering the possession of the quality or the carrying on of the activity as occupying only certain portions of that history --- though there again (on the temporal side) we have to distinguish between occasional or intermittent properties and properties which persist throughout the thing's history.

And perhaps the point may best be made in this way, that as soon as we recognise the differentiation of the identity of the subject (i.e., the subject's complexity),[1] failing which it would be complete in itself, or perhaps as soon as we recognise existence, which may be taken to involve continuance or duration --- (as soon as we do that), we are necessarily introducing the notion of something containing something else, or, what comes to the same thing, of something being alongside something else,[2] and therefore in the very fact of giving an account of qualitative predication we are necessarily introducing relations which are not qualitative predication --- we are necessarily, in fact, introducing spatio-temporal distinctions and connections.

---

[1] MN: Rel^n bet be^g & nt be^g (Y): "contrad^n", chge. — EN: this appears to be shorthand for "Relation between being Y and not being Y: "contradiction", change".
[2] MN: phases.

Lecture 22 Relation: problems of Russellian logic; relational arguments; conjunctive and disjunctive arguments.

Bk II, Ch. IV. *Relations*.

Predication as relation in the primary sense, from which we *go on* to secondary sense (juxtaposition, disjunction).

With regard to the question whether predication is a relation or not, we may say that even if predication is distinguishable in important respects from other relations, still the proposition has two terms and there are different ways in which the two terms may be coupled or uncoupled, and it does seem that we should have a sufficiently general sense of *relation* to cover these types of connection, even if there were a *special* sense for "after" and the like.[1] The question is acute in connection with the Russellians; with them it is a question of a distinction between a *logic of relations* and a predicative logic with insistence on the S-P form. And in taking the substance-attribute view of the proposition[2] (though I would reject distinction between substance [63] and attribute, still I am insisting on predication in the sense of qualification, of a predicate *describing* the subject), I would seem to be coming down on the side of a qualitative logic and leaving out relations. But even if it is hard to work this view out in full, I still think that the original or primitive type of issue is a qualitative one (whether or not a thing is *of a certain description*, or of a *special kind*) and that relations come in later. Question whether the treatment of the proposition as a relation isn't bound up with the class view --- or a view akin to that, as in Russell's *types* of propositional relation, membership of a class, inclusion of one class in another, identity etc. --- and whether it makes sense to say that there is a *relation* between a thing and its descriptions, between X and "being of the kind Y", where X is said to *be* Y, i.e., when *X is Y* is asserted. That there *are* class

---

[1] MN: Coext^n: in some sse, - same thing. (Any other "rel^n" even if symmetrical in no sse, - same thing.) — EN: this appears to be shorthand for "'Co-extension': in some sense – same thing. (Any other 'relation', even if symmetrical, [is] in no sense [the] same thing.)

[2] EN: "of the proposition" is written as MN, inserted in the text.

relations, definable by groups of propositions, is a different point. Perhaps on the whole it is best to say that predication is *not* a relation, that there isn't a "relation" between X and *going on in the way of Y* when X is going on in the way of Y; best to keep relation for that whose terms are *distinct things*, different locations (which would cover the case of whole and part) --- while admitting that predication *involves* relation or implies that there are relations within (and without) the situation which it specifies. It is then for the "qualitative" logician to show how we pass from qualitative assertions to relational assertions, how relations in the strict sense are included in the field of his logic, even if they are in some sense "subsequent" to qualities.[1]

Relational Arguments. The doctrine of relational arguments (Russell, Bradley etc.) is an attempt to show that there are arguments other than the syllogistic, because in syllogistic argument the same term (in the first figure, the middle term) functions now as subject and now as predicate and this is clearly in line with a qualitative logic (or *substance-attribute* logic, if it is remembered that substance can be attribute and attribute substance); and it is on that account that the devotees of a relational logic insist on types of argument other than the syllogistic.

In my logic I have recognised (as non-syllogistic arguments, yet starting from qualitative assertions) the conjunctive and the disjunctive arguments --- of the forms AaX, AaY therefore AaXY, and AaX, BaX therefore (A or B)aX, respectively. And I think these types of argument are connected with the relational theory and with the fact that any propositional logic must give some account of relation(s). And here I would say that *just as*,[2] in discussing identity and treating it as *being a subject*, I contended that a subject is not a proposition and so we have to go from identity to difference, and yet that a subject in some sense has to

---

[1] EN: the last four sentences of the paragraph are enclosed in square brackets.
[2] MN: *just as* – all this/*so* (next page).— EN: this MN is an indication that the first clause of the comparative "Just as...., so....", is the entire sentence beginning with "in discussing" and ending with "very first one"; and that the second clause starts on page 64 of the manuscript.

be understood, in addition, as propositional, as something not simple but complex the relation of whose constituents could be expanded (could be made explicit) and thus there might be some sense in saying that all the other categories are involved in the very first one, **[64]** *so* we might take conjunction and disjunction as illustrating the sort of thing we could *mean* by this complexity, the conjunctive term indicating the possibility of a propositional expansion of a given term as in the notion of "defining proposition", the class of *men* being defined by the proposition *some animals are rational*, and the disjunctive term indicating what is meant by (spatial) extension and by things being alongside one another, indicating the combination of *parts* as distinct from the combination of qualities, both types of combination being involved in what we mean by the complexity or the *spatio-temporality* of a thing or term. It is not going beyond the predicative (subject-predicate) logic to recognise that the same subject has many predicates and the same predicate many subjects --- and recognition of these facts leads straight into the theory of relations.[1]

The disjunctive term especially, then, gives some indication of how in terms of predicative logic we can take account of extent or quantity, and we can consider the matter further in connection with what is sometimes taken to be a peculiar type of argument, viz. quantitative argument, the sort of thing which is thought to constitute mathematical reasoning, reasoning working especially with relations of equality but also to some extent with relations of inequality. What I want to argue is that, in spite of what most mathematicians believe, this reasoning is syllogistic or at any rate can be taken syllogistically, and we can approach the matter first of all by taking equality and inequality of classes as typical of equality and inequality in general. (Of course, just as in the case of the extension-intension formula, we are concerned with the two cases of coextension and inclusion, there being no real sense in talking about equality and inequality in the cases of intersection and exclusion.)

---

[1] EN: this sentence is enclosed in square brackets.

The argument that if A=B and B=C, then A=C (an argument for which compilers of geometries think it necessary to have an axiom) is seen, if we take "equal" or coextensive classes to be representative of equality in general, to be syllogistic in character. A=B is represented by the propositions AaB and BaA. B=C is represented by the propositions BaC and CaB and from these propositions we get the syllogistic conclusions AaC and CaA, which, as before, represent A = C.

If this version of the argument is defensible, it depends not on an axiom but on syllogistic reasoning.

I have here represented the equal quantities by the same letters as I have used for the coextensive terms, and it might be argued that this shouldn't be done, that when we say that two things are equal in quantity or two quantities are equal the terms that are coextensive should be expressed rather differently --- that we mean something like this, that all things measurable by means of A are measurable by means of B, and vice versa; and this might be important in the case of inequality **[65]** because it might be argued that in one sense of measurement it is the larger quantity that measures the smaller number of things. But without going into the details of this, we can at least see that whenever two quantities are equal there can be said to be two classes of things which are coextensive and whenever one quantity is greater than another there can be said to be one class which includes another, and so there will be no logical confusion, no serious danger of misunderstanding, if we do not make the translation in each individual case and if we even use the same letters for the terms as for the quantities. (I won't bother in the case of inequality to consider the view that the thing should be put the other way round. Any reversing would work the whole way through.)

If that is the position, then, we can similarly give a syllogistic justification for the rule that when A is greater than B and B is greater than C, then A is greater than C (A > B, B > C, therefore A > C). We can take this as before as meaning that there is a class A which includes the class B (BaA, AoB) and similarly there is a class C which is included in the class B (CaB, BoC) --- and then the argument is: A>B represented by the propositions BaA and AoB, B>C represented by the propositions CaB and BoC, and these propositions giving the conclusions CaA and AoC, which represent A>C. It is from the two A premises that we get the conclusion CaA and it is from the A premise in one line and the O premise in the other (i.e., in either of two ways) that we get the conclusion AoC; and these two conclusions, signifying that the class A includes the class C, are translated as before into A>C. That is the syllogistic justification for the rule regarding things greater than other things, the rule that, in Russell's terminology, *greater than* is a transitive relation.

Now we noticed that there were two ways in which from the data we could prove AoC, and that means that to get the conclusion we were aiming at (to get the conclusion we *reached*) one of the two O propositions was superfluous. We could from the three premises that BoA, CaB and BoC have concluded that A includes C, i.e., we could have got that conclusion just as well even if it had happened that AaB --- that A was coextensive with ("equal to") B instead of including it. We can leave that possibility open, then; we can have --- if A is *greater than or equal to* B (i.e., if A is *not less than* B) and B is greater than C, then A is greater than C. And similarly, if A is greater than B and B is not less than C, A is greater than C: i.e., BaA, AoB and CaB imply CaA and AoC, even if it happens that BaC.[1]

So that, as well as having found a formula for *equal to* and for *greater than*, we now have one for *greater than or equal to*; (namely, for A→B, BaA — the A proposition); and thus the argument *If A is greater than or equal to B and B is greater than or equal to C, A is greater than or equal to C* is represented by AAA in the first figure (Barbara).[2] **[66]**

So we have found that these various types of quantitative reasoning which were held either to depend on special axioms or to emerge from direct observation but in either case to be non-

---

[1] NT: A→B, B>C ∴ A>C; and A>B, B→C ∴ A>C. — MN: A ≥ B (A is greater than or equal to B) BaA.
[2] MN: BaC, CaB ∴ CaA.

syllogistic, can be represented syllogistically; and it is possible that other types of relational argument given as examples of the breakdown or limitation of syllogistic logic (Bradley, Russell) can be coped with by syllogistic logic --- though of course we had (have?) to understand how to do the translating, how to express given relations by means of ordinary propositions, but that may not be essentially different from "putting into logical form". And the strain of the position is eased, I would argue, by the fact that we are recognising the qualitative proposition itself as a spatio-temporal situation and hence as involving from the outset spatio-temporal relations, relations of containing and being alongside of and following, and so forth.

At any rate, since mathematical reasoning is regarded as one of the largest and most important exceptions to the reasoning recognised in syllogistic logic, it is important to see how it itself can be treated syllogistically and above all not by having recourse to axioms as all-pervasive major premises (or "principles") any more than to the syllogistic dictum as a major of this sort, but simply by reference to the concrete facts that we are considering in each case.

Lecture 23 Quantification of the predicate – relational arguments.

I had been suggesting a way in which mathematical or quantitative arguments could be expressed syllogistically, viz. by assuming that *equal classes* represent equality, etc., and I was saying that the ordinary way of dealing with these matters --- trying to turn the given argument into a syllogistic argument *by means of a dictum* (as major premise) --- is not more successful than it is in the case of syllogism. Thus if you take "Whatever is true of a class is true of every member of that class" (which is often taken as the dictum), then that is not really an original major premise on which the Barbara syllogism can be based (on which the validity of a particular Barbara syllogism can be established); it is the *form* of the Barbara syllogism itself --- and just as easily as you could see the correctness of that dictum you could see the soundness of a concrete syllogism in Barbara, the point being that it is the *syllogistic premises* that prove *the conclusion*, not anything outside the syllogism that proves the whole syllogism. In the same way, then, as I have indicated, "things that are equal to the same thing are equal to one another" is not a general major premise for all equational arguments but is merely a way of stating the *form* of such arguments; and that means that we can directly see the validity of any concrete argument of that kind just as easily as we can see the soundness of the so-called axiom. (I suggested to you, of course, that the form would be more fully and exactly expressed as two AAA syllogisms.)

Now a connected question is that of the quantification of the predicate, [67] which is an attempt to turn the proposition into an equation, thus doing away with the important distinction of function, the important *order*, of the terms in the proposition, for of course, the assertion *All A are some B*, meaning that a part of B and the whole of A coincided, would be equally expressed by saying that *Some B are all A* --- both would mean that, in our terminology, B *includes* A. Of course, the cases of intersection and exclusion would not lend themselves in the same way to equational treatment; the doctrine of the proposition as class relation does not exactly coincide with the doctrine of the proposition as equation, because if e.g., you expressed intersection by saying that a part of A coincided with a part of B, that would be perfectly consistent with the whole of A coinciding with the whole of B, i.e. with coextension --- in fact, the coincidence of part with part would *follow* from the coincidence of whole with whole --- so that we could not really express intersection equationally; and that is still more evident with exclusion, where the question is not of coincidence but on non-coincidence.

And that brings us to the vital point in criticism of either the class-relation view or the equational view of the proposition, viz. that it does not give us a means (or gives us at best[1] a most cumbrous and roundabout way) of denying a proposition because, in fact, the denial of a class relation isn't itself a class relation, and the denial of an equation isn't itself an equation [but the denial of a proposition must be a proposition --- a proposition must be an *issue*]. Thus to say that the relation of coextension does not hold between A and B is not only to leave us with the disjunction of (choice among) four different possibilities, but the very assertion of that set of possibilities is an assertion of a different kind from the one [from][2] which has been taken the type of proposition --- the equation or class-relation or whatever it may be --- and thus the theory in question breaks down.

And this matter of contradiction of the form in which we can say that a given assertion is false, is the crucial point in the criticism of any view of the proposition other than the predicative view, of any attempt to find a copula other than *are*; because while we can find a symbol for denying that B is greater than A, viz. Bnot>A (alternatively, $B \leq A$ — B is less than or equal to A), in order to understand what these forms mean, in order to see how they contradict one another, we have to come back to the subject-

---

[1] EN: the text here reads "least", with "least? *best*" written above it.
[2] EN: the text here reads "from the one which has been taken the type of proposition", "[from]" has been added.

predicate form.[1] We can always say of course *It is false that* so and so, but that only leads to fresh complications; it means that we are taking "so and so", and a number of other things, as belonging to the class of things that are false, of course there is no such class. Similarly with the *existence* interpretation of the proposition --- to say that *XY exist* and *XY do not exist* are contradictions is to say that we are distinguishing existing things from not-existing things, and there are no not-existing things. It is to come back to the predicative form, with the unsound treatment of "existing" as a predicate; and the attempt to express the four forms in **[68]** this way suffers from the further defect (a connected one) that it is only by reference to the predicative form, to the possibility of saying that a thing which is X is also Y, that we can understand what XY means. Similarly in the negative case: if people represent the assertion *All men are mortal* by the assertion *There are no non-mortal men*, it is only by reference to the S-P form that we could understand what is meant by combining those two terms or by being unable to combine them.

It is in connection with relations that it is specially urged that the copula *are* is not universal; it is said that we are only forcibly reading into various assertions and that we could just as easily say *ArB*, where *r* might be any relation at all. And, in general, that sort of theory is shown to be false (is defeated) by *contradiction* --- by the fact that where we have an assertion of any character, where we have any series of symbols PQR, to *contradict* that assertion we have to introduce a *not* at some point, and that *not* breaks the complex up into parts, one of which is the subject and the other the predicate; or, as it is commonly put in terms of discourse, an issue is a question of whether something can or

---

[1] MN: If B ≤ A is BaA, then Bnot->A is BaA, so B>A shd be BoA. [It s ass^{md}, w qnt^s, t intsec^n (& excl^n) is *impos*: t it s a qn of *ei^r* eq^{ly} *or* | be^g gtr n • oth.] [Hce BoA → AaB!]. — EN: the first sentence in square brackets appears to be shorthand for "It is assumed, with quantities, that intersection (and exclusion) is impossible: that it is a question of either equality or one being greater than the other". The second sentence in square brackets is shorthand for "Hence ⟩*Some B are not A*⟩ implies ⟩*All A are B*⟩ !" This implication depends on the translation rules given in the first sentence of the MN, and on the assumptions stated in the second sentence.

cannot be said of something else, i.e., of whether one term is attributable to or *predicable* of another.

And while contradiction is our main point in the criticism of non-predicative views, implication is another important point; and that can be applied, e.g. to the class-relational or equational view of the proposition, for if we say that *All A are all B*[1] the question how we are able to draw inferences from that is bound up with the *distributive* use of the sign of quantity, for we are certainly not supposed to argue X is A, (All A are *all* B) ∴ X is *all* B. But if we rule out the *all* and simply conclude that X is B, we have to do the same in the first (major) premise; we ought to see, in other words, that an attempted *collective* use of "all" has no place in our argument. The sign of quantity goes with the subject, it is used distributively, i.e. by *all A* we simply mean the various A's, not all the A's lumped together in a collection; and quantification fails because it is an attempt to have two subjects in one proposition, thus confusing the functions of the two terms and obscuring the nature of denial, which depends upon which of the terms is subject and which is predicate, i.e., on what is being asserted of what else and thus could equally significantly be denied of it.

And an important point here is that the content of these proposed special forms or special interpretations can all be expressed by means of our four forms without any ambiguity or confusion, that "All A are all B" can be expressed by the two propositions AaB, BaA; and the trouble is with people who, when they get additional information about certain things, try to pack it all into the formula they started with, instead of using several formulae for the several pieces of information they have, and thus introduce ambiguities and difficulties where none need have been. Thus when people ask, or think it desirable to know **[69]** "Whether the predicate of an A proposition is distributed or not," meaning (where the proposition is AaB) whether it is also true that BaA or not, whether the given (original) assertion is "true of all B" as well as of all A, they show that they don't understand

---
[1] EN: emphasis added.

what is meant by *all* as well as what is meant by *distribution*, because to say that B is distributed in this proposition means that any part of B's extension can be substituted for B without loss of truth, means that when AaB and XaB ("X belongs to the extension of B") it would equally be the case that AaX (X substituted for B in AaB); in other words, the whole of A would coincide with any part of B --- which is certainly not what they mean; and the *invalidity* of arguing in this way (AaB, XaB therefore AaX) is precisely what we mean when we say that the predicate of the A proposition is *undistributed*, so that B would be undistributed in AaB even if it were also the case that BaA. [Theorists in question too busy wondering about what is *true* to be careful about what is *said*.]

Lecture 24 Relational arguments (continued).

We have been discussing the question of the reduction of relational arguments (e.g. quantitative relations) to syllogistic form. The first point is that if we are going to have formal validity, then we should have to have an argument similar to the syllogism, or it might be better to say that we have to know what sorts of argument of a transitive type are valid --- what relations, in other words, are transitive; we couldn't tell merely by looking at the argument *ArB, BrC* ∴ *ArC* that it was valid (as we could by looking at AaB, BaC therefore AaC, whatever A, B and C might be) --- it would depend on our particular knowledge of the relation (r) in question whether we took the conclusion to follow from the premises or not. Clearly there are some relations in the case which we *couldn't* argue in this way (e.g. *next* to, *father* of); we cannot validly argue A is next to B, B is next to C, ∴ A is next to C, or, equally, A is father of B, B is father of C, ∴ A is father of C. That is a conclusion which in the second example would always be *false* (if the premises are true) and in the first example would be false in the case of most series --- in all, in fact, except where you have a series of three arranged in a ring;[1] and the question is just *when* we can have our special knowledge of special relations expressed in some way so that we can without further ado that the conclusion follows from the premises.

Now of course theorists maintain that we do this by setting out a formal principle like (expressing it roughly, for brevity) "things which are equal to the same thing are equal to one another" and using it as the "major" or first premise in an argument; so that we should have, for example, first the *particularisation* of that principle in the form "things which are equal to C are equal to one another" (that would now[2] become our major premise), then "A and B are things which are equal to C", *therefore* "A and B are equal to one another" **[70]** --- though we couldn't very well make the step from the general principle to its formulation with special reference to C by inserting a premise, "C is the same

---
[1] EN: here a drawing of such a ring is given as a MN.
[2] EN: the text reads "*not*", with "now?" written above it.

thing". However, we can see what the general form of such an interpretation of the reasoning would be, viz. that when certain types of relation exist some other type exists, or that all sets of terms such that some relation holds are such that some other relation holds; (that would be the type of our major premise); then our minor premise would be that A, B and C are a set of terms such that the first-mentioned relation holds; and our conclusion would be, therefore they are a set of terms such that the last relation lives. It is along such lines that people generally attempt to syllogise relational arguments.

But there are two objections to that sort of procedure, *first*, that the statement that a number of terms fulfil certain conditions is ambiguous until we have assigned to each of the terms its precise place in the set of relations in question, and in doing that we get away from the syllogistic form again; *secondly* (a point I made before), that the supposed general principle which is taken to justify the form of argument in question, like the dictum of the syllogism simply *is* that form of argument, the only difference being that instead of putting symbols for the various terms we simply leave blanks. (Perhaps there is not even that difference, because in the dictum we have somehow to make it clear that the two premises have a common term and that their other terms reappear in the conclusion; so it is not just a matter of the *form* (quality and quantity) of the three propositions, not just a question of leaving blanks, but involves indicating in another way than by assigning a specific symbol *which* of the blanks have to be filled up in the same way, by the same thing or content --- and which in different ways: which have to have *different* fillings or content. What has to be done, then, is something *equivalent* to the indicating by symbols of a form of argument.)

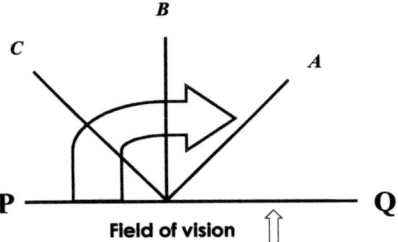

Accordingly while we might think that full analysis in any given case would disclose syllogistic reasoning, we might not be able to conduct that analysis in certain cases. We can do so in the case of equality and inequality, however, by translating these into coextension and inclusion; and it might be possible to argue that in every case of a transitive relation one or other of these forms of translation was possible --- one or other, I say, depending on whether the relation was reversible (symmetrical) or not. For instance, if we take the argument A is to the right of B, B is to the right of C, ∴ A is to the right of C, we might contend that that is only a special case of the *greater than* argument; such arguments of course being relative to a certain *point* and *direction* of view, we could take the one to the right as indicating a greater range of some sort than the one to the left (e.g. A than B, B than C --- a greater swing *from P*) --- e.g. a greater turning from a postulated "extreme left" position – **[71]** so that all we have to know is [how][1] this relation of greater and less *goes with* or *corresponds* to the relation "to the right of" (or a relation "greater than" corresponds to "to the left of" -- so long as we keep the type of correspondence consistent throughout an argument); and in whatever precise way we formulate our terms, we shall be back to syllogistic argument as in the case of unequal quantities. And of course we still have exactly the same *complication* of the argument (≥): viz. that when A is to the right of B and B is *not to the left* of C, then A is to the right of C (it being always assumed at the outset that all the terms, A, B, C etc belong to the same range or fall within the same "perspective", point of view): i.e., we should have "not to the left of" meaning "either to the right of

---

[1] EN: the text here reads "all we have to know is to this relation", "[how]" substituted for "to".

or level with" just as "not less than" means "greater than or equal to" ($\geq$), and we should have it indicated, as before, by an A proposition without an accompanying O. And even if we didn't think it possible to speak of a precise position which was the extreme left, we could still comprehend, it might be argued, the statement that A is "further from *the left*" than B.[1]

Now that again could be expressed by saying that there are more positions to the left of A than there are to the left of B, because all positions to the left of B are to the left of A but some positions that are to the left of A are not to the left of B (e.g. B itself). Or putting the position the other way round (eliminating the term "left") we can say that A is to right of B (ArB) when and only when all things to the right of A are to the right of B ($R_A a R_B$) and some things to the right of B are not to the right of A ($R_B o R_A$). At any rate, there you have the two propositions required for a relation of inclusion. And now, if we say that C is not to the right of B (C not-r B), we have, as before, that all things to the right of B are to the right of C ($R_B a R_C$); and taking that with each of the two (other) premises in turn, we can conclude that all things to the right of A are to the right of C ($R_A a R_C$) and some things to the right of C are not to the right of A ($R_C o R_A$), giving us the conclusion that A is to the right of C (ArC). (It is assumed that A, B and C are points in the given range.)

ArB corresponds to $R_A a R_B$ and $R_B o R_A$
Cnot-rB corresponds to $R_B a R_C$, ($R_B a R_C$)

These give the conclusions $R_A a R_C$ and $R_C o R_A$ which correspond to ArC. Thus we have the argument *ArB, Cnot-rB, ∴ ArC* represented by two syllogisms.

Now it might be argued that in making this transformation, particularly in passing from *A is to the right of B* to *All things to the right of A are to the right of B* we are begging the question, that we are assuming, not demonstrating, the transitiveness of "to the right of". But the point is that, in making that transformation,

---

[1] NT: i.e. we know the *swing*, even if not the extreme points.

we are not giving a *definition* of "to the right of"; we are observing a set of interrelations in a field of vision and then seeing how our argument can be founded on what we observe (have observed) [1] --- i.e. looking at the field and seeing what is meant by **[72]** moving round from the left, we can see that in order to go beyond A it would be necessary to pass through B but that in going beyond B it is not necessary to pass through A: that is, whether or not it is said that these things are part of what we *mean* by "to the right of", they are certainly things that can be grasped *along with* the grasping of the relation "to the right of". And if that is so, then the syllogistic representation of the argument is quite legitimate. (We see that "to the right of" involves these two (further) interrelations and that they involve it.)

This raises the further question whether syllogism itself is in a similar position, whether it can be said that one can observe in one situation the whole truth of syllogism (or of "the syllogistic principle", *the form of* [syllogistic] *implication*). It may seem hard to do that but, if not [i.e if it *can't* be done], how can we justify the principle of syllogism? We would have to say that we got our belief in syllogism in some way other than by observation: and it would be very hard to justify that.[2] The point also could be made that the argument BaC, AaB therefore AaC "assumes and doesn't demonstrate" the "transitiveness" of the relation "a"; what, as before, the argument demonstrates is *AaC*. Similarly, then, the putting of the "angular" argument in syllogistic form doesn't demonstrate the transitiveness of "to the right of" but shows more clearly how the particular conclusion is demonstrated[3] --- or brings out the relation (resemblance) of that demonstration to other demonstrations. Failing that, or failing some way of simply *seeing* the validity of the process,[4] the "argument" would be simply arbitrary; we should have no reason for saying that it held for this sort of relation and not for some

---

[1] MN: (classes — ord^r) (when & only when), cf. p → q → r — *sequence*.
[2] EN: the first three sentences of this paragraph are enclosed in round brackets. The remainder of the paragraph is enclosed in square brackets.
[3] EN: corrected in the text from "demonstration".
[4] MN: distrib^n.

other sorts of relation (say, being five miles distant from) if we couldn't see the whole situation and see the *difference* between one sort of relation and the other. It is no objection, then, to any way of setting forth the argument that it implies that we can *see* transitiveness; for, if we couldn't, we couldn't set forth the argument (argue in that way) at all.

What now confronts us, then, is the question whether in every case of a transitive and irreversible relation we should not make the translation in this way, whether we shouldn't say, in other words, that we must have the direct recognition of that complication of relations, that we must, in knowing that P is an ancestor of Q, either know at the same time or at least have the opportunity of knowing that all ancestors of P are ancestors of Q ($A_P a A_Q$) and some ancestors of Q are not ancestors of P ($A_Q o A_P$), e.g., P himself; whether in fact the position is not that we *observe* the relation to be transitive and then that our argument on that basis in regard to the assertion of that relation in particular cases or between particular beings is of a syllogistic character.[1] [Just as "to the right of" implies an outlook --- a *range* of directions from a point and a *direction* (of turning) among members of the range --- so, it can be said, "ancestor of" implies a series of generations and a direction of descent; and argument concerning it has the same character as argument concerning a time-series or the time-relations of a set of events.] [73] This transformation, then, which enables us to conduct the argument syllogistically, is what has to be taken as an object or a possible object of our observation. Of course, here as elsewhere we must remember that observation can be mistaken --- i.e., observation in so far as it is concerned with the conclusions that do follow from given premises is as capable of being mistaken as other observations are.[2]

We have, then, a method of dealing with relations that are transitive and either reversible or irreversible --- i.e., of putting them into syllogism in either case. There are more complicated relations (e.g. A is an aunt of B, C is a child of A, therefore B and

---

[1] MN: A is before B = all events before A are before B & some events before B are not before A (also A is *not after* B = an A prop^n).
[2] EN: the last sentence of this paragraph is enclosed in round brackets.

C are cousins) which it might be difficult, and at any rate cumbrous, to put into syllogistic form. There are also, as I pointed out, conjunctive and disjunctive arguments which we recognise as valid but which are certainly not syllogistic. But I am suggesting that the same sort of priority that belongs to the predicative form of the proposition (the attribution of a quality to a thing) can be said to belong to the syllogistic form of argument, in which if A qualifies B and B qualifies C, A can be said to qualify C.

Lecture 25 Predicative logic: the distinction of quantity

Having shown you the sort of way in which relational argument could be assimilated to qualitative argument, especially syllogistic argument, I want to tackle the matter in a more general way and advance some considerations which support the predicative view and reject (are opposed to) any sort of relational copula, unless the ordinary copula is called a relation

I have already stressed the importance of contradiction as well as implication in dealing with supposed exceptions to the ordinary procedures of predicative logic and I may just remind you of the sort of argument I've put forward in upholding the doctrine of the four forms, viz. that we are confronted in discourse, or in consideration of what makes discourse intelligible, with the notion of an *issue* --- something about which people can dispute --- and then that in order even to disagree people must have a certain measure of agreement, that they must have a *point of agreement* or, as we say, a common subject that they are disagreeing about, and then they must have *a point of disagreement* (they must have) opposing views of what can be said of the subject; and the possibility of these things depends on the recognition of the propositional subject (the point of agreement), the propositional predicate (the matter of dispute in relation to the subject), and the positive and negative forms of the copula, indicating the two possibilities of affirming or denying the predicate of the subject. That gives us, then, those three essential constituents of the proposition (subject, predicate, copula) and the distinction of *quality*.

Then the distinction of *quantity* is arrived at from a consideration of the convertibility of terms, of the fact that any predicate may be a subject and any subject a predicate, or, in the terminology we started with, any point of agreement may be a point of disagreement and vice versa [there must be agreement about what the point of disagreement *is*; **[74]** what it is whose application to the subject we are disagreeing about]; especially, then, that the subject is a general or descriptive term having various instances, which leads again, with some reference to contradiction, (and implication?), to the distinction between universal and particular, it being perhaps possible, at least in the order of knowledge, to assign some priority to the universal, to treat *where A is, B is* as meaning *wherever* A is, B is --- or, as we put it, *all* A are B --- and then to see that the contradictory of that will not be the universal negative but the particular negative. As before, subject is not an absolute place but a sort of thing: a *content*: hence has extension, can "expand" into instances. Note that the supporters of relational theories take the *subject* for granted: don't see that it's a sort of thing, equally capable of being a predicate, and thus that the first and "most natural" proposition is one which has *two* such terms. Their inability to see this is connected with their belief in "individuals" --- which can only have *external* relations to one another,[1] the *predicative* "relation" being possible only between sorts of things: hence for them even the predicative proposition is an assertion of a relation (external) like *membership* or *inclusion* etc.[2] It is in some such way, then, that I suggest we can, from the notion of an issue, arrive at the four constituents of the proposition: subject, predicate, copula and sign of quantity, or at the four forms of propositions, A,E,I,O.

Now these are quite general considerations, i.e. they should apply to any assertion whatever and thus to what we call the assertion of a relation, so that when we say that A has the relation r to B, we are presenting people with the issue, or with the possibilities, of A's having the relation r to B or not having the relation r to B; it is a question of the possibility of saying something about A just as much as if we said *A is x*. Well, then, A is the subject and *related in a given way to B* is the predicate, and if we are going now to insist on the convertibility of terms, on treating this predicate as a possible subject, then we shall insert the sign of being a subject, commonly the word *thing*: we shall say "A is a thing having the relation r to B" and treat *things having the relation r to B* as something to which in its turn predicates can be applied. And that means that we are treating all terms as qualitative, the distinction between *thing* and *quality* being

---

[1] MN: Hume.
[2] EN: the last three sentences, beginning with "As" and ending with "*inclusion* etc", are enclosed in square brackets.

merely the distinction between a term functioning as subject and the same term functioning as predicate, the only point, when we give what could be called a "relational term", being that we don't specify the qualities in question --- that we mean *the sorts of things, whatever they may be*, that have the relation r to B.

And if that sort of view is sound, it means that instead of treating a relation as an alternative form of copula, as another way besides the predicative (besides predication) of coupling two terms, we shall treat it as *falling inside terms*, as part of the material, never part of the *form*, of the proposition. And that view is in accordance with the position put forward in the previous[1] lecture [75] that we cannot tell without special empirical knowledge whether a given relational argument is valid or not, whereas we can tell from the form of the syllogism whether it is valid or not even if we know nothing whatever about the terms except that they are terms; even if we only know that there is one sort of thing called A, another called B and another called C, and have no acquaintance with A,B and C themselves, we still know that the syllogism AaB, BaC therefore AaC is valid. This would be followed up in the view that we haven't got *logical form*, we haven't reached what the argument really is, until we *could* tell from its form alone whether it is valid or not; so that the syllogistic forms are the strict logical form of the arguments involving the relations *greater than*, etc.[2] To say that relations exist inside terms is perhaps a special way of emphasising the fact that relational terms are *subjects*,[3] or of emphasising the complexity, and particularly the quantitative or extensional character, of things, which I have already linked with the conception of the subject as locating. At the same time this is in accordance with the suggestion by Alexander and others that we should regard a relation as a whole situation i.e. where the relation falls *within* something not *between* some things, though in detail it would of course be different to treat ArB as a term and to treat rB as a term i.e., *A* having the relation r to B and *something* having the relation r to B.

---

[1] EN: the text here reads "last", with "previous" written underneath.
[2] EN: this sentence is enclosed in square brackets.
[3] EN: the text here reads "*subjects*", with "things which" written above it.

Now these considerations are relevant to a question that gives Alexander some difficulty, the question of the *sense* or *direction* of a relation, the question of a relation and its converse (Russell), the converse being the sort of relation that must hold in the opposite direction to that of the given relation, as in the case where A is before B and B accordingly is after A, *after* being the "converse relation" to *before*: the difficulty, then, of distinguishing between A has the relation r to B, and, B has *the converse of the relation r* to A (A r B, B $\overset{\text{U}}{\text{r}}$ A), which it might reasonably be argued are only two sets of symbols for the same assertion. Alexander has to say things like this (Bk II, Ch. IV, p. 243): "The propositions, A is the mother of B, and (the same) B is a child born of A, describe precisely the same fact, but they describe it in the light of general relations of maternity or filial relation." But we can say that in exactly the same way (with the particular restricted sense of "filial" in question, i.e., *born of*) these two "general relations" describe precisely the same facts and so it is not clear how we could get a different "light" in the two different cases. Considering then the distinction between A precedes B and A succeeds B,[1] Alexander says (p.243): "The quality of the situation is the same but its direction is reversed." But that illustration is not really important because we are considering two quite different and, in fact, incompatible relations that might hold between A and B. And when Alexander comes back to the question of the relation and the converse relation we find him making this admission in the case of two assertions, 'Edinburgh is north of London', 'London is south of Edinburgh',[2] that "the difference is not indeed a verbal one though perilously near to it, but a difference of aspect or description, what Aristotle expressed by saying that the two things *are* the same, but not in their *being*."[3] **[76]**

That is a difference which I think few of us would acknowledge [cf. however, coextension and difference in "intent"] even if we found it possible to admit in general the possibility of being

---

[1] MN: Does he mean *B succeeds A*? (Probably *not*).
[2] EN: single inverted commas added.
[3] NT: p.243, italics in text.

"perilously near" to a merely verbal difference without being precisely there. In fact, it bears out what I have said, that on the relational view the distinction cannot be made, whereas on the predicative view it is perfectly obvious, viz. that we are treating Edinburgh as one of a class of things north of London and London as one of a class of things south of Edinburgh, so that we have two quite distinct statements even though each is true if the other is true. In the case of mother and child there is a certain complication in that only one being can be the mother of a given child, on the other hand many beings can be children of a given mother --- a point that Alexander's parenthesis "(the same)" is perhaps intended to cover --- so that again clearly the two assertions are not the same. But, finally, even if the relation were what Russell calls one-one, that is something that could be known only as a matter of empirical fact and not as a matter of logical form, and we could still see the difference between the two statements of the relation and the converse relation on the predicative view, the difference namely that we have two propositions with different terms. To say that is not to prejudge the question of the difference between two equivalent propositions with the same terms, say E and its converse (AeB and BeA). The point we should have specially to emphasise there would be that they have different subjects, that the point of agreement or point of reference is different; and if it was thought that the same could be said about the two statements of relation, it has to be pointed out that it is only in the AEIO forms that we *have* a subject in the required sense, i.e., that one of the two terms which has the function of *locating*.[1] Relational statements, then, have to be *put* in the AEIO forms; that, as noted, is how we see how they are denied or what the dispute is about when they are disputed.[2]

---

[1] EN: the text here reads "*location*", with "locating?" written as a MN.
[2] EN: last sentence enclosed in square brackets.

Lecture 26 Universality: there are no universals nor particulars; 'system' in Hegel; optimism in Idealism; the 'concrete universal'; the notion of system; the systematic thinker.

Universals. (On the question of universals and relations I might comment on G.F. Stout's article --- *AJPP*, Sept, 1940.[1] On the question of universals, see reply to Merrylees June, 1929.[2] This might be more closely related to what I want to treat in Alexander.)

With regard to the question whether there is such an entity as a universal, Alexander says (Bk II, Ch. III, p.208), "Strictly speaking, there is no such thing as a particular or a universal"; but since he does not conduct the discussion with reference to the proposition, a good deal of the force of *this* (or of his discussion)[3] is lost, and his discussion might be taken to imply that there *are* such things as universals. He continues (loc. cit.): "All things are individuals. But every individual possesses particularity which separates it from others of the same kind, or under that same universal; and it possesses universality which converts its bare particularity into individuality. Universality is thus a categorial character of all things." If you take universality and particularity as *predicates* of things (that is connected with the theory of the categories as predicates) it would be hard to say what "possessing particularity" is but *being a particular* --- and similarly with universality. But if you connect your theory with the proposition, particularity will be the capacity for being a subject and universality will be the capacity for being a predicate. [It might still be argued that these are *predicates* of any term, but passing over that difficulty] if we treat these two characteristics as possible functions in propositions **[77]** (as *actual* functions in specific propositions) we are not faced with Alexander's

---
[1] EN: this refers to G.F. Stout, "Things, Predicates and Relations", *AJPP*, 18, 1940, pp.117-130.
[2] EN: this refers to Anderson, "'Universals' and Occurrences". (ENMW: reprinted in *Studies* pp 155 – 121.)
[3] EN: in the text the parenthetical phrase is written above "*this*".

difficulty: i.e., we have a possible way out, in which we say that, instead of there being particularity on the one side and universality on the other, a thing has both particularity and universality, i.e. it can be a subject and it can be a predicate in a proposition; and this view is more concrete than Alexander's.[1]

Any expression you use is subject to criticism. I use *sorts of things* as equivalent to *terms*, signifying that any term is capable of each of these two functions and there are no bare generals or bare particulars. At the same time there is one danger in connection with particularity into which we do not fall with regard to universality. Many people will deny that there is such a thing as *a universal* and yet assert that there is such a thing as *a particular*[2] (I have done this.) You could point to a thing and say it is a particular, but could not point to a thing and say it is a universal. All this may be connected with the suggestion of a certain "priority" of identity or being a subject, with the tendency to have a philosophy of *things*, instead of sorts of things or situations.[3] Still, we have to recognise that the general notion of "a particular" has no meaning; we can speak about (point to) *a particular man* but there is no question of whether or not a thing is *a particular*. That is connected with Stout's wrongly attributing to me the view that a thing is identical with the sum of its qualities (or predicates). I do not think there is any such complex whole. I would say that when we know a thing, we know it as a such and such (e.g., as a man and having various other properties) but the notion of the totality of its properties is one (notion) we do not possess. It is not merely that we do not know the totality but that we are speaking loosely if we even speak about the totality. That position is partly supported by the point I am now making, that even in speaking of a thing as a particular at all we are speaking of it as a particular instance of a certain kind, as a thing of some sort, and that any issue is concerned with things of some sort; and so when we are dealing with a thing as a man,

---

[1] ENMW: Anderson's use of brackets at the start of this sentence is confusing and can be either be ignored or retained while still rendering an intelligible meaning to the statement.
[2] MN: & have said there is nothing but particulars.
[3] EN: this sentence is enclosed in square brackets.

then there are a great many of his characters that we are not concerned with and may not be concerned with at any other time.

It is very difficult to formulate these points clearly, but we might say --- to be a particular is to be a particular something, as is indicated by the very word "particular" which has relation to the word "partake of" and to the notion of "being an instance of": and "being an instance of", on any obvious view, is just *predication*. "Socrates *is an instance of* man" is the same assertion as "Socrates is a man". It might be possible for us to think of Socrates without thinking of him as a man, but we must think of him as *a something*, as of some kind, if we are to think of him at all. On the other hand, I would say that the notion of a *totality* of characters belongs to the logic of totality or system, the Hegelian logic, and that although thinkers like Stout, for example, have many apparent differences from Hegel, actually the same Idealist strain can be traced in the thinking of all of them. **[78]**

One aspect of this Idealist strain is *optimism*, the notion of things working together for good, and in that connection you get a close link between Kant and Hegel. The notion of system or unity as a regulative idea has a great deal in common with the Hegelian notion of system as an actually governing principle, the point being that Kant avoids some of the difficulties by maintaining that systematisation is a way in which we have to think rather than a way in which things have to be. You get a trace of the same Idealism in James in spite of his avowedly pluralist view, when he thinks that things are gradually *becoming* unified, even if they have not become unified yet.

This notion of system or totality is the same as the notion of the concrete universal, of all things (all characters of a thing, e.g., or all the members of a class) being under a simple governing principle or all being manifestations of the same central idea. (Criticism of concrete universal will be given later. It is really opposed to a propositional view and that is why I reject it in "Universals and Occurrences".) For a propositional logic there would be no essential unity either of a thing or of a class. To say various things are all men does not imply that they are united in *humanity* (they are manifestations of human nature). On the contrary they will be related in ways we could call quite accidental or "irrational". There is no simple principle of which all these other characters are manifestations (expressions), no central character to which all the variations contribute. There is no assignable reason why a person of such and such a character should have certain other characters; there will be *some* "implication" or connection of characters, we may be able to say X is Y, ∴ X is Z, because Y is Z, but there will be no character which necessitates *all* the (other) characters of X.

With regard to the notion of *system*, I have often spoken of the distinction we draw and must draw between having a number of opinions and having a position. Even if we deny axioms or first principles[1] from which a body of beliefs can be demonstrated, we all do recognise the distinction between a "scatter-brained" individual (or an eclectic thinker) and one whose views exhibit some *coherence*. What account, then, can a pluralist or empiricist give of "system" (in this sense), of holding a "position"? One point would be that such a person (systematic thinker) recognises universal connections and especially *causal* connections, though we all do that to some extent and it may be questioned whether we would define *a position* just in terms of more or less (seeing of connections). Still, that is one line of distinction --- the person who is (perpetually) surprised as contrasted with the person who has inferred. But, trying to get a more definite criterion, we might suggest that having a systematic view or having a position involves having a logic. It involves also, of course, having a fair amount of positive information, but gaps in a man's knowledge do not lead us to call his view unsystematic; the point is that he has certain ways of tackling apparently diverse questions, and that might be partly covered by his *having a logic* so that his ability to see contradictions, e.g., leads him to appear to have **[79]** knowledge in a field in which he is actually uninformed. It is in connection with logic, then, that we get one possible view of what systematic thinking might mean, viz. that while it will always involve a knowledge of universal propositions and causal

---

[1] MN: fundamental tenets.

connections it especially involves classification --- that is, that the systematic thinker is the man who recognises genera and species, who makes divisions and of course connects them with one another, and who will thus have a conception of a field of investigation in a way that the non-classifying thinker cannot have.

But then again the systematic character of a person's thinking seems to have something to do with social importance, not just with the fact that he links different questions together by means of a classificatory scheme, but that he has a special interest in current questions ("the questions of the day") that he links them together and makes some kind of policy or, at least, what we call an "outlook". The questions of the day, of course, will fall within a number of ordinarily distinguished fields, but, then, any two fields will have something in common, and the distinguishing mark of the systematic thinker, the person who classifies or, more generally, who has a logic, will be the fact that he emphasises, *brings out*, such common features. Whatever may be the importance of the social factor, it is the factor of logic that is the decisive one; it is it that supplies a common background for inquiries and leads to their being embraced in a single inquiry; i.e. in *certain* cases, because of course there is no thinker so systematic that he can make all his inquiries parts of one inquiry --- though that is what the *idealist* would be maintaining or, more exactly, that all inquiries are *necessarily* parts of one inquiry.

Suggestion above regarding *apparent knowledge* of a field coming from logic (e.g., recognition of contradiction). It could be argued that "system" (in other than the idealist sense --- and partly even in it) means the possession[1] of an *apparatus criticus*, a knowledge of certain main *types* of error and fallacy: e.g., relativism and the various types of "material fallacy". (Still *classification* but classification of views and errors.) This would still have a partly *social* character --- the types of confusion to which men are most prone.[2]

---

[1] EN: the text here reads "position", with "possession?" written as a MN.
[2] EN: this paragraph is enclosed in square brackets.

Lecture 27[1] Notion of the 'term ': both particular and universal; the universal as concrete or abstract (Moore-Russell view); universals as governing principles – connection with social activity; Cornford and 'Moira' – criticised by Taylor and Burnet; Parmenides on the Pythagoreans; Heraclitus

The essential position that I put before you is the notion of *the term*, of that which can equally qualify and be qualified, that which would be at once particular and universal. An interesting matter in connection with this whole question is what leads people to make this distinction, to set up the universal as a supposedly distinct entity, whether it is the theory of an abstract or of a concrete universal. An interesting point again is the relation of the Idealists' views on universality to their views of mind; how their notion of the mind-dependence of things is worked out within the doctrine of the universal as in some way governing particulars.

On the other side there is the *universalia post res* position --- the conception [80] of the abstract universal in which *insistence* is put on its being arrived at by a process of *abstraction*, separated (from particulars) by mental operation; and that is closely connected with an instrumentalist logic, with the notion of the concept as something we employ in the ordering of the material we are concerned with --- that is to say, *we* do the ordering by means of concepts and other instruments of thought, whereas on other views it is the *universals* that do the ordering, they are themselves the governing principles --- and that is manifest, at least, in the doctrine of the concrete universal whether or not it comes in in doctrines of the abstract universal.

For instance, the theory of forms at first sight looks like an abstract theory; the form is the pattern to which things can conform to a greater or less extent; but yet the doctrine of the *form of the good* comes very close to the theory of the concrete

---

[1] NT: Read *Universals and Occurrences*, [*AJPP*] June 1929; a little of the same in *Realism and Some of its Critics*, [*AJPP*] June 1930.

universal, i.e., it is essentially a governing or organising principle, a principle of unification by the establishment of the proper order or hierarchy. And if we took that view of the supreme form or *form of forms*, we should have to take it in some degree of the lower forms as well.[1]

There are traces of both positions in the Socratic theory. The doctrine of forms is not simply Bosanquettian logic (the *concrete* view) but the form of the good comes close to that, and the *Republic* throughout is dealing with principles of organisation, of proper order or hierarchy, which might be a way of trying to meet some of the difficulties of the (earlier) view as it appears e.g. in the *Phaedo*. So whether you agree with Bosanquet or not, a contradiction of the interpretation of the *Republic* along Idealist lines is worth entering on.

Then there is the Moore-Russell doctrine of the abstract universal, but it also is not an instrumentalist doctrine; universals are not just concepts. You simply get a dualistic theory of different levels of reality --- existence and subsistence --- so perhaps there you get the best example of a doctrine of the abstract universal. That sort of rationalism leaves a great many problems unsettled: problems which it does not even discuss;[2] whereas Absolute Idealism and instrumentalism are at least trying to tackle the difficulties; and it would be in recognising considerations of that kind that one could see how much less Moore and Russell have been able to form a school than idealists or pragmatists. There has been a school deriving (considerably) from Russell but it owes its success to the element of instrumentalism in it (Cambridge school).

If then we recognise the existence of such examples (such possible views of universals) we can say that doctrines of universals are connected with the notion of ordering or arranging things, whether on what we may call the lower level of *our* adjustments of things for our purposes or on the higher level of the operation of independent *governing principles*, and in that

---

[1] MN: the forms making particulars "what they are".
[2] EN: the text here has ":", changed to ";".

way we can see a connection between doctrines of universals and "mentalism" (mentalistic doctrines) because it is from our experience of the mind's disposing and arranging of things that we get our general notion of disposing and arranging. And in that way, I would suggest, we get not merely a kinship between doctrines of universals and doctrines of the mind-dependence of things, **[81]** but we might actually be able to say the former are derived from the latter, at any rate from some notion of the *human* disposal of things, because the question to begin with may be social rather than individual --- the real content of the [doctrine of] governing principles may be the interrelations of forms of human activity.[1]

Cornford in *From Religion to Philosophy*[2] follows the modern anthropological line and connects the doctrine of Moira (destiny) with social arrangements, i.e., with the notion of social division, of different social *provinces*, Moira being the distribution or apportioning of things according to their provinces, the allotting of them to different forms of social activity; and the primitive gods are just personifications of those different departments of social life. Now some doubt might be cast on the direct connection that Cornford tries to establish between this allocation of powers and the theory of forms, but at least we could have this general conception of a governing principle as being derived from, having its original content in, a particular form of social activity such as sowing, reaping, hunting, war etc.

Taylor and Burnet differ from Cornford. They would say he makes too sharp a distinction between the Olympian and the Dionysian aspects of Greek religion. [Cornford *doesn't* say that science derives from the Olympian and mystical philosophies from the Dionysian strain: he *runs together* the science and the mysticism.][3] I should say that in dealing with the pre-Socratics Cornford over-emphasises the religious side of their work and

---

[1] NT: ("forms and human activities": AJB & TAR)! — EN: these initials refer to A.J. Baker and T.A. Rose.
[2] EN: this refers to Francis Macdonald Cornford, *From Religion to Philosophy: a study in the Origins of Western Speculation*, (London: E. Arnold, 1912).
[3] MN: Check.

Burnet over-emphasises the scientific side --- at least showing an understanding of the *scientific importance* of the work of, e.g., Anaximander; an importance which Cornford seems not to see at all. There is more to be said for the sociological interpretation than for the psycho-analytical: the Freudians ignore the sociological except where it can be understood in psychological terms and they neglect logical questions. It is all right to explain why errors are made but you have first to decide whether the doctrines in question are false or not; it is idle to begin by looking for "complexes", etc. Cornford begs the scientific questions in his treatment of [the problems as] sociological or anthropological questions; but Burnet ignores the motivation.[1]

You would first of all then, have the notion of social content; the notion of a "governing" principle would be of social origin; the notion of the proportioning[2] of powers with reference to the main recurrent types of social activity (e.g., war). It would only be at a later stage that you would have individual(istic) interpretations coming forward --- e.g., the notion of a device or instrument a person could employ for a[3] particular purpose. It is, I think, fair to say that this notion is involved in Parmenidean criticism of the Pythagoreans. When Parmenides insists that *what is not is not* (that there is no such thing as not-being), he is rejecting the view that even if it is not *real* it might be *useful* (a useful *concept*), a theoretical device enabling us to distinguish one unit from another, so that even if the unlimited doesn't exist it might be a useful way of thinking for us. [82]

As you see from the *Parmenides,* Parmenides specifically rejects the view, in relation to the forms, that what does not exist in reality may nevertheless be a *thought* in our minds that we employ for the ordering or understanding of things; and he points to the fact that when we are thinking in this manner we are thinking *something*, we are attributing reality to forms and not simply using them to *deal with* reality (and how we could use them if they didn't have that reality would be a further difficulty),

---

[1] EN: this paragraph enclosed in round brackets.
[2] MN: [Moira] (distribution).
[3] EN: the text here reads "his", with "a" written above it.

and if they are not real then we are simply wrong, we are advancing error, not knowledge, by believing in them. (Present-day psychologists talk a great deal about "concepts" and "working principles" and ignore the objective content of these concepts; they ignore the fact that they are not treated as having a twilight existence. It is worthwhile considering the foundation of such attitudes.)

Generally, then, the acceptance of governing principles would be an example of that *dictating to nature* that Heraclitus condemned, of the endeavour to impose some particular order on the facts, to have it (reality) as we would like it to be, which for Heraclitus is to substitute an object of phantasy for reality;[1] but the persistence of that attitude would account for the persistence of the belief in governing principles and thus at once for the belief in universals and the belief in the supremacy of mind.[2]) **[83]**

---

[1] NT: References: Gilbert Murray; Jane Harrison, *Themis*; Cornford; Anderson, "The Perfect Wagnerite — EN: the reference here is to (1) Gilbert Murray, *Five Stages of Greek Religion: studies based on a course of lectures delivered in April 1912 at Columbia University*, 2nd ed. enlarged (London: Watts & Co., 1935); (2) Jane Ellen Harrison, Themis: a study of the social origins of Greek religion (Cambridge: University Press, 1912); (3) Cornford, F. *From Religion to Philosophy*. See Lecture 27; (4) John Anderson, "The Perfect Wagnerite", *Manuscripts*, 13, 1935; pp.25-38. ENMW: 'The Perfect Wagnerite' reprinted in Cullum, G. and Lycos, K. (Ed.) *Art and Reality* (Sydney: Hale and Ironmonger, 1982) pp 135 – 146.

[2] EN: the text here reads "mind(s)", with "(s)" crossed out as a later correction.

Lecture 28 Alexander on Universality as a plan: synthetic character of the proposition; the categories as universals.

Book II, Ch. III. Universal, Particular and Individual.

(Weaknesses connected with the use of the conception of the "point-instant" and with the treatment of Space-Time as "stuff".[1] Alexander's whole treatment of categories is unsatisfactory --- unsystematic --- parts of the argument very *slight*).

Alexander is especially concerned in this chapter with universality. His main contention is that the universal is a plan and that it is a spatio-temporal plan, that universals are "habits of Space-Time" just as (a) man's qualities can be identified with his habits or ways of behaviour. The latter is the view I should myself put forward, but it is another thing to talk of Space-Time itself as *behaving* in a certain way and the point serves to bring out the confusion of the *fundamental stuff* doctrine, because there is no way in which Space-Time behaves everywhere and anywhere, there is no general character that it has unless we call the *categories* its general character,[2] and on the other hand there is nothing in Space-Time itself to show why a particular "habit", a given universal, should crop up at one place and time rather than another. The doctrine, in fact, suffers from the same sort of weakness as the philosophy of Anaximander with its attempt to get the determinate out of the indeterminate, it being impossible to decide where in the Boundless a given separation will take place --- impossible in fact that separation should occur at one place and not at another unless there were a qualitative distinction[3] between these two places prior to the separation.

Whatever qualities (universals) were habits of, then, they would not be habits of Space-Time. Alexander says (p.213) that "empirical universals like dog or tree or justice are possible

---

[1] MN: also *enjoyment*.
[2] NT: Question also of geometry ("properties of space") and "primary qualities" generally. — MN: "formal" v. material (hence *less* substantial).
[3] EN: the text here reads "(a) qualitative distinction(s)", with "(s)" crossed out as a correction.

because Space-Time is uniform and behaves therefore on plans which are undistorted by difference of place and time"; but clearly Space-Time is *not* uniform in respect of these universals, it does not always and everywhere behave doggishly, justly etc,[1] and it is not Space-Time that can explain why these forms of activity take place when and where they do. The real point underlying this argument[2] is the same as that which is made when we speak of the *synthetic* character of the proposition: i.e. just as we can learn only from experience that a certain subject has certain predicates, so we can learn only from experience that a certain predicate has only certain subjects. There is nothing in a description by itself to tell us where it will be located, nothing, as we may put it, in a quality to tell us what will be its particulars --- that is to say, what will be the peculiarities of its subjects apart from their having this common quality [nothing in a genus to tell us what are its species --- this is what the doctrine of the *concrete universal* denies] – **[84]** but even so, if we take the subjects concretely, if we are talking about things and not about pure space-time, then there actually is something to prevent certain qualities being in certain places, there are subjects which do not admit of certain predicates; in other words there are true E propositions.

And this confusion which is involved in the "stuff" theory is even more clearly indicated when Alexander passes from empirical universals to what he calls "the most comprehensive of all universals, the categories themselves" (which "are *a priori* plans of configuration"[3]). He has here a doctrine of highest kinds which of course fails to solve the problems (get over the difficulties) of substantialist philosophy; and, having spoken of an empirical universal as a plan of empirical determination, he has to speak of the categories as "the key plans of all plans of empirical determination"[4] --- an expression which, I suggest, is meaningless. Incidentally he remarks that, while other categories

---

[1] MN: arboreally.
[2] NT: the "indifference of Space" --- Bosanquet, *Philosophical Theory of the State*, Ch. XI, pp. 283, 4: borrowed from Hegel?
[3] MN: p.215.
[4] MN: *ditto*.

are universals, universality itself is not a universal "any more than (we can say that) the empirical universal dog is a dog"[1]; but the comparison, I would say, is not a fair one, and universality, if it is a category and if the categories really are pervasive characters of things, would have to be a universal. (Note that Alexander's doctrines of highest kinds, stuff, etc., lead straight to --- or, perhaps better, are indicative of --- substantialism.)

In using the word *plan* to describe a universal, Alexander distinguishes plan from configuration (speaking of a plan *of* configuration); e.g. the configuration of a person, which varies from moment to moment, "remains within the limits of"[2] a plan which persists. I suggest that *plan* and *configuration* are conceptions we cannot really distinguish --- in fact, that Alexander could not in any way distinguish universals and particulars: a point which he seems to make at the beginning of the chapter though he afterwards goes back on it. (Cf. Joseph on the *particularity* of plans: "But I was thinking of a plan to dye one's whiskers green.")[3] *Any* expression that Alexander cares to use to distinguish universals from particulars will admit of particularity just as much as of universality. In trying to distinguish his theory from the theory of forms Alexander raises the question of the kind of reality that universals possess, and says "Half the difficulty, or perhaps all of it, disappears when once it is admitted that particulars are complexes of Space-Time and belong therefore to the same order or are of the same stuff as the universals which are plans of Space-Time"[4]. If universals and particulars are of the same stuff, one might imagine that there was no difference whatever between them, that all things made of space-time must be particulars (and there are no universals); but if this is not so (i.e. if there *is* a difference between universals and particulars) and if particulars are actual space-times (or "complexes of space-time"), then the universals which are said to be "plans" **[85]** or which we could call qualities (of particulars), would not themselves be space-times, would not be of the same

---

[1] MN: *ditto*.
[2] MN: p.210.
[3] MN: cf. X is of a particular *kind*.
[4] MN: pp.220-1.

stuff as particulars, and in fact would not *belong* to the particulars [would, like the forms, "hover (or float) over" the particulars, without our being able to connect such and such a universal with such and such a particular; or would, like Moore's *good*, be "non-natural"]. Thus while, on a propositional theory, we can see that the same thing can qualify and be qualified (can, if we like to put it so, be universal and particular), on a substantialist theory --- on a doctrine that things are composed of a uniform stuff --- we cannot give any account at all of qualification, we cannot recognise any sort of difference between one part of the substance and another.[1]

---

[1] NT: *Proc. Arist. Soc. Supp. Vol.* for 1926 --- Symposium on Universals: F.P. Ramsey etc. Also earlier proceedings; also Ramsey in *Mind*, criticising Stout. Kemp Smith, "The Nature of Universals", *Mind* 1927. — EN: the references here are to (1) F.P. Ramsey, "Universals and the 'Method of Analysis'" (contribution to a symposium with H.W.B. Joseph and R.B. Braithwaite), *Aristotelian Society Supplementary Volume* 6, pp. 17-26, July 1926; (2) "earlier proceedings" probably refers to a symposium on "Are the characteristics of particular things universal or particular?" between G.E. Moore, G.F. Stout, and G. Dawes Hicks in *Aristotelian Society Supplementary Volume* 3, 1923, pp.95-128; (3) F.P. Ramsey, "Universals", *Mind*, NS34, 1925, pp.401-417; (4) Norman Kemp Smith, "The Nature of Universals (I)", *Mind*, NS36, 1927, pp.137-157; "The Nature of Universals (II)", *ibid.*, pp.265-280; "The Nature of Universals (III)", *ibid.*, pp.393-422..

Lecture 29 No pure particulars: colour; plans; the concrete universal.

It is only in respect of persistent characters that we say the same thing lasts a certain time. Actuality of repetition. Any subject would have duration, which is divisible, and hence repetition: not only is repetition (of universals, kinds) possible, but it is actual in any subject.

This is connected with the point previously made that there is no such thing as a pure *particular*, that we speak only of a particular X, a particular man or colour --- though actually in those two illustrations you get two different meanings, viz, that in the case of "a particular man" you have what is called *an individual* (i.e. you have a number of occurrences of a certain sort, the sort we call manhood, which together form a continuous process, any one of which, in other words, is part of a total history which we call the history of a man), whereas when we speak of "a particular colour" we mean something like *red*, i.e. we mean a species of the genus *colour*,[1] where the various occurrences of redness *don't* add up to one single history, to one continuous existence. Nevertheless you do have the same relation to the universal in the two cases (the relation that can be called *exemplifying*) and you do have *repetition* in the two cases, so that even what we call an individual (or the individual man, X) is a species i.e. at once is an instance of the universal and itself has instances, but there is the additional fact that these instances are continuous with one another, making up what we could call in some sense a *single* instance of the universal.

On this question of colour Alexander has a curious point in the footnote to p. 216; discussing the question of a "space of varying curvature",[2] he says that "while there is good meaning in the universal contained in the varying curvatures of curves in our space, it is difficult to see what is the universal element in the varying curvatures of the supposed space which itself varies in

---

[1] MN: coloured???
[2] MN: cf *Empiricism* on maths and non-Euclideans.

curvature. **[86]** The supposed universal is rather comparable to colour in relation to the various colours, red, green, etc. There is no element colour in these of which red and green are variations. Colour is a collective name rather than a class one or a universal. Such a universal curvature is nothing then, as before, but a bare thought; and no conclusion can be drawn from the supposition of my critics" (casting doubt on his view that "there are universals because there is uniformity or constant curvature"). As regards colour, we may ask why, if red, green, etc, have nothing in common,[1] we should collect them together; or how we *could* speak of them by a collective name, how we should know what that name took in and what it left out (covered and excluded). What Alexander says of colour could be said of shape or, indeed, *any* universal; there is no "element" that we can pick up and say "That is the *shape* of the thing". It is true no doubt that we seldom if ever say, when we are presented with a thing, "It is coloured" (though we do sometimes say "It is colourless") because so little would be distinguished from anything else by colour (the genus) whereas much can be distinguished by presence or absence of a species (say, red). But if we take *red* we could be confronted with the same problem --- whether it is just a collective name for various "shades of red", because we cannot from a "shade of red" extract a particular "element" and say *That is its redness*. And if we took that view (collective name) we should be confronted in turn by the question what is meant by "an exact shade of red" --- whether this covers a range of colours or is confined to one mathematical point on the spectrum. The point is connected with the association with colours of rates of vibration; and what would be intended by an "exact shade" would be one whose vibration-rate was a precise number. But even if it were conceded that you could recognise such an exact shade (even if it were not the case, *as it is*, that any colour-name you use applies over some range, however short), even if every time you said "That is X" you were referring to something whose rate of vibration was the precise number *A* without a hairsbreadth of deviation (which you actually *couldn't* do), there would still be variations possible: the thing's being X would not be *all* about it,

---

[1] MN: if colour is not a character of particular colours

as is indicated by the fact that things "of the same colour" are distinguished by brightness and so on. But, secondly, it may be questioned whether we do have a term X of that kind (it may be asserted that we don't) whether every colour-term we use doesn't cover some range, even when we qualify the simple colour-names and speak of royal blue, bright red, salmon, etc. the suggestion is, then, that the theory of "exact shades" is of a rationalistic character (i.e. involves the doctrine of *whole natures*), and that the same may be said of Alexander's doctrine of the collective name, which incidentally comes very close to Stout's theory of universality, the theory of the *distributive unity* or *disjunction* that constitutes[1] a kind.[2] **[87]**

An expression like *plan* doesn't give a basis on which universals can be distinguished from particulars, and the same applies to the notion of *law* which Alexander uses in his discussion (with special reference to Bosanquet) of the theory of the concrete universal: i.e. that you have particular laws just as much as plans. Also, though I myself have spoken of qualities as ways in which things go on and also of laws as ways of working of things, still the law is the whole proposition and not simply its predicate, in any ordinary usage --- though, whichever way we take it, it isn't a question of a *governing principle* as the word "law" would suggest. Of course any expression we use in explanation of these categories, just as in explanation of the proposition, will be open to the accusation of obscurity or alternatively of tautology --- you cannot explain predication by anything other than predication, and if you say a predicate is a *way of behaving* you are merely suggesting the use of an adverb instead of an adjective (the man *behaves justly* instead of the man *is just*) and you are not really altering or amplifying the logical meaning. What you might really be doing would be emphasising some particular example of the thing you are talking about, an example which might strike the hearer more forcibly than other examples would do and thus bring the meaning home to him; and of course it might be said it was important to show him that linguistic differences had not real or logical differences corresponding to them, that the *very same*

---

[1] EN: the text here reads "illustrates(?)", with "constitutes" written beneath it.
[2] MN: Berkeley/no *description* possible.

meaning was expressed either adjectivally or adverbially, though it is perhaps not clear how that recognition of identity would establish what the actual meaning was. The point we were insisting on might be that everything is susceptible of these different modes of treatment or has those different aspects, though there still our language might be accused of vagueness.

At any rate, we certainly have in the theory of the concrete universal an example of the notion of a governing principle, a principle which draws things together or unifies them, or more exactly which takes them as themselves unified, as such that in any one we can see all the others. Thus on Bosanquet's view you don't see what is involved in attributing manhood to one individual unless you can see what are the capacities of man in general, what are all the things that a[1] man can be and not just what are the things any man *must* be. Human nature, in other words, is not something separately attributable to each man but is the system which unites them all, of which they are various expressions, and we don't really understand one expression without understanding all of them. Of course, as Alexander points out, such a system, such a uniting of all the members of the human race, is not what we mean by the universal *humanity* --- it is on the contrary, **[88]** *an individual*, assuming that we were able to make the collection at all, and it would be *false* to say of that united entity "This is a man." Nevertheless, this notion of a total humanity realised in all its parts is analogous to the notion of a total mentality realised in all its acts; the notion, i.e., that the I or ego is present in every single one of my acts. It is that assumption which permits this theory of concrete universality (totality) to be formulated, and the demonstration of the falsity of that assumption is bound up with rejection of the *cogito* and demonstration of the falsity of the theory of the ego.[2] [1] **[89]**

---

[1] EN: the text reads "any", with above it "a".
[2] NT: It links up with the whole of the Hegelian position. The doctrines of Bosanquet are particularly important on this matter, but the theories of Stout and Cook Wilson are more akin to Bosanquet's than appears at first sight. Cf. Kemp Smith's article. — EN: This refers to Norman Kemp Smith, "The Nature of Universals (I)", *Mind*, NS36, 1927, pp.137-157; "The Nature of Universals (II)", *ibid.*, pp.265-280; "The Nature of Universals (III)", *ibid.*, pp.393-422.

Lecture 30[2] **Idealist doctrine of the concrete universal** : **Hegelianism and Leibniz; the concrete universal of 'humanity'; Alexander's 'system' similar to the concrete universal.**

The doctrine of the concrete universal is bound up with the Idealist theory of mind, with the notion of mind exhibiting *through and throughness*, of the universal of mind running through and organising all the particular manifestations. It is connected with the notion of the person, the I or ego, and has the emptiness of this conception which has only a relational content and has to be filled out by being treated in terms of the things related to it. The position then is that the possessor (owner) of a great number of experiences is at once identified with and distinguished from them, that you can treat it as something abstract or as something concrete, enhancing the whole of experience. The doctrine of the *owner of experience* (the personal pronoun) would not be possible unless there was a qualitative reference somewhere, unless there was some entity related to that experience which had a quality of its own. That is needed for the distinction, but for the connection it is lost sight of, and we have something[3] *an object* of mind and *constituting* the mind, i.e. experience gives the concrete filling to mind. The common idealist notion (Caird, Hegel) of the inseparability of subject and object is evident here[4]. You have the rejection at once of "the

---

[1] NT: *Principle of Individuality and Value* (Lecture II, The Concrete Universal) p. 37 "The ultimate principle, we may say, is sameness in the other; generality [class as contrasted with world] is sameness is spite of the other; universality is sameness by means of the other." "Thus the true embodiment of the logical universal takes the shape of a world whose members are worlds." p. 41 The whole is truth "... the *power* of the concrete universal --- its capacity in the way of unifying experience." p. 46 "The universal is just that character of experience which overcomes the 'is not' by reducing it to an element harmonious with and corroborative of the 'is'. It is 'the self in the other?'". p. 75 Some inwardness is outwardness absorbed. (Shakespeare!) — EN: these extracts are from Bernard Bosanquet, *Principle of Individuality and Value: the Gifford lectures for 1911 delivered in Edinburgh University*, (London: Macmillan, 1912).
[2] NT: In connection with concrete universal and G.F. Stout, see also his article in *AJPP*, 1940.
[3] EN: the text here reads "something", with above it "at once?".
[4] NT: cf. "The Knower and the Known".

abstract subject" and of "the abstract object", and some expression like *experience* covers the whole, having a subjective and an objective aspect ("aspect" being another idealist device for overcoming oppositions or "unifying differences"). So the implicit distinction and absence of the explicit distinction are required to make the theory possible (plausible). And on that view *I* am the universal of all my experiences instead of the general notion "experience of mine" which ordinary logic would seem to require as that universal, and so (as we've noted) this unity of all the experiences is supposed to be found in each of the experiences; and these experiences are supposed to run together, to belong to one another, to have this kind of through-and-through connection.[1]

I have often pointed out the very close connection between Hegelianism and the doctrines of Leibniz -- the notion of the relation of perceptions to a subject, each perception being an expression of the subject and in that way an expression of all the other perceptions: i.e., it is all or any of the others with a certain degree of clarity. Hegel praises Leibniz for being the first philosopher to make the formal step from extensive unity to intensive unity (from substance to subject) and that is what "subject" for Hegel means, viz. this through and through expressiveness, each aspect or part being the whole raised to a certain power. But although such theorists talk about "unity in difference" etc., they are left with just as many unexplained differences as the theorists who have begun (and continued) with bare and unmediated distinctions. **[90]**

Now this sort of doctrine of universality requires that the particulars should be taken not just as separate instances of the universal but as forming some sort of system or totality, as being *collected* in some way. When *I* am said to be the universal, or the unity, of my experiences it is not a question simply of a relation between this universal and any experience we like to take, but of those experiences actually hanging together, having connections, making up various minor totalities within *the* totality; and you get

---

[1] MN: It's an entity (substance).

the same notion of system or totality in any subject the Idealists inquire into. For example, in inquiring into social facts Bosanquet takes *society* as a concrete universal of this kind, i.e. as something manifested in each social phenomenon, something of which each social phenomenon is an "expression" and in which the various social phenomena hang together --- and these may be appear to be some force in taking society as such a totality: there *is* a question of the various connected factors in a complex situation, only the conception of them as various manifestations of a single entity does violence to the facts in the sense that it rejects or explains away social conflicts,[1] it treats opposition of interests as something merely apparent and having to be transcended in a "rational" view of the matter. In that way you get the monistic as against the pluralistic view of society, and in the same way you get monistic versus pluralistic views of mind: and the treatment of mind as this sort of totality prevents the recognition of mental conflict, assumes that there is one pre-eminent interest which is being satisfied, or for which satisfaction is being sought, in all mental (human) activities; and there again the notion of "reason" assumes the reconcilability of all interests.

Now one particular difficulty of this view can be brought out by considering the Idealist treatment of the universal *man* or *humanity*. Men have to be treated not merely as various instances of a certain kind but as forming a system or totality (a notion illustrated in the common expression "mankind"), but then that system is indistinguishable from *society*, and we actually find Bosanquet identifying social system or harmony with psychological (mental) system or harmony: we find the Hegelians generally treating the social as mental even if they call it *objective* mind: and this sort of thing is inevitable just because the alleged unities (i.e., at once totalities and governing principles) don't really exist, so that we can't really distinguish them --- and of course that brings us on to the well-known difficulty absolutists have in preventing their alleged Absolute from absorbing every distinct thing that could be talked about and that was supposed to be its manifestation, just as Socrates has

---

[1] MN: also *indifference*.

difficulty in preventing[1] the form of the good **[91]** from absorbing all the realities that are said to come under it.

Now in spite of Alexander's rejection of the concrete universal, his contention in effect that a system or totality is a *thing*, (a particular, not a plan for particulars), we find him making statements which come very close to the same doctrine. Thus in discussing (p. 231) the doctrine of *class-concepts*, abstractions taken apart from all variation in things, and corresponding conception of laws of nature as "abstractions of the common elements in the relations of things to the neglect of the variations of those relations", Alexander says that "it is evident enough that useful as such abstractions may be and are for artificial or provisional purposes, they have nothing in common with universals as plans or laws of construction, for these so far from neglecting the wealth and variety of their particular instances are the formulae which hold the instances together, not merely in our thinking but in fact": and he goes on to say that, in the actual practice of the sciences, a class "is not a bare collection of particulars which happen to agree in certain important respects, but a group determined by their constitutive formula". So that the only difference between Alexander and Bosanquet here is that Alexander takes the universal as the determining formula and Bosanquet takes it as the group so determined, or rather as at once the formula and what it is the formula of.

But actually such a "classification", as we call it, i.e., a recognition of species with their differences, is not the universal, is not the character which constitutes the genus. We are concerned with that universal (that *term*, speaking more accurately) when we speak of the class in a general way, i.e. when we speak of the various X's as contrasted with X; and when we speak no more definitely than that, we are only distinguishing X as a subject from X as a predicate, and if these are the same term, we are not really distinguishing the class from the[2] universal or setting up any system. When, on the other hand, we

---

[1] EN: the text here reads "just as in Socrates it is impossible to prevent (just as Soc. has difficulty in preventing)".
[2] EN: the text here reads "the", with "its" written above it.

make an actual classification or division, then we are not simply expounding the genus or universal, we are finding a set of relations between that term and other terms; and if we make those other terms (the species) something inherent in the notion of the genus, then we are adopting the doctrine of the concrete universal and cannot stop short of the Absolute which is the universal of everything --- with all the difficulties of that view. (Space-Time as a universal stuff is an Absolute of the Idealist kind.[1]) To avoid these difficulties Alexander would have to return to the "abstract universal" in the sense of what is *common* to things and doesn't in any way embrace their variations. **[92]**

---

[1] MN: Ql^s (varieties) as inher^t in Sp. T.

Lecture 31 Stout's theory of universals criticised.

Reading list on universals

Plato: Phaedo, Republic
Aristotle: Metaphysics
Bosanquet: Principle of Individuality and Value (Ch. II, The Concrete Universal)
Bosanquet: Logic[1] (Bk I, Ch. V, VI[2]; Bk II, Ch. X[3])
Bradley: Principles of Logic.[4]
Hegel: Logic (Trans. Wallace) esp. Ch. II & IX.
Prichard: Kant's Theory of Knowledge (Chs. II & VII)[5]
Kemp Smith: The Nature of Universals (Mind, 1927 --- three issues --- especially for criticism of Bosanquet --- Essentials of Logic)
Hoernle: Universals (Mind 1927) (Close to Absolute Idealists)[6]
Cook Wilson: Statement and Influence (esp. Vol. II)[7]
Kemp Smith: The Fruitfulness of the Abstract (Proc. Aust. Soc., 1927-28: supplementary to above articles: not very good)
Johnson: Logic (esp. Part I, Ch. XI)[8]
Stout: The Nature of Universals and Propositions (Proc. Br. Acad., Vol. X: Studies in Philosophy and Psychology)[1]

---

[1] EN: this refers to Bernard Bosanquet, *Logic, or The Morphology of Knowledge*, 2nd ed. (Oxford: Clarendon Press, 1911).
[2] EN: this refers to Bosanquet, *op.cit.*, Vol. I, Chapter V "Singular and Universal Judgement", and Chapter VI "Universal Judgement (continued)".
[3] EN: this refers to Bosanquet, *op.cit.*, Vol. II, Chapter X "The Relation of Mental States to Judgement and to Reality".
[4] EN: this refers to F.H. Bradley, *The Principles of Logic*, 2nd ed., 2 vols. (London: Oxford University Press, 1922).
[5] EN: this refers to H.A. Prichard, *Kant's Theory of Knowledge* (Oxford: Clarendon Press, 1909).
[6] EN: this refers to R.F.A. Hoernlé, "Concerning Universals", *Mind*, NS36, 1927, pp.179-204.
[7] EN: this refers to John Cook Wilson, *Statement and Inference, With Other Philosophical Papers*, ed. A.S. Farquaharson (Oxford: Clarendon Press, 1926).
[8] EN: this refers to W.E. Johnson., *Logic, Part I* (Cambridge: University press, 1921).

Russell: Problems of Philosophy (poor)
Russell: Principles of Mathematics (good)
Stout: More about Universals (Proc. Arist. Soc, Supp. Vol XV)[2]
Stout: Things, Predicates and Relations (AJPP, 1940)
James: Principles of Psychology (Ch. XII, Conception)
Moore and Others --- Proc. Aust. Soc., Supp. Vol III
Joseph and Others --- Proc. Aust. Soc., Supp. Vol VI
Ramsey: Universals (Mind, Oct 1925) (Criticism of Stout, some points Stout can't get over) (My review of Foundations of Maths, AJPP Dec 1931)
Anderson: Science of Logic (Dec 31) --- also dealing with Robinson and Cook Wilson Proceedings of Sixth International of Philosophy (Section on Doctrine of Subsistence and Essence: My view in AJPP, Sept. 1928)[3].
Whitehead: Principles of Natural Knowledge, Part II
Whitehead: Concept of Nature, Ch. VII[4]
Anderson: "Universals" and Occurrences AJPP, June 1929
Anderson: Realism and Some of its Critics, AJPP, June 1930
Merrylees: Participation. AJPP, March and September 1929 (idealist influence of Ross and Joseph).[5]

Stout's theory of universals comes back to taking resemblance to be more primitive than qualification; we see that objects resemble one another and then qualify them in the same way, we don't first

---

[1] EN: this refers to G.F. Stout, "The Nature of Universals and Propositions", (Henrietta Hertz Trust Annual Philosophy Lecture), *Proceedings of the British Academy*, Vol. 10, 1921-1923, pp.157-172.
[2] EN: this refers to G.F. Stout, "Universals Again", *Proceedings of the Aristotelian Society Supplementary Volume XV*, 1936, pp.1-15.
[3] EN: this refers to John Anderson, "*Proceedings of The Sixth International Congress of Philosophy, Harvard University, Sept. 13-17 1926*, Ed. E.S. Brightman, New York: Longmans Green and Co., 1927", (review), *AJPP*, 6, 1928, pp.223-228.
[4] EN: the reference here is to (1) Alfred North Whitehead, *An Enquiry Concerning the Principles of Natural Knowledge* (Cambridge: University Press, 1919); (2) Alfred North Whitehead, *The Concept Of Nature*, (Cambridge: University Press, 1920).
[5] EN: the reference here is to (1) W.A. Merrylees, "Participation (I)", *AJPP*, 7, 1929, pp. 37-49; (2) W.A. Merrylees, "Participation (II): The Logical Significance of Participation", *AJPP*, 7, 1929, pp.188-203.

see the quality (in each) and then say the objects resemble one another. This I consider to be a quite impossible view because things differ from and resemble one another in all sorts of respects, and to say A is *like* B is a meaningless **[93]** assertion until you specify in what respect they are "like".

The assertion of a resemblance between A and B is only an assertion of the disjunction of A and B, i.e. of the existence of the term *A or B*. If you say AaX, BaX ∴ (A or B)aX, then you are saying A and B form a class which is X. If you do not specify X (do not say A and B are alike in being X) but only say A and B are *alike*, that leaves you with the subject of a proposition and the possibility of a predicate; i.e. you have not yet made an assertion. More exactly, when you say "*A or B* is a term", you are saying something because you are *implying* something; to say that something is a term is to say that it has an opposite (that its opposite is a term); now the opposite of (A or B) is (not-A and not-B), and so you are implying that some not-A are not-B. In other words, (A or B) wouldn't be a term if A and B together added up to everything, and that comes back to the position that there are no predicates of all things (that any real term has an opposite). The existence of the opposite, then, and so the truth of *Some not-A are not-B*, is conveyed when you say that A and B are alike or A and B form a class. But it is still not specific information about *A and B*; and the notion of likeness cannot be prior to the notion of likeness *in some particular respect*[1] and so cannot be prior to the specification of a particular quality. It may happen that we say "A is like B" when we can't *say* in what the resemblance resides, cannot *name* the quality, and even haven't a "clear idea" of it. Cf. "he looks like a soldier" or "this poem reminds me of Tennyson". But unless the common qualities were there, there would be nothing to remind us; it is the quality that has affected us even if we can't yet single it out, even if it is still "vague"; and in *learning* qualities, in discriminating them from the complexity of the things we observe, we have to begin with vagueness and uncertainty. It may be the repetition of a quality that forces it on our attention, but still it is of something that is in

---

[1] MN: Mere assertion of "likeness" leaves questions open; to recognise likeness we must 1st be able to recognise qualities.

each particular that we are passing the judgement --- we are saying "A and B have a common quality, though I can't *yet* say what it is". As before, likeness *means* likeness in some *respect* i.e. in some quality.[1]

Stout's doctrine of relational propositions (relational properties?) in the *AJPP* article doesn't get anywhere. He is just using other words for relations and is inventing a name for two different situations or taking them together when there is no justification for doing so (viz. relational and qualitative propositions). There is no justification for speaking of "an enveloping relation". If we are speaking about the whole situation *ArB,* then that in a sense is something that envelopes A and B but it doesn't really *characterise* A and B; in fact, in using the expression "enveloping relation", **[94]** we are only saying again that the situation A and B exists.

Even if you say there are "necessary relations", in the sense that there are some relations such that if the thing didn't have them it wouldn't exist, this does not justify *characterising* the thing by the relation, bringing the relation into the nature[2] of the thing itself. We should simply say that such a relation is necessary, and leave it at that. (Nothing *added* by speaking of "character-complex" or "envelope relation".)

(Next term I'll discuss the category of number, with some reference to Russell's views. Russell, especially in *Principles of Mathematics*, treats mathematics or the science of number as something other than an empirical science, in that knowledge of numbers is not knowledge of groups --- as I would say it is. [A rather dubious statement as Russell in that work builds on the basis of enumerable "classes".[3]] The question of number will be taken with the questions of order and quantity.)

---

[1] EN: the last three sentences of this paragraph are bracketed.
[2] EN: the text reads "character", with "nature" written underneath.
[3] MN: cf. remark in next lecture.

Lecture 32 Order of the Categories: Quality and Quantity; Universality and Quantity; the category of Number - begins with integers; integers characteristic of groups.

Order of the Categories. I should like, before taking up the theory of number, to make a few preliminary and tentative points in connection with the question of the order of the categories. The order of the categories is prominent in Hegel, where you get the mechanism of thesis, antithesis and synthesis, each thesis being the point of departure for a new movement of thought and where you get a development from the category of bare being through all the others to the Idea where the movement of the whole set of categories ends.

Without adopting the notion of antithesis and the *resolution* of antithesis (for if there is a real contradiction, it is impossible to resolve it, and apart from that, it is simply a matter of recognising distinctions), still some sort of theory of the alteration of categories is possible and would replace the notion of *antithetic* categories with that of relational or *dyadic* categories (cf. *Philebus*) --- those that involve a reference to two terms and distinct from "qualitative"[1] categories. (A great number of problems in all this.)

Categories of quality.[2] The categories we have dealt with form a series of that kind (alteration of positive single[3] and dyadic) and we might call them the categories of quality. First of all you have the positive category of *identity*: then you have *difference* which of course would be dyadic because you need two terms for difference. Then you have *existence* which even Alexander, though he doesn't subscribe to the doctrine of thesis and antithesis, refers to as "identity in difference" [synthesis], then you have *relation*, again involving two terms, and finally you

---

[1] EN: the text here reads "'qualitative'", with "*positive*" written beneath it, and "(descriptive)" written beneath that.
[2] NT: linked with the qualitative proposition.
[3] ENMW: This word is only partially legible in the manuscript. It appears to be 'simple' with 'positive' written above it, although George Molnar thought it might be 'single' (as contrasted with dyadic).

have *universality* or quality (*being such*) --- which is in a manner a return to identity ("being a predicate" as an *aspect* of "being a subject"), **[95]**

[handwritten: Identity, Existence, Universality / Difference, Relation } Dyadic categories on the right.]

There you have the whole set of *categories of quality* which I have related to the categorical[1] proposition, while suggesting that further problems --- of relation, juxtaposition, etc --- are raised.

Categories of quantity --- A similar set of categories of quantity is suggested. I start tentatively with the category of *universality* and then take *particularity* as the first dyadic category, in the sense that no such thing as mere particularity can be found --- it is always a question of being a particular something, something *being an example of* something else. [X is an example of Y: two terms.] And that of course gives us the notion of *classes*, and leads on to the positive category of *number*, on the understanding that number primarily refers to groups, to a collection of members of a given class; and then from number we pass on to the conception of *order* (from cardinal to ordinal number, as it is put some mathematical theories), which is clearly dyadic --- which *holds between* terms. And so again to the positive category of *quantity*, which is connected with the mathematical theory of "real number", (especially exemplified in spatial *continuity*), as contrasted with *integers* in the first place and with *rational numbers* in the second place.[2]

[handwritten diagrams: Universality, Number, Quantity / Particularity, Order | or: Particularity, Number, Quantity, Order, Intensity]

[A doubt suggested here as to whether universality should be included in the categories of quantity, and whether we shouldn't start with the "right-hand side" (dyadic) category of particularity and finish with the "right-hand" category of *intensity*. I afterwards came down definitely on the side of including Universality (connecting link between the two groups) and *excluding* intensity from this group --- *quantity* becoming the connecting link between (common member of) --- this group and a *third* group.]

Whether or not we include universality among the categories of quantity, it is important to observe their relation to universality, in the sense that all considerations of quantity, all measurement, involve(s) singleness of kind, involves a common quality, something that the quantity is a quantity of; for even if we sometimes count things which we say are not of the same kind, even if we enumerate, say, the fruits on a plate where some are apples and some are pears, the differences are irrelevant to the enumeration **[96]** --- it is only in recognising that each is *of some common description* that we could undertake the counting at all or assign any meaning to it when we have completed it.

I am arguing then that consideration of number (and this is conceded by Russell in *Principles of Mathematics* whether or not he holds to the position in later works)[1] begins with integers and that these integers are characteristic of groups, i.e. of some recognised set of members of a given class or, if you like to put it so, of instances of a given universal. Now that does not mean, as I have urged in criticism of the Pythagoreans, that the discrete is prior to the continuous, that you can build up continuity out of separate units, because of course each of these so called units is itself continuous, which implies that there is no such thing as an absolute unit, that there is nothing which is *just one* but only what is *one X* (one apple, e.g.) and as such already exhibits spatial continuity, as I said, and it is on that point (the notion of the "just one") that Pythagoreanism breaks down. But even so, even if we

---

[1] MN: see previous note, p. 94 — EN: this refers to the last paragraph of Lecture 31.

cannot make continuity out of original units, it may still be the case that considerations of number arise in connection with separate members of a class (for us, the question of membership of a class is simply that of the truth of a proposition itself already involves spatio-temporal continuity); and so while we can come from the question of number to the question of quantity, to the question i.e., of the *numerical* representation of something which has continuous gradations and does not change by units, it is on the one hand from the counting of groups that we get our numerical apparatus [and it is with reference to some *unit* that we measure quantity] while on the other hand this does not involve any *denial* of continuous gradation, any attempt to reduce the continuous to the discrete, to have a progression *by jumps* (so to speak) seeing, as I said, that continuity is present in the very first thing we take as a unit.

In measuring continuous quantity we of course decide on our unit quite arbitrarily, decide that such and such will a *foot* or such and such will be a *pound*, but unless we adopted such units we could not measure quantity, and we can still go on recognising that these units are not absolute, that they are arbitrary. Still there is a distinction of types of consideration here: there is the question of integers or whole numbers which is more closely connected with the question of qualitative descriptions --- "this is *an* X" or "this goes on in an X manner"; and there is the question of quantity which is more closely connected with the question of spatial extension, of things (as I said) being alongside one another instead of qualifying one another, i.e. with the notion of the *compound* as contrasted with the *complex* --- two types of consideration between which, as I have argued, there is no sort of opposition, which are both covered by the theory of things as spatio-temporal.[1] **[97]**

This sort of exposition is in line of course with the treatment of mathematics as an observational science just like any other science, and is opposed to the treatment of it as a science of a higher kind (perhaps as an *intuitional* science), to the view e.g.

---

[1] MN: Distinctions were removed l.f., brought in again in further complic[ns].

that $2 + 2 = 4$ has nothing to do with actual groups, with the recognising, say that two apples and other two apples are four apples; and it seems to me that the difficulty of any such doctrine of "rational mathematics" is not only to see how we could ever find out that two and two are four, but also how we could ever apply that mathematical knowledge to actual things, how we could ever know what the rational entity "two" *means* in terms of apples or whatever it might be. It seems clear to me that if it is (to be) possible to *apply* mathematical science to physical facts, then it must be possible to *refute* mathematical theories by reference to (if the recognition of) physical facts; and that brings us back to the position that it is really physical facts that mathematics is concerned with, while on the other view it would seem (to me) to be impossible to refute or criticise any mathematical theory[1] whatever, to raise the slightest objection to anyone's saying that $2 + 2 = 5$. (There is the contention that you have various "languages" in some of which $2 + 2 = 5$, and that it just a matter of arbitrariness (that certain people only agree to *say* that $2 + 2 = 4$). This is plausible because the notion of *arbitrary units* has been extended --- though consideration of the fact that you can shift your units so that what was previously 4 is now 5. But you can never shift your units so that *the sum of 2 + 2* becomes 5; $2 + 2$ in the old units may be 5 in the new units, but $2 + 2$ will never be 5 in the *same* units.)

---

[1] EN: the text here reads "theory", with "view" written above it.

Lecture 33 Rejection of category of 'whole and part': Alexander's haphazard treatment of categories.

Again the suggestion, later abandoned, that second group should start with particularity.[1] You could describe the second set of categories as mathematical, as contrasted with (the first set) the categories of logic; and then the third set would be the categories of physics.[2]

In Bk II, Ch. VIII, Alexander treats the questions of (1) whole and parts; (2) number. That is, he links the question of number with that of whole and part, and that illustrates the distinction between his line of thought from mine, since I connect number with particularity or take particularity (and not whole and part) as the starting-point for a theory of number.

I am very dubious about whether we should recognise a category of whole and part. Taking it as simply referring to the relation of inclusion [containing], one would say that that is involved in the conception of *quantity*, something admitting of more and less; and distinguishing, as I was doing, the conception of quantity as continuous from number as working with the distinct unit, one would certainly say that this *more and less* is directly involved in the consideration of quantity. And it may be very important[3] for *mathematical theory* generally to come on to the notion of *real number*, i.e. to attempt a correlation [98] of numerical values with a continuously varying quantity as against numbers varying by one(s), but that wouldn't alter the fact that your integers are the originally apprehended numbers and that the application of number to the continuous is never complete or exact, that you can never represent continuous variation numerically any more than in the Pythagorean doctrine you can represent the change from one configuration to another by a configuration, so that even if we should describe (characterise) $\sqrt{2}$, for example, as a real

---

[1] EN: this sentence is enclosed in square brackets.
[2] NT: the physical categories.
[3] EN: the text here reads "very point", with insertion mark between "be" and "very" and "the?" written as MN, and (presumably subsequently) "point" crossed out and "important" written above it.

number and consider it as having a place on a line just as definite as the place we could assign to 1 or 2, we could never exhibit the *passage* between $\sqrt{2}$, and another number on the line, say $\frac{7}{5}$ or $\frac{7}{12}$, we could never exhibit it, particularly, by any numerical expression.

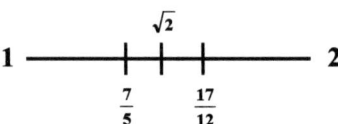

And that is why I emphasise (in the case of the Pythagoreans) the impossibility of accounting for *geometry*, or spatial continuity, in terms of[1] *arithmetic*, or definite integers --- why, in other words, the two conceptions of quantity and number can never be identified, however they may be correlated, and why, in my opinion, Alexander is wrong in making the conception of whole and part the starting-point for a theory of number. Of course even among integers we have this relation of more and less, but we do not have the continuous passage between the less and the more; and it is definitely with continuous space and time that Alexander links number, saying, for example, (p. 313) that "number is the constitution of a whole in relation to its parts; and it is generated in the concurrent or correspondent distinction of parts in space and time within a spatio-temporal whole" and again that "All existents are numerable or possess number, because in occupying a space-time they occupy parts of space in correspondence with parts of time."[2]

Taking that then as one source of misunderstanding --- the confusion of number with quantity --- I would also say that the notion of whole and part can mean something other than quantity

---

[1] EN: the text here reads "in terms of (by means of) (by) *arithmetic*".
[2] MN: convertibility -- fr not^n of X-ness to not^n of All X. (Unvl *pred* → unvl *prop^n*) hce *class*. "Be^g X" as *plac^g* ins^d of *char*. — EN: this appears to be shorthand for: "convertibility --- from notion of X-ness to notion of All X. (Universal *predicate* → universal *proposition*) hence *class*. "Being X" as *placing* instead of *characterising* ".

or that which includes and that which is included, viz. the sort of thing that Alexander recognises in the category of *substance*, what we call the *constitution* or *composition* of a thing; and once those two categories of quantity and substance have been recognised, then there is no room for a category of "whole and part" (or, perhaps better, "wholeness"). Now this alternative sense of the term *whole* is indicated in the common assertion that a whole is something more than the sum[1] of its parts, other assertion no longer seems paradoxical when we realise that a whole is not the sort of relation among things that we call a *sum*, that when we, as it is said, *enumerate the parts* of a thing we are not thereby describing the thing, or describing the whole of the thing, because we are leaving out the essential question how these parts, each of which is quantitatively included in the whole, are related to one another; [99] and that inter-relation of parts is one of the things we mean by the *composition* of a thing, though we also mean an interrelation of qualities, which is not the same as an interrelation of parts --- an interrelation of things *predicable* of the whole, which a part is not. (You could not predicate *an arm* of a man, as you could *rationality*. In a "substance" you have both complexity of qualities and compounding of parts.)

This interrelation of parts, then, is not what we mean when we speak of a sum, not what we mean by the conception of *addition*[2] --- the notion of addition being simply what is conveyed by the logical expression "or" (as in *A or B*), *A or B* being the logical sum of A and B, though in *mathematical* addition you require the further consideration that A and B exclude one another. Colloquially (in ordinary usage) we use 'and'[3] for both disjunctive and conjunctive relations, and would say that man is composed of head *and* arms *and* trunk *and* legs, whereas logically we should say head *or* arms *or* trunk *or* legs: i.e. that *H or A or T or L* are his parts. But the point is that while that expression 'or'[4] does convey what we mean by a *sum*, that sum (or disjunction) does not convey what we mean by a human body.

---

[1] EN: the text here reads "same", correction added.
[2] MN: cf. "drops of water".
[3] EN: in the text here "and" is underlined.
[4] EN: in the text here "or" is enclosed in round brackets.

If a human body were dismembered and parts lying around in various places, the logical sum would be the same but there would no longer be what we call *a human body*.

The paradox arises, then, out of simple confusion as to what is meant by addition (or by a sum), and as a special point it should be understood that the constitution of a *substance* (or what we call a "whole") does not merely depend on the being together or juxtaposition of the various things we can recognise as parts, but depends on their being together *in a certain manner* --- in the case of the human body, on the members being united to the trunk in a certain particular way. (This illustrates the confusion. The view I am putting forward is that Alexander's *category of whole and part* is a mixture of the categories of quantity and substance, and that quantity does not convey what we mean by *number*, even if it is closely connected with it.[1])

Now we find that, having said that all existents are numerable, Alexander goes on to deny the point I made in the last lecture, viz. that enumeration implies singleness of kind. He says (pp. 313-314)[2]: "It matters not whether the parts be equal or unequal, homogeneous or heterogeneous in the qualities; or whether the wholes are of the same extent of space-time or not. A group consisting of a man and a dog is as much a two as a group of two men or two shillings; though its parts are unequal in quantity and different in quality; and as much two as a group of two elephants or two mice which occupy as whole very different quantities of space-time. To arrive at the number of a whole of individuals we have to abstract from the quality or the magnitude of the individuals. Their number concerns only the constitution of the whole out of its parts or resolution of the whole into them." **[100]**

You can say in general that Alexander's discussion of the categories is very ragged; the argument does not build up into a whole. Take Hegel on the order of the categories, the unfolding of The Idea: even if Hegel is wrong, he has a theory of how the (order?) ought to be worked out. Again, in the starting point I

---

[1] MN: & substance doesn't convey it at all.
[2] EN: the text here reads "(pp.313,4)".

gave you, the proposition, you have some kind of principle or test, and there is a question of *common form* of the argument at any two given stages. Alexander throws categories at you haphazardly – cf. my description of his work, in the "Non-Existence of Consciousness", as "a mighty fragment".[1]

In talking in this way Alexander is assuming in a quite unempirical manner *the absolute individual*, assuming that there is a special reason for calling a man *one* and a dog *one* and hence a man and a dog *two*; whereas actually we could number the things in a given situation in any manner at all --- there is no such thing as *the* number of things in a given (in any) situation, and we should call a man and a dog *a pair* only if we had as our starting-point some at least vaguely conceived common quality;[2] and that would bring us back to the doctrine of the disjunctive term again, to the fact that "A is like B" amounts only to presentation of the term *A or B* and that this is still incomplete until we have said that *(A or B)aX*, until we have found a common quality in which their likeness resides. Now if the notion of disjunction requires for its completion the notion of a common quality,[3] then addition (as against Alexander's view of the notion of enumeration or the possession of number in general) takes its departure from the possession of a common quality though of course we don't need the same quality for every enumeration --- and that is why we can have general propositions like $2 + 2 = 4$, abstracted if you like from the common quality, but we certainly can't have *an absolute individual* or *pure unit* abstracted from the[4] quality.

---

[1] EN: this paragraph is enclosed in round brackets.
[2] MN: animality, e.g.
[3] MN: & also of a *thing*: of a quality which belongs to a "whole" and not to its parts [cf. q^n of the singular prop^n: one man etc].
[4] EN: the text here reads "the", with "a" written underneath.

Lecture 34 General remarks about the categories: Alexander has no method of discovering the categories; the natural order of the categories; criticism of Hegel.

Leaving aside till next lecture further consideration of Alexander's view on number as presented in the passage quoted (Bk II, Ch VIII, pp.313-314)[1] I should like to say something about the categories in general.[2]

Alexander's work is unequal because he has no method of *discovering* the categories: e.g. he doesn't make *the proposition* generate the categories.[3] I have tried to place them in what appears to be their logical order (an order in which they would be placed from the outset). There may be some resemblance between Kant's *schematism* and what I am trying to do with the proposition. Compare also Hegel's *Logic*, in which categories are multiplied in a reckless manner, yet in which there is a definite *order* (the categories **[101]** being unfolded from the Idea in its barest or most abstract form to the Idea in its most concrete form) and a definite *method* (that of thesis, antithesis and synthesis), with my straightforward (positive) and dyadic categories.[4] Alexander begins with the most abstract categories, of identity and difference, but thereafter neither follows any definite order nor has any clear principle. He said in his Synopsis that we have two consummate guides to the categories, Plato and (to a lesser extent) Kant. To take persons as guides would be no great theoretical advance; he should take facts (or a feature of them) as guide. Thus he presents the categories in an unequal and haphazard way --- all complicated by his language of "contemplation and enjoyment" and by his doctrine of "point-instants". So I in some measure follow Alexander (in regard to

---

[1] EN: the text here reads "(pp.313,4)".
[2] NT: (Suggestion, in regard to passage from universality to the categories of quantity, that quantity is more closely connected with the notion of a subject than with the notion of a predicate --- the notion of a predicate being more closely connected with activity.) — MN: Omit [not much in this]. — EN: the "this" in the MN refers to the sentence in the bracketed NT.
[3] MN: Order of the categories.
[4] MN: alternating.

192

what are categories) but determine independently the order of presentation.

I follow what I think is the natural order: but an important general question about the conception of "the order of the categories" is how far this is an objective order, an order of the categories themselves (how far they can be said to *have* an order), and how far merely a convenient order of presentation. If you pass the phrase in which I describe the categories as "conditions of existence" or as constituting the *form* as distinct from the *matter* of the proposition, then you wouldn't from these descriptions get any notion of order: no one category would seem to be prior to any other: and although both in my exposition and in ordinary logical discussion you get a certain priority given to the subject {term} of the proposition,[1] still the subject is not really prior to the rest of the proposition: the whole proposition[2] would be the least that could be understood and there would be something abstract about concentrating on different parts of it[3] and, eg, treating identity as specially the function of the subject. Of course if one says there is no objective order but only a natural order of exposition, that would be a difficult thesis to maintain; it would be hard to show why it should be convenient for us to take a particular category first if there were no reasons in the categories themselves why it should be first. That sort of doctrine (of the order of the categories as having a pedagogical character, as being incidental to learning rather than to truth[4]) would push us in the direction of an *instrumental* view of the categories in general, a treatment of them as modes of our thinking rather than as modes of reality or being --- whatever "mode" in the connection might mean.

The only reason for the order I adopt (viz. analysis of the proposition) I have already given; I can give no supplementary reason here, but still I think *there really is an objective order of*

---

[1] EN: the text here reads "the subject of the proposition".
[2] EN: the text here reads "the (whole) proposition".
[3] MN: separately.
[4] EN: the text here reads "than (to) truth".

the categories, and that this is a problem,[1] and that Alexander, because he makes no attempt to establish a rigorous order, has to that extent a defective theory. Hegel of course makes his categories come round three times (1) as categories of being, (2) as categories of essence, (3) as categories of the notion, each slightly modified from its previous form --- the threefold appearance being connected with Hegel's conception of thought in its immediacy or in itself (being), **[102]** thought in its mediation or in its externalisation, as it goes out into Nature (essence) and finally thought in its return into itself, its re-internalisation (notion), though in that return it is supposed to bring with it all it has gathered in the stage of mediation. And while there might something *corresponding* to all this in a true theory of categories, our criticism would be that the *pure categories*, the *categories of nature* and the *categories of spirit* are not different at all and so we can reduce Hegel's categories to a third of their number.

It is very hard in general to distinguish the categories on the view that each of them is involved in anything there is (any occurrence; anything that *is or occurs*); that is to say, each one is exactly where every other one is; and in the matter I was discussing with you, the approach to the categories of quantity through the theory of classes, through the numbering of groups, (on the view that that is the proper approach) continuous number (so called "real number") comes after integral number and rational number, but, as I said, this does not involve the attempt to base continuity on the discontinuous because the units with which we began are already continuous and of course exist in a continuous spatio-temporary medium. Now the first representation of this conception of continuity is to be found in the category of *existence*, is to be found, then, in the copula; and if that view is taken, then we shall have to say that *in the category of quantity*, where we get continuous number or measurable continuity as contrasted with measurement by units, *a notion of continuity* which was implicit in the conception of existence *is now made explicit* or definitely brought out. For the matter of that

---

[1] EN: "and that this is a problem" written as MN and place of insertion indicated.

we might say that all the subsequent categories are implicit in the category of existence or even in the first category of identity, in the sense that if we were to realise fully what is involved in existence or identity we should have to bring in all the categories --- which seems to bring us back to (the question of) an expository order as against a real order; and in other case we find it very hard to distinguish categories --- so that we have here a very difficult problem: not surprisingly, since it is the central problem of philosophy.

And perhaps the solution would lie along some such line as this, that the different categories would correspond to *different logical procedures*, forms not merely of statement but of argument, procedures the possibility of which was involved in any situation whatever,[1] and that it would be the task of the thoroughgoing logician to bring out these connections in detail. I had been thinking of the earlier set of categories ("categories of quality") in connection with the *constituents* of the proposition, though of course recognition of these constituents involves us to some extent in recognition of different *forms* of assertion; at the very least, in recognition of the distinction of *quality*, whereas it might be that the distinction of quantity was more closely connected with the "categories of *quantity*",[2] that the question of particularity or instances, and with it the question of enumeration, is bound up **[103]** with the distinction we make between the logical *all* and *some*, at any rate with our recognition of quantification [different *forms* of assertion, again]. But it might be possible to connect some of the later categories with *forms of argument*, as Kant e.g. connects them with such distinctions as modality, which would either be a mere repetition of the forms already utilised [hypothetical proposition as *universal* proposition] or would involve the standpoint of argument as contrasted with simple assertion. That in its turn would bring us

---

[1] NT: Cf. the "convertibility" of the terms of the proposition.
[2] MN: (1) [in pencil] *qnt* bnd up w *djcn* (plural^y of ins ie. of prop^{ns})(juxtap^s). (2)[in ink immediately below (1)]: 1st set of categories of "quality" in that sense --- categories of yes and no, or of a simple issue? — EN: (1) appears to be shorthand for: "*Quantity* bound up with *disjunction* (plurality of instances, i.e. propositions)(juxtapositions)".

to a very important consideration in logic, viz. how far the notion of argument (of syllogism, in particular) is already involved in the notion of assertion --- the sort of question forced on us by the consideration that the raising of the question of extension, or more particularly *distribution*, in regard to a given proposition is really the raising of the question of the validity of certain syllogistic arguments.[1]

(I haven't thought that matter out --- e.g. how *causality* could be related to forms of argument rather than to forms of assertion. In dealing with the later categories, although I have not formulated any mode of generating them, I still present them in a definite order. I am suggesting that such categories as causality may have special connections with argument rather than with assertion, and we would have to consider how far the whole question of argument is concerned [connected?] with assertion. I have said that the proposition is the least we can know and that it is complex, but it is interesting to consider Idealist doctrines like Bosanquet's, which amount to the view that *argument* is the real unit of thought, and that the proposition has to be understood as a "moment" within a inferential process. That is another large question.)[2]

---

[1] MN: Bosanquet etc – argument as real unit of thought: proposition as a "moment" in an inferential process.

[2] MN: Even *difference* (or recognition of *negation* as categorial) could be connected with *procedure* of obversion, not just with simple *negative* statements. (So, as previously noted, with *conversion* and *universality*).

Lecture 35 Alexander's theory of number: enumeration; Alexander's rationalistic treatment of mathematics; Alexander's discussion of Russell-Frege theory of cardinal number.

Coming back to Alexander's discussion of number, I had criticised his statement that a group consisting of a man and a dog is as much a *two* as a group of two men and that [to][1] arrive at a number we have to abstract from the *quality* of the individual. The point is that if you abstract from the quality you abstract from the individual; you must have *one X* (one man, one dog, etc). In the given case (man and dog) you would require some such quality as animality, which would indicate the unit, before you could speak of them as two they would have to be taken as *two X-es* (though there are various things that X could be).

In the notion of the unit of enumeration (in connection with which we can get laws of number irrespective of how the unit is determined, though these laws are to be understood with reference to things *of the same quality* and not as concerned with an absolute or pure unit "abstracted from quality") you have something quite different from the quantitative unit which may be anything at all.[2] If we are going to derive number from groups of instances **[104]** or groups of members of a class, we have to have[3] some notion of what is meant by *a* member of a class. We should have to have something that enables us to distinguish between a statement such as "There are six persons in the room" or "There are two hundred slates on the roof" and a statement such as "There are twenty things on the table", the latter having no real meaning because we don't know what *a* thing (similarly, an individual) is --- we have no real unit because a part of a thing is just as much a thing as the whole, while a part of a man is certainly not a man. There might be some element of convention is our decision as to what we are going to call *one* this or that, but at least we have to distinguish between cases where a sufficiently

---

[1] EN: the text here reads "that arrive".
[2] MN: from the notion of continuous number which may relate to anything.
[3] EN: the text here reads "have ? To", with MN "have".

exact notion of the unit can be formed and cases where it cannot. In fact, one would never say, unless one were speaking very loosely or in a way which would be covered by some convention (even unspoken) "There are twenty *things* on the table"; and even if one said "There are twenty pieces of wood on the table", then granted that a "piece of wood" could be divided into two pieces of wood whereas a man cannot be divided into two men, we can still take it that what at a given time we call *a piece of wood* is something which is continuously wooded (i.e. which is wooden throughout, right up to its boundaries) and which is discontinuous with (separate from, not continued into) any other piece of wood. That might raise a difficulty in the case of blocks which are in contact (which are touching) but we do quite clearly distinguish two blocks in contact from one continuous piece, i.e. however closely they may be touching they do not constitute what we call a continuity.[1] That is, at any rate, one convention we could conceive as being adopted --- one way of intelligibly calling a thing (and being able to recognise) one piece of wood. (Cf. question of Siamese twins, raised by A. C. Jackson. They are two *men*, not one.)

Allowing for variation of conventions and dubious cases, the point is that we do have the notion of *one* of a certain sort of thing, and in that connection we have a general distinction, of whatever logical importance it may be, between a quality of a whole which is a quality of any of its parts (e.g. being wooden),[2] a quality of a whole which is a quality of only some of the parts of that whole, and a quality of a whole which is a quality of *none* of the parts of that whole (e.g. being a man); and it is the last sort of quality that is important in connection with the notion of one member of a class and is the sort of thing we assume, whether we precisely get it or not (whether we are precisely conscious of it or not), in all cases of enumeration.[3] **[105]**

---

[1] EN: the text here reads "continuity:".
[2] MN: cf. earlier.
[3] MN: Q^s of parts wh re nt ql^s of whole [$conn^n$ x $subst^{ce}$, q^n].— EN: this appears to be shorthand for "Qualities of parts which are not qualities of whole (connection with *substance*, quantity)".

This notion of one member, however exactly or inexactly we may form it, depends upon the quality in question --- if you like, on the class in question --- on what the things are supposed to be instances or members of; so that there is no question of an absolute individual, of something that is *one*, no matter what quality may be in question, or again no matter what size may be in question (Cf. Alexander on elephants, mice, etc). We might be able to take the same thing as one instance of the kind X and as made up of several instances of the kind Y; we are not tied down to this or that unit, or this or that class; but in any concrete case we have to have the notion of *one* instance and therefore of what it is an instance of.

Now Alexander, in connection with all this, seems to be tending to a rationalistic view of mathematics, to treating it as concerned with something other than observable things, for although he does say that figures in geometry and numbers in arithmetic are different kinds of empirical objects we observe for[1] themselves, his contention just before that "however much the observation of collections of things may provoke us to attend to numbers and their combinations, we no more derive arithmetical thoughts from the things in which they are embodied than we derive geometrical truths, such as that the two sides of the triangle are greater than the third side, from actual measurement of brass triangles or three-cornered fields"[2] would seem to suggest that mathematical knowledge is derived from something other than observation, that number was to be taken as something apart from the numerable (enumerable), as is at least suggested by Alexander's description of numbers as "empirical universals" (p. 314 ft), which for us can only mean sorts of things on the same logical footing as any other sorts of things. (Cf. earlier discussion of Alexander on "universals".) I would argue that, if there is a theory of number, it will be a theory of integers or whole numbers exhibited by different groups of concrete things, even if the different groups have the same number. (Cf. different groups with the same quality.) Now Alexander says that unity is posterior to multiplicity ("it is safe to say that unity is a notion posterior in

---

[1] EN: the text here reads "for?".
[2] MN: p. 315.

development to multiplicity"[1]), which would imply, e.g. that we contemplated *fours* as a particular sort of thing before we thought of *the unit*. There may in fact be a certain psychological priority; we may recognise a pattern (configuration) before there is any question of counting (enumeration); and we may see that a group (which is actually) of six sheep is greater than a group (actually) of four sheep without having considered the relation of each group to the unit (*one* sheep). But we could never *assign* a specific number to a group without having decided on a unit, and the unit is *involved* in what the person perceives (in the above discrimination, e.g.) **[106]** whether he brings it out explicitly or not. He could of course be interested in the pattern more than in the number (in the *square shape*, say, that a quartet of things can form --- and that is a quite general conception) but even then he has some interest in the *things* that form the quartet and some ground for taking each as one[2]; and it is only after classification of another sort, after recognition of *an X*, that any question of number as such can arise. Number, then, is a *secondary* ground of classification and is nothing without the unit. (There is of course no reason why it shouldn't be associated with, and have interest in it stimulated by, considerations of shape or configuration, which is a *primary* ground of classification; though, even there, when we see a constellation, a shape picked out by stars, it is because of a prior interest in a common quality of the stars --- call it brightness or yellowness.)

Alexander then discusses the Russell-Frege notion of the cardinal number as a class of classes, the number *n* as the class of classes similar to a given class. What that could (defensibly) mean would be that "the number 2" is *any pair*, not this or that pair, not a particular pair but the general notion of a pair. The expression *class of classes*[3] is hardly proper because (1) it is (amounts to) treating a class (b) as a *collection* of a certain number of members, but (2) cannot treat class (a) in the same way because

---

[1] MN: p. 316.
[2] MN: & if not, it is *shape* & *nt* no. t s in qn. — EN: this appears to be shorthand for "And if not, it is *shape* and *not* number that is in question".
[3] EN: the text here reads "*class of classes*" with "(a)" written above "*class*" and "(b)" written above "*classes*".

there is no question of our making or being acquainted with a collection of all such collections. Thus *belonging to the class (a)* of classes (b) simply means *being of the sort of* classes (b), and that means being the sort of [i.e. of the *number* of] a certain *collection* (of unit members) --- in other words, being of a certain number.[1] Thus if you remove the ambiguity of "class" (and particularly the identification of *class* with a set of individuals), you are left with the position that the number two is *any pair* (or *a* pair: Cf. Russell on denoting), that to say of a collection (a group) that it has the number 2 is to say that it is a pair. We don't have to bring *similarity* into the matter (i.e. the fact that any pair has a one-one relation to a given pair)[2]; so that the Russell-Frege position is needlessly complicated and is not any sort of explanation of cardinal number. It is important to have the idea of cardinal number and not to treat numbers as merely ordinal (1, 1 + 1, 1 + 1 + 1, etc) and that (a) may be part of what Alexander has in mind when he says that the notion of multiplicity is prior to unity and (b) is part of what is involved in the Pythagorean configurations where a specific number is identified with a quite specific figure which we can recognise by its general character (its figure or shape) without counting the units. It is important, then, to see that a group definitely has a number apart from its being reckoned one at a time; but even then, when **[107]** Alexander says that the act of counting does not explain number (even admitting, I mean, that this rules out the subordination of cardinal to ordinal number), it is, I think, part of the same procedure, the attempt to separate number from the concrete things that we can observe; and in that respect Russell, in his *Principles of Mathematics* period, in his reference to concrete groups, his treatment of number in effect as *any group* which can form a certain configuration and is much nearer the truth of the matter than Alexander.

---

[1] MN: *Not* that "All instances of pairs are 2" but that 2 is what happens in every (each) instance of a pair.
[2] MN: enough that we can see that a given pair *is* a pair.

Lecture 36 Ordinal numbers: category of order.

Even if there is no question of taking a Pythagorean view and trying to develop continuity from separate units (the point being that continuity is already *in* each unit), still in the logical order we come to the question of integral number (number made up of units) prior to the question of real number (number made of quantity).[1] Beginning with the logic of quality we get the notion of membership of a class and from that the notion of a *collection* of members of a (certain) class, a collection which has a certain number and for which you require a certain unit.

Once you have this theory of number --- of cardinal numbers, of the various positive integers --- you then get the notion of ordinal numbers, of the number-series. (Actually children at least learn the *names* of the numbers ordinally, but have to be able to appreciate cardinal number to know what these names mean.) We are said, then, to form *the number-series*, and thus[2] we have the notion of a greater and lesser number, and then the further notion of addition, which might be said to involve the conception of groups of groups, and the correlative notion of subtraction.[3] These, I say, are further notions we can form *once we have the notion of a greater or less integer*; and having this notion of groups of groups, we can also form the conception of multiplication --- the notion e.g. of a group formed of six groups, each of six members --- and of course the correlative notion of division, and from that it is easy to form the notion of fractions,

---

[1] MN: Do math^l oper^{ns} invol treat^g nos. as qnt^s? — EN: this appears to be shorthand for "Do mathematical *operations* involve treating numbers as *quantities*?".

[2] EN: the text here reads "thus??". It seems that "??" was added when the MN (below) was written.

[3] MN: 2+1 as "def^n" of 3 (the no. t comes aft 2 in • ser^s of nos) (How do we kn t there *re* such nos?) (Smth^g ord^l no dbt, in our gene^g • not^n of *succ^r* & gett^g • "no-ser^{s}") [Djcn (thus *add^g*) in • orig^l not^n of no. (?!)]. — EN: this appears to be shorthand for "2 + 1 as "definition" of 3 (the number that comes after 2 in the series of numbers). (How do we know that there *are* such numbers?) (Something *ordinal*, no doubt, in our generalising the notion of *successor* and getting the "number-series".) Disjunction (thus *adding*) in the original notion of number (?!)".

applied first of all to groups of groups but leading to the conception of a fraction or proportionate part even of a unit; so now forming the conception of rational number, i.e. of the class of numbers each of which is expressible as a ratio between two integers, we can then recognise an *order* (series) of rational numbers (we needn't in this connection have formed the conception of negative number, although we would have the notion of subtraction) which exhibits what is sometimes regarded as continuity, as *sufficient* for continuity, viz. the characteristic that between any two members of the series a third can be found, i.e. the characteristic that in relation to any two rational numbers there is a rational number which is greater than the less and less than the greater (e.g. the average of the two; or a ratio whose numerator is the sum of their numerations and whose denominator is the sum of their denominators). **[108]** That, I say, has sometimes been regarded as sufficient for continuity, but actually it does not prove *contact* between two different rational numbers (where I am thinking especially of the representation of them by points in a straight line); and without such contact [of points?!?] we do not really have continuity,[1] a continuity perhaps best described in terms of movement, viz. that there could be no movement from one rational number to another rational number *through rational numbers alone* [that is the point; that whereas between any two rational numbers there is a rational number, there is between any two rational numbers something that is *not* a rational number: where *between* means greater than the less and less than the greater][2]; and that point is reinforced (*made*, rather) by consideration of *irrational* numbers, by the fact that we can find a point on the line just as definite as the points that represent rational numbers but not itself representing a rational number --- in other words, by the *fact* of irrational numbers, numbers not expressible by any ratio whatever between two integral numbers; so that what might be called the "betweenness" of rational

---

[1] NT: No *next* points ▲ real numbers *aren't* a series. — MN: Confus^n in math^l th^y of re no.? — EN: this appears to be shorthand for "Confusion in mathematical theory of real number?".

[2] MN: Point is -- • v^y ccp^n of *order* invol^s contn^y (qnt) even if the ordered thg^s re nt contn^s. — EN: this appears to be shorthand for "Point is --- the very conception of *order* involves continuity (quantity) even if the ordered things are not continuous".

numbers (that between any two there is another) does not amount to continuity, and for the notion of *real* number (covering both rational and irrational numbers) we have to bring in quantitative continuity in space, it being of course particularly in geometry that the question of the irrational arises. Thus we distinguish continuous quantity from the series of rational numbers as well as from the series of integers,[1] and we take the category of quantity after the categories of number and order even though we recognise that actual quantitative continuity is involved in anything that from the outset we might call a *unit*. [Could possibly say that in first set of categories we work from continuity to discontinuity ("intractability") and in second set work back to continuity --- and in third set work on again to "intractability" (individuality).]

I might remark here that Alexander takes the category of order in Ch. V, after *relation*, and not in connection with number and quantity. I don't profess to have given any rigorous demonstration of the order of the categories, but we do need some sort of principle (determining, at least, order of presentation). On the other hand, there will be objectively no order in the sense that the categories (whatever we might mean by their "application") must all be equally applicable to every situation, so that what exhibits identity must also exhibit order and that which exhibits order must also exhibit identity, and so on with any other pair of categories. The fact that the conception of order has already entered into (been linked with) the general discussion of (the relations between) Space and Time is not so much to the point (entered into the discussion, I mean, particularly in connection with the three characters of Time), because *any* discussion is bound to involve the categories and the discussion of "the relations between Space and Time" might be a rough preliminary treatment of the questions which are more exactly treated in discussion of the categories. **[109]**

---

[1] MN: & still no such thg as "the" ser^s of *re* nos. [Series implies discreteness.] — EN: this appears to be shorthand for "And still no such thing as "the" series of *real* numbers. Series implies discreteness.

However that may be, Alexander makes quite an interesting point (p. 263: Ch. V on *Order*) in regard to the question of transitiveness and irreversibility which we considered in connection with his account of the relation between Space and Time, viz., that we shouldn't speak of an order among terms or an order in a certain relation unless that order is asymmetrical or irreversible as well as transitive, so that we could set up an order in terms of greater and less but not in terms of equality. (What about non-symmetrical and non-transitive? Apparently the desire is for a continued series like that of integers or pitches etc.) Admitting (?) that that is so, in this reference to *equality* Alexander is admitting that the transitive is not necessarily irreversible and thus re-affirming (?) our criticism of his account of the transitiveness of Time in which he *included* irreversibility. [We can see here how that confusion arises. He has fixed in his mind the notion of the *irreversibility* of time and so reads that into its transitiveness.]

Lecture 37 Transition between categories: logical, mathematical, physical; category of quantity - from mathematical point of view as real number - from physical point of view as solidity; category of intensity – number dependent on quality – confused conceptions of degree.

The view is taken that to speak of a relation as having *order* means that it is asymmetrical. Thus, from the case of equality, it appears that transitiveness is necessary but not sufficient for order. This is an important point for the theory of order, but it cuts across Alexander's argument about Time where he treats transitiveness as including irreversibility. His present admission supports our criticism of that argument. (A good deal of Alexander's further discussion I'll say little about; I'll treat the categories he recognises, but much of his discussion is so very slight that I'll ignore it.)

I have taken the categories as they appeared (in second set) without relating them back to the propositional theory (exposition of first set in terms of the proposition). In general we can say that while the first set of categories, *categories of pure logic*, can be expressed in terms of the proposition or correspond to different features of the proposition as such, the second set, categories of quantity (or *mathematical categories*), correspond rather to, or revolve upon, the logical term, especially the subject, indicate what we would mean by complexity or more accurately by *composition* --- are connected, if you like, with the "logic of relations" because we are dealing with things alongside one another. (I pointed out earlier some of the difficulties in connecting the logic of relations with that of predication.) We can say, then, that mathematical categories are bound up with the logic of relations and that again with the character of the subject. Now the third set of categories, the *physical categories*, emphasise the **[110]** logic of process, of events (and so with the *predicate*, as "activity"?) Naturally it would be argued that there is a transition from each category to the next and from each group to the next. And, without having worked the transitions out, I would suggest that the logic of events would be linked up with the logic of *implication* as contracted with the logic of propositions and their constituents.[1] (Alexander hasn't given much help on the relations between number, order and quantity.)

Quantity. One might take the category of *quantity* as the point of transition from the mathematical to the physical categories, just as the category of *universality* is the point of transition from the logical to the mathematical, because it does seem to be the case that the conception of intensity or degree takes you beyond (purely) quantitative considerations and involves qualitative considerations. Where it was purely a quantitative matter it would be the category of *order* that was in question: i.e., you would have your capacity of being greater or less --- an example of order, not of intensity. Then, with regard to quantity being the turning-point (or term linking --- common to --- the two sets)[2] you have the question of different interpretations of the category of quantity according as you look at it from a mathematical or a physical point of view. From a mathematical point of view, quantity is just the same as *real number* --- that which has continuous measurement (I have already argued that you get *a continuity* in real number which you do not get in *rational number*, which I linked with the category of order[3]) --- whereas quantity or the continuous, from the *physical* point of view, might be regarded as *solidity*, as what in fact we mean by "matter", what, with the Atomists, we distinguish as the *full* from the *empty*. In lecturing on Haeckel and 19th century materialism[4], in 1st year, and comparing them with the Greeks, I suggested that "matter" couldn't mean any *quality* but only solidity or "space-filling" --- though, of course, it requires a quality, something qualitative, to have this space-filling character, but it can be any quality whatever and there is no quality common to all others, on

---

[1] MN: argument.
[2] NT: Logic : Identity to Universality; Mathematics: Universality to Quantity; Physics: Quantity to Individuality.
[3] MN: i.e. you cd get no pt on the line wh *wasn't* a real number. ["Real number" *means* point on a line?]. — EN: this appears to be shorthand for "i.e. you could get no point on the line which *wasn't* a real number. "Real number" *means* point on a line?"
[4] EN: The text here reads "materialism", with "(molecular theory?)" Written above it.

which all others are "founded", or belonging to all things. Space itself (also Time) has mathematical quantity, but only what is in Space (and Time) can have physical quantity as well.[1]

I suggest that matter can be no more than solidity (cf. Locke's treatment of this, of impenetrability, as a "primary quality") and consequently that it is meaningless to regard things as composed of matter, to speak of matter as the stuff of which things are made up, i.e., if that, space-filling, is all we can say things have in common, then if we ask [111] what any particular thing is composed of, it would be the peculiarities and not this common feature that we expected to receive as the answer. And the ordinary doctrine of materialism, as the attempt to say what is the real substance of things as contrasted with their accidents is untenable, since we cannot say that there is any such order among the characters of things or that things are made of their common features and not their peculiarities. And of course the very existence of chemistry as a science (without going into the fields of biology and psychology) shows that things are recognised as composed of *different* materials and takes away all meaning from the question *what it is that they are all composed of*. The only possible answer to that question would be one that we would never want to stand by, viz, that they are composed of the solidity or space-fillingness; yet physics might quite well investigate the characteristics and proceedings of things *as* space-filling (Time would be understood there as well) irrespective of what their *peculiar* characters might be. (If we take quantity on the mathematical side we should be taking it as it applies to the "void" as well as to the "full", to continuous space as well as to the space-filling, whereas quantity in the physical sense is restricted to the space-fillingness of things, to things as space-filling. There is no antagonism between the two conceptions. If we take the categories of characters of things in general, then their mathematical quantity and their physical quantity would in some sense be the same, although we are emphasising different connections in the two cases.)

---

[1] EN: The last sentence of this paragraph is enclosed in square brackets. The penultimate paragraph is enclosed in round brackets.

The notion of real number could not be arrived at from any development of the notion of integral number as rational number can, but only from continuity in Space-Time.[1] To form the notion of real number you have to be thinking of (have the notion of) spatial continuity as e.g. in a line. Although you have that continuity already in your unit, still it is brought out in a more definite way in the theory of real number.

Intensity. Starting off, then, with quantity as the first of the physical categories and taking it to involve the notion of something which is continuous (which has the same continuity as the real numbers), I would pass on to the conception of intensity or degree, which again Alexander discusses in no very thorough manner, referring to but not specially elucidating *Kant's* theory of intensity. And I would argue that intensity differs from order in that the conception of order is independent of quality. When we say things are in a certain order we are making no presumptions as to their quality [the members of the series could have any qualities at all] whereas in the case of intensity we are: and again, as Alexander himself [112] says, we can say that intensity is *correlated* with quantity but cannot be simply *equated* with it, in the sense that where there are differences of intensity there are corresponding differences of quantity but to recognise a difference of intensity is not necessarily to recognise a quantitative difference: e.g. we speak of one note as *higher in pitch* than another and we know that the difference between higher and lower goes with a difference in the number of vibrations in a given time in the two cases, but to recognise difference of pitch, to recognise say a higher note, is not in general to recognise anything about rates of vibration.

Of course it might be argued that this is a question of exact measurement, that when we recognise one distance as longer than another (which would certainly be called a *quantitative* difference) we are not recognising[2] it to be longer by such and such an amount, and that similarly *hotter* or *louder* or *higher* in

---

[1] EN: "as rational number can, but only from continuity in Space-Time" is written as a MN, with an insertion mark in the text between "number and ".".
[2] EN: the text here reads "recognising", with "finding" written above it.

pitch could be described as quantitative differences even though they do not require any exact measurement, even though we may not know at all how much one thing is hotter, louder, etc, than another or have even *attempted* to determine a unit. Nevertheless there does seem to be a definite distinction between merely spatio-temporal comparison, as in *longer* or *faster*, and the kind of comparison that is involved in these other cases. We could never express hotter or louder *simply* as a distance or a rate or in merely spatio-temporal terms, nor again could we express these differences in terms of one another, the point being that some particular sort of *quality* is involved in each case, though of course under particular conditions there could be *connections* between different types of variation --- a sheet of metal could become brighter as it got hotter, and so on --- whereas if intensity were reducible to simple quantity, it ought to be possible to express hotter in terms of louder and vice versa, and so with any similar pair of terms.

I have argued of course (e.g. in "The Meaning of Good") that there is a great deal of confusion in the conception of *degree*, that it would always be wrong to speak as if, when two things had a given quality, one of them could have it in a higher or more eminent degree than the other; I have argued that if it is proper to speak if X and Y as *green*, if *X is green*, is a complete statement, then it must be improper to speak of X as *greener* than Y --- or, if it is proper to say that A and B are simply *good*, it must be improper to say that A is *better* than Y. But, granting that point, granting in general that we can never have a comparative of a strictly positive term, it may still be the case, and I have been suggesting that it *is* the case, that where we *can* properly use a comparative, qualitative considerations are involved – **[113]** or, more accurately, that while there are comparatives that have a purely spatio-temporal meaning, there are others that have also a qualitative component; and thus if we say that *louder* is significant, that will mean that *loud* cannot be a quality, that *X is loud* cannot be a complete statement, and yet, I suggest, it will still be the case that, when we say X is louder than Y, there are certain qualities of X and Y that are involved in the comparison.

(Alexander on *Quantity and Intensity*, Bk II, Ch VII: very brief, and doesn't distinguish between the two types of cases --- taking *speed* e.g. as a case of intensity. Note that he doesn't think there is any such thing as colour in general: Cp. Bk II, Ch. III, p. 216: so that, for him, it must be a matter of intensity or place within a certain range or scale --- comparable to *pitch*.)

Lecture 38 Measurement of sensation: Weber's law; 'threshold of consciousness'; cognitionalism in psychology.

Bk II, Ch. VII, p. 307, *note*: reference to Weber's Law.

The position is of an attempted measurement of sensation (a "psychophysical" problem), particularly the measurement of sensation in relation to stimulus. The "Weber-Fechner" law amounts to this: that sensation varies as the logarithm of the stimulus; or that while the stimulus increases in geometrical progression, the sensation increases in arithmetical progression. Of course many people have maintained that this assumes an exactitude that never could be obtained in these investigations, that in particular the whole attempt to set up a *unit of sensation* is one that cannot be successful; and the essential point here is that what is really being investigated, what these theorists are dealing with when they set up this correlation, is *people's powers of discrimination*.

There is of course first of all the question of a "threshold of consciousness", of the amount or intensity of stimulus required in order that any sensation may occur, in order that (the stimulus or the impression) should rise above the threshold of consciousness or, as we would say, in order that it may be noticed. Obviously it would be a different "threshold" that was in question according to the type of stimulus that was being applied, though it might be argued that the noticing of certain kinds of things is intimately bound up with (is promoted perhaps or again is hindered by) the noticing of some other kind of thing; and it may be remarked here that the attempt of experimental psychologists to be "scientific" by isolating particular factors, by trying to separate sensitivity to red, let us say, from every other sensitivity and from any other mental or physical condition, is a mistaken one, just as scientists in general are mistaken in thinking that they can "isolate" factors, though the psychologists here are losing in company with the non-experimental psychologists, viz. in their *cognitionalism*, in their assumption that cognitive powers can be taken by themselves --- in particular, can be taken apart from the emotional life --- a cognitionalist view which of course is in line with the whole **[114]** trend of Cartesian and post-Cartesian philosophy.

The main point, then, is that there is a different threshold according to the kind of stimulus in question; and of course it would be different for different minds; one mind might have far greater capacities for noticing colours or again for distinguishing colours than another; and of course that is recognised in these studies --- you do have experimental studies of tone-deafness, colour-blindness, etc. But even that is qualified by the fact that the same mind will not have the same discriminatory powers at all times, a point that again has been allowed for by those investigators in studies of the influence of fatigue, e.g. but what I say they haven't allowed for is the way attention and discrimination are rooted in the whole emotional life, this being something which can be brought out much more clearly and definitely on a Freudian than on a pre-Freudian basis (and most psychological schools would still be pre-Freudian in their outlook).

Such considerations, then --- quite generally, the rejection of cognitionalism --- would lead us to cast doubt on the assigning of a particular value to powers of knowing or distinguishing (discerning) this or that, would lead us to see how such powers could change independently of a change in the apparatus (particularly the physiological apparatus). But even without carrying the argument as far as that, even without challenging cognitionalism, we can find certain fundamental weaknesses in Weber's law; i.e. admitting quantitative measurement of the stimulus and its variability along a continuous scale, we cannot admit a similar scale (similar measurement) on the side of sensation; we can only regard as arbitrary the decision that the *difference of intensity of sensation* in the case of two things that the person in question can just distinguish *is a unit*, i.e. we have no reason for saying that each[1] of a successive set of discriminations while the stimulus is being steadily intensified, is quantitatively equivalent to every other, and at the same time the

---

[1] EN: the text here reads "that in the case of each", with "in the case of" encircled (marked to delete).

absence of continuity (or what we can *call* the absence of continuity) on the psychological side is opposed to the very notion of units here, since by a unit we mean not something indivisible but something continuous and divisible.

The suggestion is that you have (say) a stimulus A which is recognised and, supposing you have some unit on the side of the stimulus and stimulus A+1 is applied, then the mind wouldn't notice the difference between A and A+1 (wouldn't *discriminate* the stimuli) but would only notice the difference when the stimulus had been increased to A + B. So then, calling the sensation from the stimulus A "X", we arbitrarily call the sensation on the occasion of the stimulus A + B (when the first discrimination is made) "X + 1". That is the way in which this "unit" is established; and at all the intermediate points [115] (between A and A+B) you will still be said only to have the sensation X --- or a sensation of the *intensity* X; it is only when the stimulus reaches a certain mind that the discrimination is made and that a "sensation of higher intensity" is said to have occurred. (Cf. loudness of noise, amplitude of electric current; there are any number of possibilities of continuous increase of stimulus; and in each case, over certain ranges the mind would not distinguish --- wouldn't be able to say that an increase had taken place.) The further suggestion of the theory then is that, when you went on to A + B + 1, the mind wouldn't distinguish it from A + B (would still recognise it as, or have the sensation, of intensity X + 1) and the same might be the case with the addition of further units of stimulus; but at the point at which *further* discrimination was made, it would be said that the intensity of sensation had been increased by one more unit (that it was now X + 2), and what the law says is that the stimulus must have increased in the same *proportion* as in the case of the previous discrimination (between A and A + B), so that we should have, following the terms A and $A + (1 + \frac{B}{A}) [= A + B]$, the term $A(1 + \frac{B}{A})^2$ --- which is $A + 2B + \frac{B^2}{A}$. That is what is meant by the assertion that the sensation is as the logarithm of the stimulus --- that where A *just* gave the sensation X, and A + B *just* gave the sensation X + 1, $A + 2B + \frac{B^2}{A}$ would similarly be the minimum stimulus for sensation X + 2; and the decision to say *X + 1* and *X + 2* would be made on the basis of successive discriminations (or noticing of increase).

It is clearly arbitrary to speak of a "unit sensation" under these conditions. It is assuming of course that there is a specific entity "the sensation" in each of these cases, something that would be distinguished from mere *knowledge of the stimulus*; and here it may be argued that the only fact we have at our disposal is the fact that certain discriminations are made. We are just able to distinguish one stimulus from another --- that is what has happened, but that gives us no ground for speaking of a *unit sensation*. The real outcome, then, of the law is that discrimination, the noticing of a difference between this and that; is not in terms of the absolute or arithmetical difference but is in terms of the *ratio* (geometrical difference) of the two things in question; so that the general assertion would be that we distinguish two things of a certain class as to their amount or intensity when and only when the ratio of one to the other (of the larger to the smaller) does not fall below a certain level; and of course that is exactly what we should expect --- we should expect things to be distinguished in accordance with the proportion that one bore to the other and not according to the absolute amount of difference. **[116]** And when Alexander suggests, referring of course to experimental work, that this holds only within certain ranges, he can be answered, I think, by saying that it is in not the same type of question that is at issue in the two sets of cases. [There is, however, *also* the question of greater discriminatory "keenness" in certain ranges --- of ranges of notes, e.g. where we are quite at a loss (too high or too low for us to make out much about them), even if, over our "good" range, it is *intervals* that we specially pick out (recognise).]

Alexander is talking about the estimate of just perceivable differences of lengths of line as measured by the eye; and he says that, with lines of moderate length, the just perceptible difference follows Weber's law and is approximately a constant fraction of the length; but, he goes on, "when the differences of length are larger we tend to equate not fractional but absolute differences:

e.g. the difference of 5 and 7 inches seems equal to that of 10 and 12 inches, not that of 10 to 14 inches, as it should if Weber's law held."[1] Now of course it was *just perceptible differences* that were in question from the beginning and there would be very few people for whom the difference between 5 and 7 inches would be a just perceptible difference; but even so when (for brevity) we equate 7-5 and 12-10, it is because we are thinking separately of these differences, whereas if we were really thinking about the *whole* of the lengths in question we should equate 7-5 to 14-10. All Alexander is saying is that we can consider other things than proportions, which is obviously true. It is still the case that when we are considering two things[2] as wholes we are much more likely to think of their proportions than of their absolute difference of length, whatever it might be. In fact, that is obviously the case, e.g. in the recognition of musical relations; we recognise two intervals as the same even when they (the intervals) differ by an octave or more, and of course "the *same* interval" means they have the same proportion between rates of vibration, whereas the same *arithmetical difference* between rates of vibration would, musically speaking, mean nothing to us at all.[3] The notion of arithmetical difference there would be, so to speak, an artificial one, whereas the geometrical difference is a natural one. (You get the same relation here as the relation of stimuli which are just distinguished. What is called *a number of tones of difference* between two notes --- say, "two tones"; a major third --- is the ratio of the two rates of vibration.[4]) So that Alexander's solution (the one he takes from Ebbinghaus) that in the one case we are considering the lengths intensively and in the other case as extensive quantities, doesn't seem to meet the case or be really to the point unless we identify an "intensive relation" with a proportion, **[117]** and then that comes back to the point I have already made, that proportion or relative intensity [and note that it may be proportion of "extensive" or spatio-temporal characters like length or speed] is not the only thing we can

---

[1] MN: 307, n.
[2] EN: the text here reads "things", with "(two things)" written above it.
[3] NT: What about "difference-tones"? Is that arithmetical or fractional?
[4] MN: $\frac{5}{4}$.

consider in any given situation, but that there will always be *something* which calls forth our powers of discrimination and recognition, and that we can recognise (or find repeated) a ratio or proportion where we should be quite incapable of recognising a mere arithmetical difference.

Lecture 39 Category of substance outlined; category of intensity continued.

Substance. Alexander's theory of substance is slightly connected with Kant's: There is a closer connection between his and Kant's theories of causality. Alexander conceives substance in relation to the First Analogy: and Kant's point about the performance of *substance* might rather be related to the point I made about *quantity*, as space-fillingness. We can agree with Kant that a change is a change of something, not a matter of complete novelty; but what is constant through that change will not be constant through *all* change, will not be *permanent* but will itself pass away in other changes. There is no permanent subject of all change --- the "permanent subject" could only be *Space* which *doesn't* change: isn't "that which changes". I link this criticism of Kant with my discussion, in connection with the position of Parmenides among the pre-Socratics, of what is meant by *becoming*. It requires the notion not merely of novelty but of replacing --- of a change taking place *in* something constant: constant through that change. Becoming is not just Y coming to be but $\underline{X}$ *which was not Y* becoming Y (not simply Y appearing where there was previously not-Y): and X itself will be a state of *some subject* which *was* not X and became X.)

Intensity (cont). I was arguing that expressions of degree are not just quantitative distinctions; that there is a real distinction between degree and quantity because in the former quality comes in (quality essential to *intensity*). You could speak of quantity, e.g. the distance between two things, without implying that the distance is occupied by a third thing; i.e., you could speak of it in terms of pure Space-Time. But you couldn't speak so of intensity because it involves quality.

Even so, the intensity is not *the intensity of* a particular quality (having a quality in greater or less degree); what we get is a number of quite different qualities which can be arranged along a certain scale and correlated with quantities. Of course, we can recognise the range, the differences of intensity, without having any exact knowledge of the quantities. Differences of musical pitch were recognised before the Pythagoreans made their discoveries about the harmonious intervals, and in turn these relative quantities or ratios were recognised before any exact quantitative measurement could be given, before it could be said what it was a quantity of. And to know that what is being measured is rate of vibration is not to know the octave, let us say, any better than we know it before. In the same way **[118]** you could have recognition of a range of colours without having any knowledge of the quantities involved (again, the rate of wave-motion); so that, as I said, intensity is not to be reduced to quantity any more that it is to be equated to quality. It appears as a quite peculiar type of relation [dyadic] involving both quality and quantity.

Seeing, then, that the taking of *green* (say) as a quality implies that there is no such thing as *greener*, and on the other hand that the recognition of degree of brightness (relations of brighter and duller) implies that there is no such quality as *bright*, but, (seeing), nevertheless, that such qualities and intensities can be closely connected, we may ask whether intensity is bound up with *all* qualities, whether *every* quality exists in a range like the range of colours and the range of tones;[1] and it may be argued, I think, that even if intensity is categorial, even if it is in some sense a feature of all occurrence, it is not necessarily a feature of all quality --- taking quality as just *being such and such*, being of a certain kind (character).

On the other hand there may be a basis here for quite important distinctions, distinctions between those qualities which do exist in ranges and those which do not; and this may be the same distinction as that already suggested between those qualities which, if they characterise a whole, characterise all its parts and those qualities of a whole which characterise some only, or even none, of its parts. e.g., *yellow* -- when we say a thing is yellow, we would also say any part of it is yellow;[2] on the other hand, humanity --- when we say a thing is human or is a man, we *don't* say any part of it is human or is a man. Now yellow is one of

---

[1] MN: Phaedo.
[2] NT: Alexander wouldn't: cf. his theory of substance, etc.

those qualities but exist in the colour range, whereas there is no qualitative range in which humanity exists. (In spite of the attempt of some biologists to get a continuous series of animal types culminating in man, there would never be any real continuity in any such series.) It is possible, I say, that these two distinctions would coincide (that the qualities existing in ranges would be "through and through" qualities and the others not); and in that way we might be able to account for the distinction between substance and attribute, to see that the through and through qualities are the ones that would be considered *attributes* and the others substances, that no one, e.g., on being asked what a given thing is composed of, or what is its substance, would answer *yellow*, whereas he would say that *humanity* is the substance or, if you like, the constitution of a man.[1]

And that raises the further question, whether such a substance could always be described in terms of what we may call the "pure" qualities and spatial and temporal relations between them --- which would mean that substance was the same sort of thing as I had previously referred to as *relations in the*[2] *extended* sense as against relations in the strict sense (viz. spatio-temporal relations). **[119]** I don't want to press the point, but I would suggest that our knowledge of what I am now calling a substance does involve a knowledge of spatial relations (juxtaposition, etc) and perhaps temporal relations (certain types of succession) as well, in addition to simple *qualities*; so that a merely qualitative description of man, e.g., would be something we would never look for and would never enable us to *identify* a man. We call man in that rough definition "a rational animal"; but then whatever may be meant by *rational*, animal at least would be a substance in the same sense as man --- and this attempted distinction might cast some light on the general theory of classification where even if, as I've suggested, the genus and the difference would both have the same class relation to the species (viz. inclusion), still the difference in a good definition could be

---

[1] MN: Are these "range qualities" the same as the usual "secondary qualities"? (i.e. qualities of *matter*; everything space-filling enters into these ranges, whatever else it does, or "is like")?

[2] EN: the text here reads "an", with "the" written above it.

expressed in terms of qualities in that narrower sense I've suggested ("pure qualities"), while the genus would be a *substance* in the sense I've suggested.

Now I don't think this development of logical theory really cuts across a propositional logic, really involves a hierarchy of terms or a distinction among kinds of prediction. It would still be just as possible as before to use either of the terms in such a defining complex as the subject and either as the predicate --- if we call the defining complex QS, it will still be just as proper to say QiS and QoS as to say SiQ and SoQ, and it will still be just as significant, even if false, to say QaS. The distinction is one *supplementary* to the predicative theory, not in opposition to it; and indeed it may be observed that if there was not to be such supplementation we should have stopped at what I've called the categories of quality; there should not have been any more categories unless we were going to make distinctions or indicate connections which were not indicated by those early categories --- and indeed it is in terms of predication, together with the notion of whole and part (i.e. with the quantitative categories which we regarded as involved in the complexity of the propositional subject) that we have actually made the distinction.

And that position, if it could be made good, would bring out a very important point in the criticism of rationalistic theories --- that the trouble with them is not that they make certain distinctions but that they make them at the wrong stage, make them here as a variant of the proposition, of propositional form, instead of as something supplementary to it, recognise in general *kinds of propositions* when the single propositional logic fully permits of the making of the necessary distinctions of kind. (That is, they are real distinctions if they are put in the right place. The rationalist aims at a real distinction of kind but takes it as a distinction in the proposition.[1] **[120]**.

---

[1] MN: Kinds of assertion: assertion of attribute (attributive) versus assertion of essence (definition).

Lecture 40 The categories related to the proposition: Idealism as a philosophy of degrees: category of Substance.

The last lecture might appear to be a modification of the propositional view, but I suggested that whatever distinction there may be between substance and quality, still your propositional theory (conversion, etc) would remain unaffected.

I suggested that we get first of all a set of *categories of quality* related to the four forms of the proposition (covered by the constituents of the proposition and the distinctions[1] of quality and quantity[2] then the *categories of quantity*, making explicit what was implicit in the first set of categories, viz. spatial spreadoutness or juxtaposition --- and I suggest that it was already in the conception of subject as a region in which things went on, i.e. that it wasn't anything new, not opposed to the categories of quality; and I would suggest here that there is still good reason for taking the categories of quality first, then the categories of quantity, and finally the categories of *action* (process)[3]; and in connection with the development of further categories from the categories of quality, I think it should be said we have to make some distinction between relational assertions and qualitative assertions, even if the former take the predicative form (if they both take the same logical form) and that while in my logical discussions generally I have emphasised qualitative considerations while at the same time presenting it as a situational logic (while in this way I have identified things and situations) it might be better to take things as a species of situations, to say that things are situations but situations are not necessarily things, and then your predicative logic or logic of quality would be concerned with the qualities of things, while your logic of quantity would bring in situations in a wider sense and would be

---

[1] EN: the text here reads "relations", with "distinction" written above it.

[2] NT: Actually, the distinction of quality (affirmative and negative), there was some suggestion that the distinction of quantity might be connected with the *categories* of quantity. — EN: the text of this note reads "the relation of quantity", with "distinction" written above "relation".

[3] MN: Categories of quality: X is or is not Y. Categories of quantity – classes (genera & species).

applicable to pure Space and pure time apart from their being filled with things or processes, though it would still be the case that consideration(s) of situations arose out of consideration(s) of things, that to understand a thing we had to think of it was existing in situations, in particular as having spatio-temporal relations to other things, and also as having situations existing within it, as having spatio-temporal relations between its parts. (What I am doing could be viewed as a correction of over-emphasis. I have not given enough attention to relations or to relational proposition as contrasted with straightout qualitative prediction. I am suggesting that all I say now is quite sufficiently in accord with a situational logic.)

I was suggesting that in connection with intensity you could distinguish between quality, in a narrow sense, and substance by saying that the former existed in a certain range and the latter did not; also that humanity might have to be expressed in spatial and temporal relations as well as qualities; so in the notion of substance you have situational and qualitative considerations [121] and you have them generally in the categories of action or physical categories.

Now that distinction I made (in last lecture) would be one that was not made by Idealism. We could characterise Idealism as a philosophy of degrees, or of "perfections" to use the Cartesian or scholastic term, so that humanity, e.g. would be the expression of the Absolute with a certain degree of adequacy, it would be reality raised to a certain power, and everything, every characterisation we could possibly give, would come somewhere in that range. (Cf. Hegel, Kant, Bradley). Of course Hegel cannot really *consistently* range all characters in one series, just as Alexander with his theory of "complexities" of Space-Time cannot do so but fixes his levels arbitrarily in terms of the existing division of the sciences. (Alexander's evolutionist optimism is of course a *variety* of Idealism and one which helps to confuse and conceal the importance of his Space-Time theory - -- confuse it e.g. by the treatment of Space-Time as the "stuff" of which things are made.) Hegel cannot really arrange everything in that serial order, but he has to try to do so, and the same applies to Leibniz with his continuous series of monads from the lowest to the highest, where (apart from difficulties as to the series itself, the difficulty of two monads interchanging their positions in the scale and the alternative of no change taking place at all) we can say that there is a great deal of empirical fact which this series cannot possibly cover.[1] Idealism is a philosophy of degrees and if Alexander were a consistent evolutionist he would have to take the same sort of line; and he does speak of greater and less complexity, and even of the categories as having greater and less complexity, but he cannot make out this distinction in any consistent sort of way.[2]

Substance. Now Alexander's discussion of substance (Bk II, Ch VI, Section A) seems to me to be a thoroughly confused one --- one in which he confuses the category of substance with several other categories, e.g. when he says (p. 269), proposing to take substance in a spatial sense though recognising that temporal questions also come in, "For simplicity and brevity it will be enough to speak of substance as a piece of Space which is the scene of succession without stating the same thing in terms of Time in the reverse order" (i.e. a piece of Time which is "spread out"), where without challenging this simplification, without insisting on an equal emphasis on Time, we can say that this is to make substance indistinguishable from identity. And when he goes on to say (p. 270), "A thing or complex substance is then a contour of space (i.e. a volume with a contour) with which take place the motions correlated to the qualities of the thing; and the complex substance or thing is the persistence in time of this spatial contour with its defining motions," we can say that there is here some confusion between substance and quality, occupation of a certain limited part of continuous Space that the term contour in fact is thoroughly misleading and that **[122]** it is not a question of (as he goes on to suggest)[3] yellow and other qualities being "contained within the contour of the atom or molecule of gold." He would seem again to be introducing the mere notion of a subject or identity, though in its quantitative

---

[1] NT: The two criticisms might run together.
[2] EN: the last sentence of the paragraph is enclosed in round brackets.
[3] MN: p.270.

aspect of *containing* predicates, whereas if we are thinking seriously of gold as what we call a substance, then yellow or any other essential quality is not merely within it but helps to constitute it, is *part* of the "contour", if we like to use that word, and not just inside the contour. In fact, it would be better to reject the term contour, and, in thinking of a substance as a complex of qualities, to consider it as having a form or formula of combination, a formula which I suggested would cover not only qualities but spatial and temporal relations among them.[1] Admitting that, the notion of a contour or extreme boundary is of no special importance in this connection.

We need not bother about the term *correlation* between a motion and a quality, though it suggests what I had previously commented on, Alexander's failure completely to shake off parallelism, the suggestion of a quality as *standing above*, or hovering over, what it is attributed to. (Just another example of the incomplete *thinking out* of Alexander's position; he is bound, in that connection, to have some *arbitrary* views --- such as this one of a substance being a contour.) His confusion is further indicated in his reference to our own mind as a substance, where he refers to "the activities of mind" changing "from one moment to another according to the objects which engage it"[2], this reminding us of the relational and thus[3] insubstantial character of his own view of mind, the impossibility of his describing it except in terms of *a field of consciousness*, i.e. of its taking in various distinct objects of attention which do not really have any substantial unity; and this again being connected with the view of substance that he goes on to --- that its qualities do not interpenetrate but that it is "a space of a certain contour stippled over", as he puts it "with qualities",[4] the qualities, or the motions correlated with them, going through the given space but all somehow missing one another, which seems to me like an account of *several* substances, one for each quality, and not a

---

[1] MN: cf. H_2O etc. & chemical theories of spatial arrangement of *elementary* constituents. *That* is "substance".
[2] MN: p.270.
[3] EN: the text here reads "so", with "thus" written above it.
[4] MN: pp.275-276.

single substance --- seems to show, in fact, that in spite of all Alexander says about complexity he doesn't really admit complexity at all; and it is possible, I say, that this theory has been partially occasioned by the remnants of Idealism in his thinking, by his relational and, finally insubstantial view of mind, so that even a non-mental substance is a sort of field like the "field of consciousness", through which various ideas or trains of thought run, that it is then a mere arena --- not just that it has a locative function but that it is a location and nothing more, a location having for a given period a certain number of tenants. Certainly the argument that Alexander does give is very far from proving that the qualities of a substance do not interpenetrate, the argument, viz, that "It can only be supposed that they do" (interpenetrate), "if qualities are treated [123] as mental creations or ideas and, because they are such, are somehow regarded as not being in space or time."[1] To say that they are supposed to interpenetrate because they are *not* in Space and Time is a quite extraordinary contention, and if what is meant is that the qualities could[2] be treated as hovering over the motions with which Alexander says they are *correlated*, then presumably what would be meant is that the motions which *are* in Space and Time are what interpenetrate; yet Alexander immediately goes on to say "But the motions at any rate which correspond to the qualities are separate from one another and differently located", a position which seems to me not merely dogmatic but to exhibit the extreme of wrong-headedness. (To me his contentions are quite extraordinary --- they have neither rhyme nor reason.)

A person could argue "The motions which are in Space and Time can interpenetrate, but the qualities are not in the motions but are in the mind, therefore they needn't interpenetrate." But how could anyone argue "The motions which are in Space and Time *can't* interpenetrate but the qualities, which are in the mind, *can*"? Perhaps the person is supposed to argue "There is no *externality* in mind, therefore the qualities can't *miss* one another"; but in Space, Alexander points out, they have *room to miss*. Even then, that would be no sort of proof that they *do* miss

---

[1] MN: p.275.
[2] EN: the text here reads "can", with "could" written above it.

one another, for there is such a thing as spatial intersection. Perhaps not, however, on the doctrine of "point instants"; no point-instant can *cross* another. Then what in creation is "complexity"?¹

---

¹ EN: each of the last four sentences of the paragraph is enclosed in brackets.

Lecture 41 Alexander confuses substance with identity: the three groups of categories – and the transitions between them; substance continued – as the constitution of a thing.

If the qualities do not interpenetrate, you don't have *complexity* --- you have a multiplicity of substances, not one --- you have an arena in which various substances carry on (occur). That is a very arbitrary doctrine, with no force whatever. It is similar to the emphasis on contour, which makes substance simply *that within which* there are various qualities, so that there is really no substance at all. (Of course, that is quite in line with treating Space and Time as *stuff*, as *making up things*.) Alexander does not really get hold of a separate idea of substance; he confuses substance with categories like quantity and even identity. The same is the case in Kant's First Analogy where quantity or matter is confused with the permanent.[1] It might be that on my view the differences among the categories would be emphasised more than in Kant or Alexander. In the latter the categories are modifications of Space-Time and you have no *proposition* to hang the categories on. It is hard enough at any time to distinguish conditions that are in every occurrence, but it is particularly hard to make distinctions from the point of view of Space-Time alone. Alexander doesn't get substance distinguished from quantity or identity. In the main he treats it as the abstract identity most theories begin with but also as the concrete identity with which on my view the categories would end --- i.e. as *thinghood* (what is involved in being a thing).[2] **[124]**

Thus he says (p. 272): "The identity of a substance is individual identity as persisting through a duration of time. Numerical identity was occupation of a point-instant or complex of them. Generic identity or identity of sort was the preservation of a plan of construction throughout repetition at different times or places. When the repetition of a plan is found in its varying phases in the duration of an individual we had individual identity. We see now that substantial identity is equivalent to individual identity."

---

[1] NT: [?].
[2] NT: Individuality.

Alexander here is distinguishing substance or substantiality from mere identity (mere power of locating) and now he is identifying it with individuality; but when we speak of *identity of substance* we certainly do not mean individual identity. We say that two things are "of the same substance" when they are of the same composition or constitution, which would support the view I was putting forward that substance is the *make-up* of a thing, is a certain arrangement of qualities in (and) spatio-temporal relations. That of course is what Alexander would call universality or plan, but this notion of plan or construction seems a very forced interpretation of the meaning of *being such and such*. When we speak of being yellow, we certainly do not have in mind any plan or build-up, even though the thing which *is* yellow may have one; and there would seem to be a distinction between being of a *sort* or being predicable and the notion of being a certain *constitution*, having a certain interrelation of constituents.

I would suggest also that if, along the lines of the distinction of things from situations, we treat things as a species of situations or treat situations as involving more than things --- as involving spaces and times as well as concrete motions --- then the notion of universality or being such and such would apply to the spaces and times as well as to the things, and that is how the category (universality) can form the bridge between the categories of quality, arising in the first instance in connection with qualitative prediction, and the categories of quantity which are fundamental to mathematical, including geometrical, science. With the physical categories,[1] on the other hand --- the passage taking place through the dual use of the category of quantity that I suggested --- we come back to *concrete quality* and that is what is emphasised in those categories of Intensity and Substance that we have just been treating. (In previous notes, two opposed views of grouping: what I now give arises from the treatment of intensity and substance.)

---

[1] MN: measurable extent and matter.

I would distinguish now the categories of quality, which are connected with the general form of the proposition (which we might call the *propositional* or *pure logical* categories), from the categories of quantity, arising from the notion of the complexity of the subject, of juxtaposition or the situation[1] and these we might call the *extensional or mathematical* categories; and again from the physical categories, which might be called *intensional* categories, categories of the concrete or of process.[2] (In a sense they are all involved in the first set; the second and third emphasise distinctions involved in the first set.) **[125]**

So you would have:-

I Qualitative[3]	II Mathematical	III Physical
Identity[4]	Universality[5]	Quantity[6]
Difference	Particularity[a]	Intensity
Existence	Number	Substance
Relation	Order	Causality
Universality[7]	Quantity	Individuality[b][8]
	a: Class	b: Thinghood (being a thing)

In the final category we return in a sense to the first, and it might be called concrete identity as opposed to abstract identity; this might involve the reconsideration of the singular proposition, though there need be no departure from regular propositional theory. It might be suggested that we need a category of *ground and consequent* (or implication) before causality, but it seems to be involved in the fourth category of each set, i.e. relation, order

---

[1] NT: Don't they arise from the notion of *class*?
[2] MN: 2nd set as *static* (3rd as dynamic). Being, Essence, The Notion! (Immediacy, Externalisation, Return!!).
[3] EN: the text here reads "Qualitative", with "Logical" written above it.
[4] NT: abstract identity.
[5] NT: relating to subject (*quantity* of proposition).
[6] NT: matter.
[7] NT: character. predicate.
[8] NT: concrete identity, thinghood.

and causality. [In what way is implication involved in "relation"? Cp. previous remarks on obversion (and conversion): these may be involved in first set and especially in relation --- or *obversion* especially in relation. More needed on these immediate inferences; they are certainly part of "pure logic" (propositional theory) but it might be said that *they* introduce juxtaposition (contrast between X and not X) as well as *class* (convertibility) and so *they* lead on to second set.] In the case of causality we do have ground and consequent, but that is not all. In the case of order we have *transitiveness* (and irreversibility).

The transition from the second to the third set lies in turning from pure quantity to quantity as space-filling. So the transition from the first to the second set lies in turning from universality as predicate (just the notion of character) to universality thought of in connection with the subject, where we come to the distinction of *quantity* of propositions[1]: i.e. universality as contrasted with particularity (*all* or *some* of the class --- and it is here, it might be suggested, i.e. with membership of class, that *juxtaposition* comes out definitely --- "implicit" in first set). In the first set you might really have only the distinction of the *quality* of propositions, and quantity might only come in the second set (*all* as an indication of a certain class; antithesis of *some* and *all*), the quantity of proposition leading on to the whole theory of quantity.

The third set should be thought of in connection with Kant's Analogies. What corresponds to causality (as I see it) is Kant's reciprocity, but it has always seemed to me that Kant's[2] category of reciprocity is unnecessary, that the Third Analogy only brings out what was obscured in the Second Analogy, i.e. the question of *spatial continuity* in causal relations; that it is not merely (purely) a matter of necessary succession in Time **[126]** but also (1) of *replacing* in Space, and not merely of phases of a particular thing but (2) of the action of one particular thing on another thing outside of it.[3]

---

[1] MN: disjunction.
[2] EN: the text here reads "(Kant's)".
[3] NT: Cf. my article on "The Problem of Causality": *AJPP*, Aug. 1938.

Substance (contd). I was arguing that in Alexander you get a confusion of categories, in particular that substantial identity should not be identified with individual identity. Another point arising in Alexander's discussion of substance is the question of the relation between the different qualities of a substance. He wants to argue that, as he puts it (p. 277), "the multiplicity of properties of a substance is not haphazard but rooted in some simple state of affairs which enables many properties to belong together within one contour and to be in part simultaneous". He connects this view with the Lockian theory of primary qualities. There has to be some reason, in other words, why whiteness and sweetness coexist in a certain[1] substance (say, sugar), and since that reason doesn't exist in whiteness and sweetness themselves --- because, of course, they can be found apart --- there must be something else in which it does exist (consist), some single explanation of why sugar[2] is both white and sweet.

Now that is coming nearer to the notion of the constitution of a thing, but it is doing so in a rationalistic manner; that is to say, if there is no reason why the white should be sweet or the sweet should be white, we are certainly not going to find a reason why something X should be both sweet and white except the fact that X *is* both sweet and white. We are going to find, in other words, that there are certain conjunctions of properties but not anything that explains *why* there should be such and such a conjunction. And the whole point of recognising the complexity of a substance is just that we have to admit the mere concomitance of a number of different properties, and the supposed *explanation* of that concomitance would on the one hand be the real substance or composition of the thing but would on the other hand be something superior to the properties --- something from which they emerged; and either, then, it would have to be the same complication over again or it would be a mysterious power *whereby* that combination existed, and in neither case would we have a clear and sound conception. It may be very important, of course, to see that some properties of a substance do entail certain

---

[1] EN: the text here reads "certain", with "given" written above it.
[2] EN: the text here reads "this", with "sugar" written above it.

others; that is one of the things we have in mind in definition and classification; but however far we may go in finding such connections or entailments, we always come back to the peculiarity of the given substance, viz. that in its case those various properties just do occur, and are found, together.[1]

This sort of complexity constituting a particular substance or type of thing is the same sort of thing as Heraclitus refers to as "a balance of tensions". [127]

---

[1] EN: the text here reads "(are found or) do occur *together*", with "do occur, and are found, together" written after it.

Lecture 42 Substance as constitution or composition – structure as harmony: Heraclitus; category of causality – Alexander emphasises spatial side – Kant emphasises temporal sequence – concomitance.

I have been suggesting a doctrine of substance as constitution or composition --- something which comes close to Alexander's "plan". If so, he can be said to confuse *universality* with substance, and he certainly confuses *substance* with the categories of identity, quantity and individuality. My position is then that we have a sequence from substance to causality and thence to individuality as the completion of the (third set of) categories, and that we don't have a separate category of implication --- rather, that it is a *type* of category exemplified in the fourth category of each set: relation, order, causality. It might be that it is the category of *relation*, those others being examples, species, further details, of relation --- though, as the argument has gone, it looks more like the category of *order*.[1] (If under *order* you include transitiveness, implication has already come in at that stage.) In causality you get necessity and sufficiency, and other relations as well; and wherever you have certain types of order (viz. transitiveness) you have implication as well --- apart from the *temporal* emphasis of causality. What is involved in "relation" is another matter. (If you say transitiveness is a type of relation, then implication comes in at that stage.) Clearly causality is a relation and a relation involving order, i.e., it takes in the two earlier "fourth" categories.

(It seems peculiar that there should be a special linkage among "fourth" categories, but if we take the third or middle categories, existence, number and substance, there doesn't seem to be much connection among them --- unless we were to say that number is *mathematical* existence, and substance is *physical* existence, as contrasted with, though as taking in, *logical* existence: continuity? --- and I've suggested that substance *takes in* number.[2] Apparent *absence* of linkage might imply imperfection

---

[1] EN: in the text this sentence is enclosed in square brackets.
[2] NT: Cf. Chemistry again.

in my presentation or *naming* of the categories. At any rate the point arises whether in the three sets of five we don't have *repetition*, if not "at different levels" yet with different references, just as Hegel's categories are *repeated with a difference* at the levels of being, essence and the notion --- of course, he has more than five at each stage. The *second* categories in my groups seem to give more promise of a linkage comparable to that of the *fourth* categories, to give a sequence of sorts, since particularity and intensity might be reckoned as species of difference[1], though it is hard to see how intensity takes in particularity --- except in the sense of *uniqueness*, of that which is in some way above measure, as contrasted with what is exactly repeated or measured. Thus universality, which at first might seems to give "intractability", might be said *not* to do so because it implies repetition, whereas particularity implies something not repeated, and similarly intensity, as contrasted with quantity or extensive measurement, implies something that escapes measurement.[2,] [3][128]

I have criticised Alexander's theory of substance at various point, and the last main criticism was connected with the hanging together of various features or components of substance, where I argued that, whatever relations of entailment there might be, still it is the concomitance of qualities *not* entailing one another that constitutes the peculiarity of the substance. (No possibility and no need of "underlying unity"; the "explanation" would have to exhibit the same disunity or variety as the substance itself; no *primary constitution* or essence.)

I had been suggesting to you (at end) that this constitution or structure is analogous to the harmony, the balance of tensions or interrelation of tendencies, that Heraclitus finds to be characteristic of any particular kind of thing; and that leads on to the question mentioned by Alexander at the end of his section on

---

[1] MN: X is *a* Y (its Y-ness is determinate a-ness is indeterminate). *Difference* is essentially indeterminate: implies absence of "common measure".

[2] MN: Escaping measurement = indeterminate = dyadic = difference.

[3] ENMW: There is no paragraph break at the beginning of this section in the manuscript. The text runs on from the previous sentence.

substance (Bk II, Ch Vi, Section A: P. 278), of the interaction of the parts of a substance which is the "reciprocal action of different substances within the whole substance", which involves "causal relations within the substance". Now to say that a substance in this way involved causal relations is not to say that the category of causality is contained within the category of substance; in some way, we should have to argue, every category involves every other category, but still they have to be distinguished, and the point is, I think, that *when we are thinking of substantiality*, even when we recognise an order of phases as well as an arrangement of parts, even when we recognise opposing tendencies, *we are not recognising causality as such*. And when we do recognise causality within a substance, we are, as Alexander puts it, recognising relations between different substances within that substance --- or, more strictly, relations between different *things* within the substance. In other words, these things, from the point of view of substance, i.e. of the substance we started with, are internal; and we are not at the point of view of *causality* until we have introduced externality, until we are considering the *interaction* of different things, whether or not they are taken to the parts of the same thing.[1] It is their *coherence*[2] that we are thinking of in terms of substance; it is their distinctness that we are thinking of in terms of causality. But still there is a natural passage from substantiality to causality in so far as consideration of (a) structure of parts and phases inevitably raises the question of external action or influence.

Causality. Now the important point in Alexander's theory of causality is the emphasis on the spatial side. With Kant the question of causality is bound up with the question of temporal sequence; in fact, the recognition of objective or absolute succession is regarded as contingent on the recognition of a rule of succession, and it is such laws or regularities of succession that constitute causality. Thus in distinguishing between the reversible or contingent order of the perceptions of the parts of a house and the irreversible or necessary order of the perceptions of the

---

[1] MN: togetherness & distinctness.
[2] EN: the text here reads "*coherence*", with "hanging together" and "togetherness" written above it.

positions of a boat floating downstream, Kant takes the recognition of the rule and the recognition of the irreversibility to be identical; **[129]** that is to say, the assertion of the absolute temporal order indicates our belief in a causal law.

Of course Kant would have to admit that our belief can be mistaken, and he would also have to consider special circumstances of the belief, because we can just as easily conceive a succession of positions in accordance with a rule such that the later is *higher* instead of lower, e.g. if the boat was being towed up the stream or was sailing up. There is no absolute connection, there, between lower and later in the case of boats in streams, and it would seem that Kant's explanation of our belief in the necessity of the given order in the given case was inadequate. [Nothing against the fact that we do hold the belief and that we may be right; but *not* (in the notion of succession according to a rule[1]) a *full* account of what it is we believe when we believe in causal connection.[2]] There is also of course the point that his explanation of the distinction between the case of the house and that of the boat is inadequate, because in whatever way we come to grasp absolute temporal order we certainly can recognise such temporal order in the case of our perceptions of the parts of the house, and in order to explain why we *don't* think that the roof is the cause of the foundation or the front of the back and so on, Kant would have to introduce distinctions which are not allowed for in his theory.

First of all, of course, he would have to introduce the conception of *concomitance*, our recognition of the parts of, the house as existing at the same time even if we don't see them at the same time, and that, along with some of the other points, involves a distinction between our acts of perceiving and what we perceive which might be supposed to be allowed for by Kant in his theory of the phenomenal self but which would imply, if they are really our acts, that we are in spatial and temporal relations with the

---

[1] EN: the text here reads "succession according to a rule", with "or objective succession" written above it.
[2] MN: Cf lecture on intractability i.e. causality is *material* irreversibility [& material & formal (temporal) are known in *conjunction*].

things perceived, that perception is simply an empirical relation between empirical things, and thus would do away with the *whole* theory of phenomena as something falling short of reality, because what they are supposed to be relative to is on no higher level. But the other point is that to distinguish the relation in the case of the boat from the relation of concomitance we require not merely the conception of absolute or objective succession, but the conception of *replacing*, the conception of a total spatial situation within which one phase supervenes on and cancels out another in a way in which one part of the house does not cancel out another part, even though *our perception* of one part gives way to our perception of another; which is to say that there is causality among our acts of perception apart from any question of causality, and particularly of sequence, among the parts of the house. (The ground is partly covered in Kant's account of reciprocity, but should be treated in connection with causality. The two essential points I have made are (1) that the account of causality requires the spatial, or **[130]** rather spatio-temporal, conception of replacing as well as the temporal conception of absolute succession, and (2) that Kant's distinctions require that our acts and the whole process of our knowledge --- or our transactions with things --- should be put on the same footing as the things we observe; that is, undermining the phenomenalist theory and implying that we are just things among others in absolute space and time. This discussion[1] is incomplete but gives the main points.)

Then we come to the point that even *replacing* is not a sufficient account of causality, that that is something already found in the conception of substance viz. in the recognition of regular phases, *of a typical kind of process*, so that to take Alexander's trite example, the phases of infancy and youth and manhood and old age are features of *the human substance*, of human nature; and though, as must be the case if causality is a category, these things wouldn't *be* without causality, they do not in themselves illustrate causality but only character or regularity. Now Alexander seems to waver between that view (replacing as sufficient) and the other

---

[1] EN: the text here reads "discussion", with "criticism of Kant" written above it.

view that causality involves not merely a sequence of phases or *change* in a thing but involves *that change* as conditioned by a different thing, by what we call *external action*, by, at the very least; some other thing's coming into certain spatial relations to the first thing. Thus, when he says (p. 283) that causality is "the continuous passage of one motion or set of motions into a different" motion or set of motions, Alexander seems merely to be saying that causality is *change*, whereas on my view to assert that X becomes Y is merely to say[1] what the effect is and not what the cause is, and thus is not a complete statement of a causal relation; but again Alexander speaks of "the very different effect produced by one and the same cause in different substances", e.g. by a stone which would break a window but would only bury itself in a cushion or mound of earth; where he seems to treat the cause as an *external*, a *different* thing, one which, as we say, is the occasion of the change in the given thing. (There are these two different lines in Alexander's exposition. In the main he emphasises the fact that one motion *issues in* another and this exhibits change and not causality. See "The Problem of Causality" for the doctrine of the field.)

---

[1] EN: the text here reads "assert", with "say" written above it.

Lecture 43 General points on the order and grouping of the categories; causality continued.

Some general points on the order and grouping of the categories.

First of all I call in question the expression I've used for the first set --- "categories of quality". It seems to me that since I've been recognising that the mathematical categories or categories of quantity apply as much to Space and Time (especially Space) as to what is *in* Space and Time[1] (e.g. "the air in this room is twenty feet across", "the space between these walls is twenty feet"; i.e., you have the quantity whether or not you recognise any *thing* between the walls --- even if it were a vacuum, still the distance is twenty feet; of course you require the walls as reference points [131] since i.e., these categories are common to both Space and Time and what *occupies* Space and Time, or is extensional; since, again, the physical categories are concerned with what is *peculiar* to the things that occupy Space and Time, and doesn't apply to Space and Time themselves (quantity as a *physical* category being taken as equivalent to space-fillingness, which I take to be the same as the notion of matter), since, in other words, these categories as contrasted with the extensional or mathematical categories could be described as *intensional* categories, it might be better to call *them* the categories of quality --- and the first set [2]of categories, as contrasted with the second set which are concerned[3] with what is common to Space and Time and what is in Space and Time would be concerned with the distinction (and connection) between Space and Time and what is in *it*, between *location* and *description* as I've put it; in other words, with the situational proposition (situation or proposition??]; and these could be called *propositional* or *situational* categories (or, as I've sometimes been putting it, *logical* categories) as contrasted with the mathematical or quantitative and the physical or what I now

---

[1] MN: what's *common* to Sp. & T. & the things that are in them. Thus a space & a line will have extent. Can speak of an extent between two limits without recognising anything as occupying that extent.
[2] EN: the text here reads "set", with "group" written above it.
[3] EN: the text here presumably has the sense of "the second set which is concerned with", or, "the second set whose members are concerned with".

propose to call *qualitative* categories. (The use of 'quality'[1] is only a way of speaking. Quality would readily be taken as *quale*, being such and such, which would {apply} to Space[2] and Time themselves as much as to other qualities. That doubt might lead me to describe the sets as (1) the categories of *fact or situation*, (2) the categories of *extension*, (3) the categories of *intension or quality*). [Question now of *relational* assertions; they would seem to come under (1) simply as being capable of being contradicted, as being *issues*. But that means treating them as predicative in the manner of already described. There would seem to be some reason for calling first set categories of *predication*, second set categories of extension, and *third* set categories of situation; at any rate, causality seems to be a situational category --- but then so is order: "situation" applies to "fourth" categories.]

The second group would be connected with a question I raised earlier --- how we can talk about Space and Time at all --- a thing which I think is really impossible on Alexander's stuff theory but which seems easier if we recognise (first) *spaces* at least as well as things, taking them both to be inherent in what we call a situation. Without arguing the point now I would take it as tending to strengthen the objections to Alexander's view of things as *made of* Space and Time, to strengthen the recognition of qualities as something quite distinct from spatio-temporality, even if they *are* all spatio-temporal or have extension and duration. It might also be noticed, in connection with the special emphasis on Space with reference to the categories of measurement of quantity, that we regularly measure Time by Space, though of course we have to know it is not just Space we are measuring --- we have to **[132]** have a sense of duration as well as of extendedness.[3]

(This new way of describing the distinction of groups --- e.g. not using "categories of quality" for first group raises many problems but also indicates how a number of points may be cleared up.)

---

[1] EN: the text here reads "*quality*", inverted commas added.
[2] EN: the text here reads "which would to Space".
[3] EN: the text here reads "extendedness", with "extension" written above it, and "(extent)" written after it.

Causality (contd). I had pointed out that in some of his formulations Alexander doesn't seem to distinguish causality from change, though in other cases he seems to insist on external action; and actually he says quite early in the section on causality, "It is immaterial, with our metaphysical conception of a substance, whether we describe a cause in popular language as a thing or substance affecting some other thing or substance and producing an effect in it, or in the stricter language of the logicians call the cause an event or process which precedes another event or process and without which the second event or process, the effect, does not exist" (Bk II, Ch. VI, Section B, pp.279-280). Incidentally, Alexander takes credit for saying "does not" instead of "would not" exist, because, he says, the only means of telling what *would or would not exist* is by seeing what *does or does not* exist. It seems to me that it would be losing all the force (of a causal assertion) to say that without the first event the second does not exist; this suggests only concomitance (that A *exists with* B) and loses the universal element in causality which is obscurely conveyed by the "would".[1] Of course Alexander goes on to speak of regarding the event not as an isolated occurrence but as a process which is continued into the effect or into which a cause is continued, so that we are not to take any two successive events as cause and effect as the earlier formulation (or the substitution of *does* for *would*) would seem to imply. But in speaking of this continuance, and even in what is his account of the logical as against the popular way of speaking, he seems to come down on the side of causality as mere change, the mere acquiring of a character by something; and that is all the more remarkable since in a later chapter he goes on to deny that change is a category.

Alexander's way of speaking also obscures the position of *universality* (necessity and sufficiency: cf. "The Problem of Causality") in causality, a consideration quite distinct from *being continued into* something (which could be taken to apply simply to particulars); there is no question of the agent *becoming* the

---

[1] MN: Any^g mt be • C. of any^g else. — EN: this appears to be shorthand for "Anything might (must??) be the cause of anything else".

patient but of (a certain sort of) agent *coming into a certain relation with* (a certain sort of) patient. That complication is obscured by the doctrine of continuance. If we do not clearly distinguish agent from patient and have no notion of the field (etc), then we get talk about a causal line or chain of causation (e.g. in Kant's Antinomies), which *becomes pointless* with the notion of a field --- and so also (pointless) does the notion of a "first cause"; **[133]** we have only contingency and interaction (anything we begin with will be complex and have various influences operating on it). In Alexander's case, the distinction of "agent" and "patient" is treated at first as merely popular language, but we get a clear expression of the other view towards the end of the section (p. 298): "But the cause does its work not by a change in itself but by leading on into something else. A cause might well remain unaltered for a time and then finding its patient produce its effect." [Not *quite* clear whether this is Alexander's own view of part of his exposition of Bradley; it *appears* to be part of his reply.[1] But note that a cause might find its patient and produce its effect and *still* remain unaltered.] If this (which comes nearer my notion of external action) is Alexander's own position, he is inconsistent --- and if the view above stated is allowed (patient, etc.), continuing into or issuing in becomes quite inadequate (it is only the treatment of causality as change). Yet Alexander ends the section by saying (p. 299: after "any instant is the *point of passage* of a motion" --- my emphasis): "To repeat on often-stated proposition continuity is the conceptual formulation of motion itself, and, hard as it may be to say where cause ends and effect begins,[2] yet if cause is itself a process and effect another and different one, the relation between the two is the transition of the one which is earlier into the later motion, or group of motions" --- where it would appear that he is abandoning the notions of agent and patient.

Coming back to general exposition, we find Alexander using a phrase like this: "Causality is thus the spatio-temporal continuity

---

[1] MN: Seems to be part of SA's answer.
[2] MN: C & e. just earl^f & later *phases* of • same proc^s (for SA). — EN: this appears to be shorthand for "Cause and effect just earlier and later phases of the same process (for Alexander)".

of one substance with another" (p. 281), or again saying (same passage) that the cause "is transformed" into the effect --- though he modifies that by saying that transformation is *only an instance* of causality, which we use from the difficulty of describing anything quite "elementary" (there would be similar difficulties about thing, substance, etc.): but still the predominant conception, as I've said, is simply that of change and not of certain *transactions* between different things (the sort of *cycle* that is referred to in the theory of sense-knowledge in the *Theaetetus*). Now this leads on to the question whether causality is *immanent* or *transeunt*, as Alexander puts it, i.e., whether it is something falling within the development of a particular thing or involves a *going across* from one thing to another; and while to begin with Alexander seems to reject the conception of immanent causality, he goes on to treat the difference between the immanent and the transeunt as one merely of convenience in description, to suggest in other words that if we took our system wide enough we could always see causality as immanent, as a matter of inner development or the working out or[1] unfolding of the character of a thing --- what I have taken to be involved in the conception of *substance* rather than that of causality. The point would be on the one hand, that we could never take our system wide enough to rule out external influences affecting its development, and on the other hand that when we **[134]** do treat such developments in a causal way or from the point of view of causality, we are thinking of the parts of the given system as different things and of their action on one another in terms[2] of *their* characters and not of the characters of the whole system.

Again that is the sort of question that is obscured by Alexander's not recognising, or not bringing out, the *universal* character of causal relations --- treating it as a question of *this causing that* instead of *this sort of thing causing a given sort of change in that sort of thing.*

---

[1] EN: the text here reads "or", with "of" written above it.
[2] EN: the text here reads "terms", with "respect" written above it.

Lecture 44 Another grouping of the categories – causality continued – Alexander neglects the universality of causal connection.

Another grouping of the categories

First group are ways in which we give an account of things as in Space and Time, as located or in situations (Situational or Propositional Categories).[1]

Second Group are ways in which we given an account of things *as* spatio-temporal, as having spatio-temporal characters or even, if you like, as spaces and times. At any rate this group would cover the cases of *Space and Time*, would help to show how it is (that) we can have a theory of spaces and times[2] themselves, and hence of something which things could be said to be *in*.[3]

Third group are ways in which we give an account of things as *distinct* from Space & Time --- in other words, as qualitative, as having what are sometimes loosely called "secondary qualities". (Primary qualities would come under the second group, being bound up with *quantity*.)[4]

What is distinctive about this scheme is that it gives a more intelligible way (than earlier schemes did) of distinguishing the *first* set from their other two.[5]

---

[1] MN: Fact (is it so or not).
[2] NT: other way round?
[3] MN: Sit^n ENMW: 'Situation'
[4] MN: Occ^{ce} ENMW: 'Occurrence'
[5] MN: Place – char^t / 4 forms & syll^m. / ③ place – char^r / ③ place (sit^n – math^l cat^{gs}) / ③ char^r (occ^{ce} / activity / phys^l cat^{gs}) — EN: "/" has been added here, to indicate that the words so separated are written in the margin on different lines, underneath one another. ENMW: In this margin note, Anderson appears to be relating the distinction between place and character to the three groups of the categories. Hence the first group of categories relates to both character and place, the second group of situational or mathematical categories to place alone and the third group of physical categories (occurrence or activity) to character alone.

Causality (contd). I have been criticising Alexander's theory of causality on the ground that, as far as his main argument goes, it is a theory of change rather than of causality, as when he says (p.284) that it (causation) "is the continuity of existents within continuous Space-Time as subsisting between substances, which are themselves motions or groups of motions". This is just an account of the passage of certain motions into others, or of their replacing of others, in spite of the terminology of "substances". Now we find on the next page (285) that Alexander insists on this *difference*, (between cause and effect), contending that mere continuance of the same uniform motion is not a causal connection; but, if causality is categorial, how is that compatible with change taking place in some cases and in others not, so that in the latter there would not, on Alexander's showing, be causality? And, apart even from that, apart from the description he would give of the two types of cases, how is Alexander going to account for the difference (for the two different types), for the fact that sometimes there is a change and sometimes not, that some motions go on as they were and other motions go on in a new form? Why (to put it **[135]** in what I think is its strongest form) is there ever change at all? And I should argue that the problem cannot be solved on the basis of continuity alone, that we have to take account of external action, that we have to have something like the Heraclitean theory of exchanges and thus see persistence as a special case of change and not as an exception to change or a different kind of thing. We should have to argue, in other words, that change is *inherent* in motion, but that in some cases we get a *balance* of changes in such a way that no alteration was apparent to us, a balance at any rate such that we would say "that is the *same thing*" (same *person* or whatever it might be) and yet we would know perfectly well that changes had been going on in him all the time,[1] that in physical terms he had constantly been giving out and taking in energy, and therefore that his persisting or remaining uniform (within the limits in which he does so, of course) would exhibit (involve) causality.

---

[1] EN: the text here reads "time", with "while" written above it.

No doubt if we were giving a detailed account of that causality it would have to be in terms of differences, in terms of something acquired or added, even if something equivalent were lost or taken away at the same time. In each causal connection that we recognised, the cause would be different from the effect and the thing acted on would have changed, and still we could see in terms of a Heraclitean or near-Heraclitean theory how this is compatible with what we call the persistence of an individual, whereas on Alexander's view (i.e., as the argument runs) we are simply recognising two types of occurrence, neither of them categorial, with no indication either of their common ground or of the basis of the distinction between them. That again is a consideration strengthening the demand for recognition of external action as essential to causality. (Third set as categories of *action* --- starting from *externality* in the form of impenetrability of space-filling.)

Again we find Alexander's looseness in the discussion of the question whether effect determines cause as much as cause determines effect; and Alexander says that this is so only in a *logical* sense, that we can only mean that when the cause and effect are precisely started they are reciprocal: "when the cause, that is, is purged of what may indeed occur in a particular case but is accidental to it, and when the effect is stated in terms so precise as to presuppose one cause only and not a choice of several; when, to take the familiar example, the death from drowning is distinguished from the death of hanging, and the two not lumped together under the general designation of death. The reciprocity of cause and effect means then that unless there were the precise effect there would not be the precise cause. But such determination **[136]** is logical and not real determination, and effect cannot be interchanged with cause except as a basis of inference" (p. 287). He goes on to say: "We cannot say in any real sense that the future determines the present, for the future is not yet and a future event introduces the order of Time. In that order the future does not determine but is determined."

Here again we see Alexander neglecting the *universality* of causal connection, speaking as if what were causally linked were simply two particular events, whereas there can be no account of causal connection at all unless we can consider the particular events to be linked as, and only as, events of certain sorts; and it may be pointed out here that death by drowning is just as much a *sort of thing*, admitting of variations, as is death in general, and that, as I have argued, the question always is --- What is our problem? What is the field and what is the property to be acquired? And on that understanding there should be just as precise a solution whether we are trying to account for death merely or for death with special features. (Cf --- previous remarks to the effect that Alexander neglects the universal element in causality. If it is a case of necessity and sufficiency we have *a certain* reciprocal relation, even though there are elements in the situation, features of the relation of causality, which are *not* reciprocal.)

Another interesting point is Alexander's distinction between real and logical determination, and especially his reference in this connection to the order of Time --- where he seems to think that the recognition of a symmetrical relation between two things keeps us from recognising at the same time an irreversible or asymmetrical relation between them. It may be quite true that the effect cannot precede the cause, and yet true that the effect *determines* the cause in exactly the same sense as the cause determines the effect. Here of course we have to grant the popular usage in which "determines" and "causes" are used as equivalent, but why a necessary and sufficient *precedent* condition should be held to determine any more than a necessary and sufficient *subsequent* condition does, is certainly not in the least apparent from Alexander's account. At least he can be said to deviate from realism in distinguishing logical from real determination, apparently meaning by the former that which permits us to infer, or use the expression *therefore*, as when he says again, on p. 291: "The only necessity which philosophy can recognise is that of inference. But there is no necessity in things except fact. Nothing is added to causal relation by the adjective necessary": and once again on p. 297 where he says: "Real grounds are to be distinguished from logical grounds, though they may coincide" and where, after treating the real ground as the complex of motions of which the event or fact is the [137] causal outcome", he refers to logic as "the science of truth, or of how our beliefs, as expressed in propositions, are to be systematised into a coherent whole at the guidance of reality."

Just what a belief would be, or for that matter what a fact or event would be, if it were *not* in propositional form is not indicated; but if propositional form is something *added* to events, then it is just a falsification of them, and if logical grounds are not real grounds, then there are no such things at all. We have Hume in the same way trying to give an account of causality as what we assert when *we* make the transition from one idea to another, when we infer; and of course the line of attack on that view is a realistic one, is the assertion that we are not just passing from some ideas to others but are recognising the actual passage of some things into others, that the relation, in other words, is part of what we know. So in the case of inferring in general, the realist has to say that the relation *implication* is part of what we know, *is part of the real or objective situation*, or else he has to deny that there is any connection at all, deny that there is such a thing as "logical grounds".

Alexander's whole view of logic and truth is normative and anti-realistic. He tries to treat propositions, beliefs etc, as distinct from things, as being in our minds or not definitely located: i.e. he holds a correspondence theory. See "Realism vs Relativism in Ethics"; conception of "force" to indicate reality or thinghood --- individuality. Loughnan[1] tried to identify my theory here with *Russell's* position.

---

[1] EN: this refers to H.B. Loughnan, "Scholasticism versus Realism In Ethics", (discussion note), *AJPP*, 11, 1933, pp.141-153.

Lecture 45 Alexander neglects the causal field: Alexander's immanentism; thinghood/individuality; reciprocity.

I had been discussing the ambiguity in Alexander's wavering between causality as change and the recognition of external action. The important point is to realise that what you may call "internality" or the development of a thing out of its own resources will not cover the ground; e.g. the Leibnizian *notion* would not provide the whole history or a single conception whose content would cover the (whole) ground. You have to recognise external action or contingency, to give an account of a thing --- contingency not implying that there is an exception to every event having a necessary and sufficient precedent condition, but that there could never be a single principle, that there is no single set of conditions, from which the whole history of a thing is derivable. You have to admit the mere fact of *collocation*, of (an unrelieved) multiplicity of factors in the development of a single thing.

And when Alexander, following Hume, rejects the notion of power or force, he is rejecting along with the *metaphysical* or *rationalistic* conception of force, of "that whereby" something happens, also (I would suggest) the logical conception, **[138]** the recognition of *agency*, of the operation of independent factors in bringing about any result. There again he, like other theorists, does not distinguish the field from the agent, doesn't see then what I would call the nature of a *causal problem* and thus incidentally the distinction between a mere question of change and a question of causality.

In my view you never would get causal laws if you took it as a question of what kind of situation is followed by what other kind of situation, or what phase is followed by what other phase of a developing situation, but only if you recognise on the one hand the developing or changing thing, the member of a field or genus, and (on the other hand) the external thing, the agent or occasion.

And it is quite interesting here[1] to note the dictum of Hume that causality is the only basis on which one can argue from one thing to a different thing, which of course would be distinguished on my view from argument based on the interrelation of the properties of the same[2] thing. The latter type of argument brings in, I've suggested, only the category of substance, whether the properties are concomitant or in temporal order, whereas the former brings in the conception[3] of thinghood or individuality, with the emphasis on force or agency. And from that point of view it would be wrong to say that immanent and transient causality are just different ways of regarding the same events. On the contrary, causality will be necessarily transeunt and the immanent development will fall under the head of substance. (Alexander denies that change is a category. I am not saying that where there is change there is --- or rather, need be --- no question of causality. Causality is categorial and so will be present wherever there is change. But this is not to deny the distinction --- the two questions are different --- and Alexander in denying force or power *is* getting rid of the distinction; i.e., he gets rid of the important [empirical?] distinction as well as of the metaphysical notion.)

The Leibnizian *notion* is an example of *immanentist theory*.[4] The same sort of doctrine is found in Hegel; the essential point in Hegel is development from inner resources, the working out of its own potentialities in the development of the Idea. (Cf. my review of "Textbook of Marxist Philosophy" in *Australian Highway*, 1938.[5] The denial of external action is used for political purposes, the upholding of the official Soviet theory against Trotsky on an immanentist basis; and it could be said that this is so far in accordance with Marxist theory that for Marx *society* is

---

[1] EN: the text here reads "there", with "here?" written above it.
[2] EN: the text here reads "a single", with "the same" written above it.
[3] EN: the text here reads "conception", with "category" written above it.
[4] MN: of the metaphysical conception of "force"??
[5] EN: this refers to John Anderson, "*A Textbook of Marxist Philosophy*, (Victor Gollancz)", (review), *The Australian Highway*, 20(1), 10 February 1938, pp.13-17. "A Textbook of Marxist Philosophy" was reprinted in *A Perilous and Fighting Life: From Communist to Conservative – The Political Writings of Professor John Anderson* (Sydney: Pluto Press 2003) pp 164 - 175

unenvironed, world history --- not of course the history of a particular country --- is society's realisation of itself, all facts are ultimately social facts: that is his "historical materialism".) The transeunt conception is quite vital here. **[139]** We can see how Alexander with his doctrine of Space-Time as the stuff of things is pushed in an immanentist direction; reality must be spun out of Space-Time (Space-Time must "involve" everything else[1]) because there is nothing outside of Space-Time to act on it.[2] Alexander would certainly say that we couldn't *predict* the later stages, you couldn't say from the beginning what was going to be unfolded (novelty, "emergence"); but still the *stuff* theory is in line with Idealism. This is associated with (is the case with) evolutionism generally, i.e., the doctrine of a single all-embracing evolution. Hegel holds an essentially evolutionist theory in that sense: e-volving, unfolding, actualisation of potentialities.[3] Such theories are really meaningless. When you say, after the event, that things became this because they *had it in them* to become this, you are not giving any explanation at all. You have, as Hume did, to accept the plain fact that the effect is different from the cause.

Alexander naturally, as other writers do, distinguishes (p. 296) the relation of cause and effect from the relation of ground and consequent, but he goes further and considers that the latter is an evisceration of the former, viz. by the leaving out of the temporal element, the element of Time. He even says that implication is a notion *posterior* to causation. Now clearly if we recognise necessity and sufficiency in causal relations we are recognising implication, but we do not at all need to go to causation for necessity and sufficiency. We have seen that this is already involved in quantitative arguments, arguments involving *equality* specifically,[4] though here it should be remembered that Alexander discusses quantity and intensity *after* discussing causality (Ch. VIII after Ch. VI), that he hasn't, then, presented extensional categories before those I have called intensional. But

---

[1] EN: the word "else" is encircled, and "?" written above it.
[2] MN: cf notion of "a universe".
[3] ENMW: 'e-volving' occurs in the manuscript.
[4] EN: the text here reads "especially", with "specifically" written above it.

whatever procedure he may follow, Alexander cannot deny that in the order of the sciences mathematics is regularly put before physics and mathematics is studied for the most part without employing the category of causality, that we consider the interrelated properties of a triangle without raising any question of what *makes* a thing triangular (a triangle) in a temporal sense, what *brings about* its being triangular, and that the absence of the temporal character from these calculations is not in general felt to be a defect in mathematical demonstration(s). It may be contended of course that the history of mathematics has been linked with the history of mechanics that mechanics has set problems for mathematics and thus led to progress in that science; we might even take the view put forward by Sorel in his *Utility of Pragmatism*[1] and maintain that it was essentially from **[140]** problems of (mechanical) engineering, from problems of practice, that mathematical problems came to be formulated. But the fact remains that the problems[2] are not worked out in mechanical terms; and the properties of a triangle, again, do not have a temporal order and yet can be recognised as necessary and sufficient for one another; so the treatment of implication as something abstracted from causality would not seem to be justified here.

The quantitative categories also had the importance, we say, of indicating how we can take Space itself as a subject of study, of covering spaces as well as things though Alexander wouldn't admit the distinction. But it is precisely one of the weaknesses of his *stuff* theory that he cannot derive things, concrete agents, from it, that the mere complication of Space by Time does not generate events, that the qualities or peculiarities of things which are dealt with by physics are distinct from the spatial characteristics which are dealt with by mathematics.[3]

Alexander has something on the notion of thinghood or individuality in his discussion of *substance*. But our discussion of

---

[1] EN: this refers to Georges Sorel, *De l'utilité du pragmatisme*, (Paris: M. Rivière, 1928).
[2] EN: the text here reads "solutions", with "problems" written above it.
[3] NT: This should be supplemented by reference to earlier lectures.

causality shows that he fails to clear the matter up. My view is that of a propositional (situational) logic, a doctrine of things both as situations and as *in* situations, according to which things can be distinguished from Space and Time, though they could be said to be *in* Space and Time, and according to which we can give some account of Space and Time themselves.

Reciprocity (Bk II, Ch. II, Section C). We find the same confusion here as before (Alexander's discussion in this section is not of very much importance) and while it is possible that the category of reciprocity could be taken as covering some of the ground of thinghood, Alexander does not succeed in bringing that out[1]. You would think you would get the notion of external action here, but Alexander thoroughly obscures that point (possibility??) (p. 300): "The transaction into which the two substances enter, so far as they constitute a closed system, is a two-sided and not a one-sided transaction. It is one in which each partner is cause and effect in turn. The situation which is the relation of the two substances is from the point of view of the first an effect on the second, but from the point of view of the second an effect on the first" and (below) "There is thus only one total situation arising from the relation of the two and it appears as an effect in B of A and an effect in A of B".

Now this sort of view is a result of a failure to keep the questions of the *change* and of the *external agent*, or the thing effected and the thing effecting, [141] clear of one another, because when we do that, when we recognise the field, we see that the question of A's action on B and the question of B's action on A are quite different ones, even if they are connected, and that it is not a matter of a passage of motions in A into motions in B and vice versa, but of a passage or change in A into which B does not enter and vice versa. It is of course true to say that the effect of B on A depends on the sort of thing A is as well as on the sort of thing B is --- that is the whole doctrine of the field --- but that is not the least reason for confusing the effect of B on A with the effect of A on B.[2]

---

[1] EN: the last three words of this sentence are enclosed in round brackets.
[2] NT: confusing what happens in two different fields.

You find in this passage (pp.300-301) the alternation between different views. Alexander identifies the different effects, or says they are the same (thing) from different points of view; and sometimes he speaks as if the fact that the nature of the changes depends on the characters of both the acting thing and the thing acted on were the[1] reason for the changes not being distinct. (This is at least to bring in agent and patient, though treating them wrongly.) But, as was apparent in our consideration of his account of causality, he must be treating causality as change because (here again) what he insists on is *continuity*, the earlier thing *becoming* the later; and he neglects the notion of the external agent. And that again is bound up with *stuff* theory; if you start with pure Space-Time, it is clearly going to be a question not of causality but of the unfolding of inner resources. So even if his Spatio (extensional[2]) --- Temporal (intensional[3]) theory[4] drives him in the direction of empiricism, you get the *stuff* theory driving him in the direction of Idealism (i.e. hints of empirical theory, complicated --- or contaminated --- by rationalist conceptions).

---

[1] EN: the text here reads "a", with "the?" written above it.
[2] EN: the text here reads "extension", with "extensive" written above it, and "extensional" written below it.
[3] EN: the text here reads "intension", with "intensive" written above it, and "intensional" written below it
[4] MN: in TAR (externality....internality).

Lecture 46 The source of the categories as the form of the proposition: the physical categories; structure and aesthetics; category of individuality.

Bk II, Ch. X: *The One and the Many* (p. 336). "Space-Time is thus the source of the categories, the non-empirical characters of existing things, which those things possess because of certain fundamental features of any piece of Space-Time" Cf. Kant's view that things in themselves are the source of phenomena. If you say things in themselves are the *source* of phenomena you are bringing them under the categories: and no matter how you express the relation you have to think of some relation or the whole distinction is meaningless. You get the same sort of position in Locke; matter is the source of ideas, of what we immediately perceive, but being a source has meaning only in terms of what we are aware of and to say matter is a source is to say it is perceived (or is unintelligible unless it is perceived). Adamson says things in themselves (Kant) have many of the features of Locke's matter.[1]

As far as I have indicated a *source* (of the categories) it has been the form of the proposition or what is involved in the proposition, the *distinction* between location and description which is bound up with the *distinction*[2] between Space-Time and what is in it. I did make the point that the mathematical **[142]** categories are concerned with what is *common* to Space-Time and what is in it, taking as the point of departure the convertibility of terms, the convertibility of location and description, the point being that since any term is capable of locating, it is capable of being treated as quantitative or extensional or as so much Space-Time. On the other hand, the physical categories are concerned with what is peculiar to what is *in* Space-Time (things) as contrasted with Space and Time themselves.

---

[1] EN: this refers to Robert Adamson, *The Development Of Modern Philosophy*, (Edinburgh: William Blackwood and Sons, 1903).
[2] MN: also *connection*?

I mentioned that, although I originally called the first group of categories the *categories of quality*, I think it is better to use that for the third group, an alternative naming being *intensional* categories, and to use categories *of the situation* (which embraces both quantity and quality) for the first group. Then we could treat the second and third groups as *differentiations* of the first group or of situations, the second group involving specifications of location (or the possibility of such specifications) and the third group, similarly, specifications of description. (That is to be taken in relation to Alexander's contention that Space-Time is the *source* of the categories.)

Now the last group I presented as

> Quantity
> Intensity
> Substance
> Causality[1]
> Individuality or Thinghood

which (last)[2] I identified with *force* --- or at any rate argued that the category of individuality is conveyed in the notion of an *agent*, agency being something over and above mere sequence, and again over and above implication (or necessity and sufficiency); and before going on to say a little more on that, I would remark that Alexander seemed, among other confusions, to confuse substance with individuality and there might be a usage of "substance" (though not, I think, the most defensible historically) in which it was identified with thinghood; but in that case we should simply have to find another word for what I have called substance --- it would still remain the central one of the last group of categories. For example, we might use the expression "structure", which is the way in which I have interpreted *substance*.

---

[1] MN: Causality is the relation: thing (agent) what can have it – in one *sense*. Similar connections in other cases?

[2] ENMW: The previous two words can be interpreted to mean "the last of which".

Now as you have seen the conception of structure is what I have taken to be the leading conception of Aesthetics[1]; and we might argue that the categories of aesthetics are part of the physical categories --- the point being that we stop, as far as aesthetics is concerned, at the category of structure, that we are not concerned there with the category of causality but in what I may call non-temporal art you have a *balance* and even in art which takes time, where there is the working out of a theme through successive phases, still the question there is of bringing out the character of the theme or subject, just as I have argued, in commenting on Alexander, that mere change, the mere succession **[143]** of phases or stages, was not sufficient for causality which needed an external agent, but could be part, or could be involved in the nature, of the substance itself.

Now of course if in that way the artist rules out causality, if he tries to show the development of something in its own terms, treating it as self-contained, it is not that he really believes that such things are impervious to external action but just that he is concentrating on a certain character, bringing out what we may call its elements or *leading features*, and thus proceeding[2] in the same way as a person *defining*, viz. giving a number of features which are necessary and together sufficient for a certain kind of thing. The scheme of interrelated properties which the classifier recognises is equivalent to the phases in which an artist works out a theme or to the features by which he builds up a structure; but such a structure as it exists in nature[3] can of course be invaded, we can have the intrusion of other factors and the breaking up of the character in question, we can have in a word *history* --- but that remains antithetical to art; and when *the artist* intrudes other factors, when in Joyce's term he is concerned with *kinesis* rather than stasis, then he is falling away from the artistic standpoint ---

---

[1] ENMW: This statement is confusing for it is the first instance in these lectures of the connection between structure and aesthetics. However in Anderson's 1942 Lectures on Ethics and Aesthetics (which he may have repeated in 1943 or 1944) there is extensive discussion of structure as the leading conception in aesthetics.

[2] EN: the text here reads "arguing", with "proceeding" written above it.

[3] EN: the text here reads "Nature", with a stroke through the "N", probably indicating a change from upper to lower case.

Index

action 26, 70, 122, 222, 223, 231, 236, 244, 247, 250, 254
  external 236, 239, 242, 243, 246, 247, 250, 251, 254, 258
activity 14, 20, 61, 70, 129, 130, 160, 162, 163, 166, 192, 206, 245, 259, 260
Aesthetics 11, 28, 104, 256, 258
Anaximander 58, 163, 165
Anderson, J. 11, 12, 14, 16, 17, 18, 19, 20, 22, 23, 24, 25, 26, 27, 28, 30, 32, 33, 34, 35, 41, 50, 59, 90, 96, 104, 108, 111, 114, 115, 155, 156, 164, 179, 245, 251, 258
arguments
  disjunctive 132, 133, 149
  quantitative 138, 252
  relational 23, 132, 133, 138, 143, 144
Aristotle 31, 153, 178
Bosanquet, B. 47, 105, 108, 121, 161, 166, 171, 172, 173, 175, 176, 178, 196
Bradley, F.H. 54, 74, 99, 100, 107, 133, 137, 178, 223, 243
categories 11, 13, 15, 18, 20, 22, 23, 24, 25, 26, 27, 28, 30, 31, 32, 33, 36, 37, 43, 62, 73, 80, 107, 109, 110, 111, 112, 114, 119, 120, 122, 123, 124, 125, 127, 128, 130, 134, 155, 165, 166, 171, 182, 183, 184, 187, 189, 190, 192, 193, 194, 195, 196, 204, 206, 208, 221, 222, 223, 224, 228, 229, 230, 232, 234, 240, 241, 245, 247, 252, 253, 256, 257, 258, 259, 260, 261
  as conditions of existence 20, 33, 35, 73, 193
  as predicates 22, 108, 109, 110, 111, 124, 155
  as relations 110, 114
  of quality 25, 182, 183, 195, 221, 222, 229, 230, 240, 241, 257
  of quantity 25, 183, 184, 189, 190, 192, 194, 195, 206, 222, 229, 230, 240
  physical 18, 22, 25, 27, 187, 206, 207, 209, 223, 229, 230, 240, 245, 256, 258
category 15, 20, 22, 23, 24, 25, 27, 28, 36, 49, 112, 114, 124, 125, 126, 127, 167, 181, 182, 183, 184, 187, 189, 190, 193, 194, 202, 204, 206, 207, 218, 222, 224, 229, 230, 231, 234, 236, 238, 240, 242, 251, 253, 254, 256, 257, 258, 261
Causality 15, 19, 25, 34, 35, 36, 37, 43, 45, 47, 48, 110, 112, 114, 123, 196, 218, 230, 231, 234, 236, 237, 238, 240, 241, 242, 243, 245, 246, 247, 248, 249, 250, 251, 252, 254, 255, 257, 258, 259
  and agency 242, 250, 254, 255, 257, 258, 259
  and concomitance 62, 232, 234, 235, 237, 242, 251

the earlier stages of the discussion any more than there is a question of our not employing syllogism in the arguments by which we present that part of logical theory which comes before our presentation of the logic of syllogism --- or, even if we *started* with the logic of syllogism, that part of the argument that came before we had completely set forth our syllogistic theory itself. That is to say, we are not involved in the Hegelian position of treating each category **[145]** as a conception under which we endeavour to think the whole of things, so that we begin with the attempt to think them all as *being* and our attempt breaks down --- the conception of *not-being* intrudes, and then we endeavour to think them all under a category which synthetises[1] being and not-being, and so on indefinitely. There is for us no question of trying to think the whole in terms of this or that conception or allowing each conception to generate its own world; but from the very beginning we have recognised propositions, recognised a variety of facts, and our later procedure at no time calls that starting-point in question, at no time tries to do away with the proposition or with the *variety* of propositions [trying to run them all together or make them all signify one fact --- the totality of things]; it merely elucidates that starting point, bringing out characteristics and relations of proposition which remain as *distinct* (i.e. as different from one another) as ever they were.

The end of the course of 1944.

---

[1] ENMW: 'synthetises' occurs in the manuscript. "Synthesises" would be the more common usage.

and reciprocity 231, 238, 247, 250, 254
category of 234, 236, 253, 258
causal field or region 25, 26, 38, 70, 129, 130, 133, 147, 158, 159, 222, 225, 239, 243, 248, 250, 254
   immanent 244, 250, 251
   transeunt 244, 251, 252
clarity 50, 52, 53, 174
cogito 17, 34, 59, 172
   cognitionalism 212, 213
complexity 15, 58, 61, 63, 66, 69, 117, 118, 122, 131, 134, 152, 180, 189, 206, 221, 224, 226, 227, 228, 230, 232, 233
compresence 14, 16, 66, 67
continuity 20, 24, 31, 39, 47, 61, 64, 70, 77, 90, 95, 126, 185, 194, 198, 202, 203, 207, 209, 214, 220, 234, 243, 246, 255
   quantitative 204
   spatial 64, 183, 185, 188, 209, 231
copula 17, 20, 23, 27, 62, 107, 109, 124, 125, 126, 139, 140, 150, 151, 152, 194
Croce, B. 50, 259
degree 15, 25, 27, 91, 161, 174, 206, 210, 218, 219, 223
   or intensity 207, 209
Descartes, R. 17, 34, 48, 52
description 18, 26, 27, 47, 56, 69, 102, 116, 118, 121, 127, 132, 153, 166, 171, 184, 191, 199, 220, 244, 246, 256, 257, 260
   function as location 127, 240, 256

development 11, 12, 13, 17, 28, 56, 66, 104, 182, 200, 209, 221, 222, 244, 250, 251, 258
   inner 244
difference 23, 25, 27, 36, 40, 45, 66, 77, 83, 87, 90, 91, 92, 93, 95, 97, 108, 111, 119, 122, 124, 125, 126, 127, 128, 133, 144, 148, 153, 166, 167, 174, 176, 182, 196, 209, 213, 214, 215, 220, 230, 235, 244, 246
   arithemetical 215, 216
   category of 124
discourse 20, 28, 34, 35, 37, 38, 110, 140, 150, 261
   conditions of 19, 35
distinction 14, 21, 22, 23, 25, 32, 33, 39, 40, 42, 43, 45, 48, 56, 60, 63, 64, 65, 69, 73, 74, 75, 77, 78, 79, 83, 87, 92, 95, 101, 107, 108, 109, 116, 120, 124, 125, 126, 128, 130, 132, 138, 150, 151, 153, 154, 158, 160, 162, 165, 173, 185, 187, 188, 195, 198, 210, 218, 219, 220, 221, 222, 223, 229, 231, 237, 240, 241, 243, 245, 247, 248, 250, 251, 253, 256, 260
   distinctness 33, 41, 42, 43, 61, 62, 64, 66, 69, 70, 75, 236
duration 70, 85, 96, 131, 169, 228, 241
Empiricism 14, 17, 19, 33, 40, 42, 83, 97, 99, 169
equality 88, 134, 135, 138, 140, 145, 205, 206, 252
Ethics 11, 12, 13, 28, 31, 35, 52, 249, 258, 259

263

Evolutionism 50, 54, 56, 66, 252
Existence 13, 15, 16, 17, 20, 22, 23, 27, 35, 36, 40, 42, 43, 50, 64, 72, 102, 103, 105, 106, 107, 109, 110, 114, 119, 124, 126, 127, 128, 131, 140, 161, 164, 169, 180, 182, 194, 208, 230, 234
   category of 23, 124, 126, 194
   conditions of (see Categories) 20, 33, 35, 73, 193
   extension 26, 27, 58, 69, 70, 74, 85, 105, 115, 116, 122, 134, 142, 151, 185, 196, 241, 255
   force 38, 46, 72, 89, 110, 114, 125, 155, 175, 228, 242, 249, 250, 251, 257, 260
Freud, S. 213
Hegel, G.W.F. 11, 13, 17, 28, 30, 31, 32, 45, 50, 72, 73, 104, 119, 123, 124, 155, 157, 166, 173, 174, 178, 182, 190, 192, 194, 223, 235, 251
   Hegelian(ism) 72, 99, 119, 124, 157, 172, 173, 174, 261
Heraclitus 18, 25, 61, 99, 100, 102, 107, 110, 160, 164, 233, 234, 235
   Heraclitean 100, 107, 246, 247
History 12, 17, 32, 50, 63, 104, 110, 120, 122, 131, 169, 250, 252, 253, 259
Hume, D. 17, 31, 34, 39, 40, 42, 43, 47, 48, 51, 101, 151, 249, 250, 251, 252
Idealism 13, 14, 16, 19, 30, 45, 72, 108, 155, 157, 161, 222, 223, 226, 252, 255

   conception of totality 45, 99, 102, 156, 157, 172, 174, 261
Identity 15, 23, 25, 27, 28, 40, 41, 45, 48, 50, 51, 52, 54, 61, 79, 104, 105, 114, 115, 119, 121, 122, 124, 125, 126, 127, 128, 131, 132, 133, 156, 172, 182, 192, 193, 195, 204, 207, 224, 228, 230, 232, 234, 260
   and difference 119, 192
   as 'being a subject' 119, 121, 122, 124, 133, 156
   as a relation 114
   category of 23, 182, 195
Individuality 18, 25, 155, 173, 178, 204, 207, 228, 229, 234, 249, 250, 251, 253, 257, 259, 260
   category of . 25, 27, 256, 257
   or 'thinghood' 25, 228, 230, 249, 250, 251, 253, 254, 258
Intensity 15, 25, 27, 184, 207, 209, 210, 211, 212, 213, 214, 215, 216, 218, 219, 223, 229, 230, 235, 252, 257
   category of 25, 27, 184, 206, 218
issue 27, 100, 113, 114, 132, 156, 195, 215
   an 113, 139, 140, 150, 151
   real 22, 112, 122
   the 22, 35, 47, 117, 151
James, W. 16, 33, 39, 40, 42, 48, 53, 54, 67, 157, 179
   'vicious intellectualism' 39, 40, 42
juxtaposition 132, 183, 190, 220, 222, 230, 231
   as spatial spreadoutness .. 222

locating whereas in individuality we are concerned with *activity*, with something (as I put it) intensional; yet at the same time it is such an active being that we should refer to specifically as a *subject* --- something which was capable of affecting other things, something which not merely *located*[1] certain activities but, as we might put it, *had*[2] those activities --- something which *operated* in these specific ways or *whose acts* these predicates are.

And here again I don't think I am departing from the distinction of functions in the proposition, the distinction of location and description, but simply insisting on the *connection*[3] on the fact that the activities are the subject's activities, that it is only so that we are able to think of it (subject) concretely. Of course that does not mean that we have to look for some kind of power or force additional to the activities themselves; on the other hand, it does not mean (it is not the case) that we have to reduce a subject to something general, to a sort or kind. Undoubtedly, as I have already argued, individuality is a species of universality, it has instances, so that, Socrates being an individual, the Socratic character is *repeated* --- it occurs now here, now there --- but again, as I have always insisted, such instances do not form just any sort of class, they form a continuous series, which members of an ordinary class (say, men) do not do.

It may further be argued that even in contrasting individuality with universality, even in contrasting the instances which form a series with those which don't, we are in the latter case as much as in the former employing the conception *an* instance, an "individual (or single) instance", and thus using the conception of individuality. But it does not seem to me that that is a vital criticism --- the criticism, in effect, that we have to use the later categories in order to understand the earlier --- because it is the point of the whole theory that all the categories are present everywhere, that all are involved in any sort of discourse, and even if we think we can *distinguish* one category from another there is no question of our *not employing* the later categories in

---

[1] MN: locates.
[2] MN: has.
[3] NT: cf. 141 above. — EN: this refers to Lecture 46 footnote 2.

and this is so in general when the work in any way refers beyond itself, when it has some kind of social reference, when it is not treated as just self-sufficient.

Now when we complete the third group of categories, when we bring in interaction or external agency, then[1] we come to the foundation of epistemological theory as well as physical theory in general; then, in other words, we come to the historical as contrasted with the aesthetic. (Here I am directly opposing Croce who considers history a definitely non-causal study, who holds that causality is alien to history, whereas I say it is the very mark of a historical question.) (as contrasted also with a *philosophical* question: question of the "permanent").

Individuality. Coming, then, in conclusion to the question of individuality and agency, I have spoken, in "Realism versus Relativism in Ethics", of certain things as forces and that is equivalent in my argument to treating them as things.[2] I am rejecting, that is, with particular reference to social theory, the view that there is anything at all which is a mere resultant, which is any kind of epiphenomenon or after-effect or exists in subordination to or relatively to something else; I am arguing that anything that can be produced is itself capable of producing or acting; and it is in emphasising this activity of things, the fact that they can act (though they can also be acted on) that I refer to them as *forces*. It is the same sort of point I am making when I speak of their *independence* and of course the particular point of this article[3] is that goods, if they exist, must be agents, that they cannot be merely *attached* to something else but must have their own modes of operation if there is to be a subject **[144]** of ethics at all.

It is possible to say, as I suggested, that the last of our categories is only the concrete form of the first, that individuality is the practical form, if you like, of identity, but the distinction is there, because in identity we are concerned only with the function of

---

[1] NT: no time to develop the point fully.
[2] MN: goods (cf Mng of Gd). ENMW: "The Meaning of Good".
[3] NT: R vs R. ENMW: "Realism versus Relativism in Ethics"

Kant, I. 30, 31, 32, 40, 43, 47, 54, 62, 72, 73, 82, 93, 104, 105, 119, 120, 157, 178, 192, 195, 209, 218, 223, 228, 231, 234, 236, 237, 238, 243, 256
Leibniz, G. 30, 31, 46, 51, 52, 54, 97, 99, 100, 104, 105, 173, 174, 224
location 20, 23, 27, 64, 108, 112, 124, 127, 130, 154, 226, 240, 256
  subject term as 23, 27, 121, 126, 129, 256, 257, 260
Logic 11, 16, 17, 19, 20, 21, 23, 25, 33, 34, 35, 36, 37, 46, 50, 51, 55, 62, 84, 85, 99, 101, 102, 104, 107, 108, 111, 112, 115, 116, 117, 119, 120, 123, 132, 133, 137, 150, 157, 158, 159, 160, 161, 174, 178, 179, 187, 192, 196, 202, 206, 207, 222, 231, 249, 254, 261
  of events 55, 62, 84, 206
  of implication 207
  of process 25, 206
  of quality 202, 222
  of quantity 222
  of relations 132, 206
  predicative 132, 134, 150, 222
  propositional 23, 37, 38, 107, 133, 157, 221
  situational 21, 33, 99, 101, 104, 107, 222
Logical Functions
  coextension 49, 95, 114, 115, 116, 117, 118, 119, 121, 125, 134, 135, 136, 139, 145, 153

contradiction 19, 53, 131, 139, 140, 141, 150, 159, 161, 182
converse 90, 153, 154
distribution 142, 162, 163, 196
exclusion 134, 138, 140
extension 26, 27, 58, 69, 70, 74, 85, 105, 115, 116, 122, 134, 142, 151, 185, 196, 241, 255
inclusion 58, 132, 134, 145, 146, 151, 187, 220
intersection 67, 134, 138, 140, 227
obverse 22, 28, 110, 112
opposition 40, 41, 42, 114, 175, 186, 221
syllogism 115, 121, 138, 143, 144, 147, 149, 152, 196, 261
Marvin, W. T. 30, 50, 54
Materialism 20, 25, 56, 57, 207, 208, 252
Mathematics 24, 30, 46, 51, 98, 100, 179, 181, 184, 186, 197, 199, 201, 207, 253
Mind 13, 14, 17, 33, 35, 38, 40, 41, 43, 45, 46, 47, 48, 51, 53, 56, 59, 60, 61, 63, 64, 68, 70, 72, 73, 77, 99, 104, 105, 106, 160, 162, 164, 168, 172, 173, 175, 178, 179, 201, 205, 213, 214, 225, 226, 229, 232
Monism 17, 40, 41, 45, 47
Moore, G.E. 13, 14, 16, 19, 30, 50, 74, 112, 116, 161, 168, 179
motion 15, 56, 67, 82, 85, 86, 87, 89, 91, 95, 225, 239, 243, 246

265

motions 67, 81, 82, 84, 95, 224, 225, 226, 229, 239, 243, 246, 248, 254
necessity 26, 50, 51, 52, 68, 69, 76, 78, 80, 82, 90, 92, 104, 122, 125, 135, 147, 181, 206, 221, 231, 234, 236, 237, 242, 248, 250, 252, 257, 258
Number 16, 24, 27, 32, 53, 56, 99, 100, 111, 117, 125, 135, 140, 144, 158, 159, 169, 170, 173, 181, 182, 183, 184, 187, 188, 190, 191, 192, 194, 197, 199, 200, 202, 203, 204, 206, 207, 209, 214, 216, 218, 226, 230, 232, 234, 241, 258
   cardinal........... 197, 200, 202
   category of.. 24, 27, 181, 183
   integers 182, 183, 184, 185, 187, 188, 194, 199, 202, 205, 209
   ordinal 24, 183, 201, 202
   rational 183, 203
   real 24, 183, 187, 194, 202, 203, 204, 206, 207, 209
objective 37, 45, 95, 117, 164, 174, 175, 193, 236, 237, 238, 249
Order 13, 15, 24, 27, 48, 49, 56, 77, 86, 91, 97, 110, 111, 124, 125, 138, 139, 147, 150, 151, 161, 164, 167, 181, 182, 183, 190, 192, 193, 195, 196, 202, 203, 204, 205, 206, 207, 208, 209, 212, 223, 224, 230, 234, 236, 237, 240, 241, 247, 248, 251, 253, 261
   category of 24, 25, 202, 204, 207, 234

Parmenides 45, 74, 111, 160, 163, 218
Particularity 24, 27, 65, 111, 113, 114, 155, 156, 167, 183, 187, 195, 231, 235
   category of 184
Particulars 50, 73, 109, 155, 156, 160, 161, 166, 167, 169, 171, 176, 183, 242
   'a' or 'the' particular 24, 35, 36, 46, 50, 96, 110, 111, 113, 121, 130, 138, 143, 147, 151, 153, 155, 156, 157, 162, 165, 167, 169, 170, 173, 174, 176, 180, 183, 193, 200, 213, 218, 231, 233, 244, 247, 248, 252, 259
Perry, R. B 30, 33, 50, 54
Plato 11, 24, 30, 31, 32, 51, 110, 178, 192
   Parmenides 163
   Phaedo 161, 178, 219
   Philebus 31, 70, 182
   Republic 51, 161, 178
   Sophist 31, 38, 61, 70, 110, 119, 129
   Theaetetus 31, 67, 244
Predicate 17, 20, 22, 23, 27, 38, 46, 47, 52, 54, 61, 64, 65, 66, 70, 77, 78, 105, 108, 109, 111, 112, 117, 121, 122, 124, 125, 126, 127, 128, 129, 130, 132, 133, 134, 138, 140, 141, 150, 151, 155, 156, 166, 171, 176, 180, 183, 188, 189, 192, 206, 221, 225, 230, 231, 260
   of the proposition 21, 22, 49, 62, 64, 68, 70, 78, 107, 108, 109, 122, 125
   as activity 38, 128

qualitative 128, 129
quantification of 138
Predication 23, 33, 38, 45, 49, 50, 52, 128, 131, 132, 152, 157, 171, 206, 221, 241
predicative relation. 129, 151
qualitative 128, 129, 131
Proposition 17, 18, 20, 21, 22, 23, 24, 25, 27, 28, 34, 37, 39, 46, 49, 50, 51, 52, 54, 61, 62, 65, 68, 70, 73, 74, 77, 78, 83, 98, 101, 107, 109, 111, 112, 115, 119, 120, 121, 122, 124, 125, 126, 127, 128, 132, 133, 136, 137, 138, 139, 141, 146, 149, 150, 151, 152, 155, 165, 166, 171, 180, 182, 183, 185, 191, 192, 193, 195, 196, 206, 221, 222, 228, 230, 231, 240, 243, 256, 260, 261
particular 24, 121
propositional 21, 22, 23, 26, 27, 33, 34, 37, 38, 39, 54, 57, 61, 62, 66, 72, 73, 75, 78, 79, 101, 107, 108, 109, 125, 132, 133, 150, 157, 168, 206, 221, 222, 230, 240, 249, 254
propositional form 22, 38, 39, 62, 66, 72, 73, 75, 107, 108, 221, 249
universal 24, 50, 158, 188, 195
Pythagoreans 63, 104, 160, 163, 185, 188, 219
Qualities 15, 21, 38, 54, 56, 57, 58, 62, 66, 67, 68, 95, 96, 99, 107, 109, 112, 116, 117, 118, 120, 122, 124, 128, 129, 130, 133, 134, 152, 156, 165, 167, 171, 180, 189, 190, 198, 209, 210, 218, 219, 220, 222, 223, 224, 225, 226, 228, 229, 232, 235, 241, 245, 253
primary 97, 165, 232
secondary ... 56, 96, 220, 245
Quality 25, 38, 54, 56, 57, 59, 61, 62, 66, 67, 68, 75, 96, 120, 121, 127, 128, 129, 130, 144, 149, 150, 151, 153, 166, 173, 180, 182, 183, 184, 190, 191, 195, 197, 198, 199, 206, 207, 208, 209, 210, 218, 219, 222, 223, 224, 225, 229, 231, 240, 241, 257
Quantity 15, 24, 25, 27, 28, 63, 120, 121, 134, 135, 141, 144, 150, 181, 182, 183, 184, 185, 187, 188, 190, 192, 195, 198, 202, 203, 204, 207, 208, 209, 210, 211, 218, 219, 222, 228, 230, 231, 234, 235, 240, 241, 245, 252, 257
category of 24, 183, 194, 204, 206, 207, 229
quantification . 138, 141, 195
Rationalism 17, 40, 41, 42, 45, 48, 54, 61, 97, 98, 99, 100, 161, 171, 197, 199, 221, 232, 250
Realism 13, 14, 16, 17, 18, 19, 20, 30, 33, 34, 45, 105, 160, 179, 249, 259
relation 14, 15, 18, 19, 22, 23, 27, 31, 33, 38, 40, 43, 48, 58, 59, 63, 66, 67, 68, 70, 74, 75, 77, 78, 79, 82, 86, 88, 89, 90, 91, 92, 93, 97, 100, 105, 106, 112, 114, 124, 127, 128, 131, 132, 133, 136, 139, 140, 143,

144, 145, 146, 147, 148, 150, 151, 152, 153, 154, 157, 160, 163, 169, 170, 174, 178, 181, 182, 183, 184, 187, 188, 189, 200, 201, 203, 204, 205, 206, 212, 216, 218, 219, 220, 222, 230, 232, 234, 238, 239, 243, 248, 249, 252, 254, 256, 257
  category of 127, 234
Relations 22, 28, 33, 41, 45, 47, 51, 53, 54, 64, 67, 68, 82, 88, 90, 92, 99, 100, 101, 104, 106, 108, 125, 128, 131, 132, 134, 137, 140, 143, 144, 148, 152, 153, 155, 176, 177, 179, 181, 189, 204, 206, 216, 219, 220, 222, 223, 225, 229, 231, 234, 235, 236, 237, 244, 252, 261
  asymmetrical 86, 205, 206, 248
  extended 68, 220
  external 16, 19, 129, 151
  reciprocal 248
  spatial 54, 62, 93, 129, 220, 239
  strict 68, 129, 133, 220
  symmetrical 67, 128, 132, 145, 248
Russell, B. 16, 30, 31, 34, 50, 82, 83, 90, 99, 100, 106, 132, 133, 136, 137, 153, 154, 161, 179, 181, 184, 201, 249
sensation 212, 213, 214, 215
Situation 21, 37, 42, 53, 75, 82, 92, 101, 102, 112, 120, 121, 125, 127, 133, 137, 147, 152, 153, 175, 181, 191, 195, 204, 217, 230, 238, 240, 241, 245, 248, 249, 250, 254, 257
  situational 21, 26, 33, 37, 99, 101, 104, 107, 125, 222, 223, 240, 245, 254
Socrates 36, 157, 161, 175, 176, 260
Space 11, 12, 13, 14, 15, 17, 18, 20, 22, 26, 27, 28, 30, 31, 32, 38, 40, 43, 54, 57, 60, 61, 62, 63, 64, 65, 66, 68, 69, 70, 72, 73, 74, 75, 76, 77, 78, 79, 80, 82, 84, 85, 87, 90, 91, 94, 95, 96, 97, 99, 101, 102, 104, 105, 106, 107, 108, 109, 165, 166, 169, 188, 204, 205, 208, 218, 224, 225, 226, 228, 231, 238, 240, 241, 245, 253, 254, 256
  'pure' 21, 54, 56, 58, 67, 69, 70, 79, 84, 120, 218, 223, 255
  as a form of togetherness 40, 64, 68, 69
  one dimensionality 76, 79, 82, 89, 90, 95
  space-filling 25, 27, 207, 208, 220, 231, 247
  space-fillingness (Solidity) 208, 218, 240
  three dimensionality 21, 75, 76, 78, 80, 82, 87, 92, 94, 95
  two dimensionality 76, 87, 90, 91, 95
Space-Time 11, 12, 13, 15, 17, 18, 20, 22, 23, 27, 33, 38, 39, 40, 44, 56, 57, 58, 61, 63, 64, 65, 66, 67, 68, 69, 70, 72, 73, 74, 78, 79, 84, 90, 95, 104, 107, 109, 111, 119, 120, 121, 165, 166,

167, 177, 188, 190, 209, 223, 228, 246, 252, 256, 257
'medium' theory 15, 21, 27, 68, 69, 72, 73, 74, 78, 80, 194
'stuff' theory 15, 17, 20, 27, 38, 56, 57, 61, 63, 66, 67, 68, 69, 72, 74, 75, 78, 109, 165, 166, 167, 177, 208, 223, 228, 241, 252, 253, 255
as togetherness and distinctness. 21, 62, 69, 75
spatio-temporal 20, 21, 22, 23, 26, 27, 38, 44, 55, 61, 62, 64, 66, 68, 70, 72, 73, 75, 99, 101, 103, 109, 116, 131, 134, 137, 165, 185, 186, 188, 210, 216, 220, 223, 229, 238, 241, 243, 245
Spinoza, B.................31, 66, 105
Stout, G. F. 11, 105, 117, 155, 156, 157, 168, 171, 172, 173, 178, 179, 181
Structure 12, 17, 20, 27, 28, 38, 61, 64, 77, 234, 235, 256, 258
Subject 17, 19, 20, 21, 22, 23, 25, 27, 38, 40, 45, 47, 49, 50, 52, 54, 61, 62, 64, 66, 68, 70, 77, 78, 99, 104, 107, 108, 109, 111, 121, 122, 124, 125, 126, 129, 130, 131, 132, 133, 140, 141, 150, 151, 152, 154, 156, 166, 169, 173, 174, 175, 176, 180, 192, 193, 206, 218, 221, 222, 224, 230, 231, 253, 260
and object 40, 45, 49, 173
as theme..........................258

Subject of the proposition 65, 121, 123, 150, 151, 155, 183, 221
and predicate 17, 21, 22, 49, 62, 64, 68, 70, 78, 107, 108, 109, 122, 125, 126, 134, 140
function of locating 23, 38, 108, 121, 129, 152, 193
Subjectivism 45
Substance 15, 18, 25, 27, 46, 49, 55, 56, 57, 58, 66, 67, 101, 104, 105, 106, 111, 118, 130, 132, 133, 168, 174, 189, 190, 198, 208, 218, 219, 220, 222, 223, 224, 225, 228, 229, 230, 232, 233, 234, 235, 236, 238, 242, 244, 251, 253, 257, 258
as constitution or composition 25, 59, 188, 189, 190, 206, 220, 228, 229, 232, 234, 235
category of 25, 189, 224, 236, 251
substantialism 20, 38, 56, 60, 111, 167
sufficiency 52, 67, 68, 69, 76, 80, 82, 90, 92, 203, 206, 234, 238, 242, 248, 250, 252, 257, 258
system 15, 16, 40, 53, 58, 84, 89, 90, 91, 97, 99, 102, 107, 155, 157, 158, 159, 172, 173, 174, 175, 176, 244, 254
systematic 119, 155, 158, 159
term 14, 20, 36, 45, 61, 65, 73, 78, 79, 80, 81, 85, 100, 101, 111, 113, 115, 116, 117, 121, 122, 125, 127, 129, 133, 134, 141, 144, 146,

150, 152, 155, 156, 160, 171, 176, 180, 181, 189, 191, 193, 206, 207, 210, 214, 223, 224, 225, 256, 259
  convertibility of terms 150, 151, 188, 195, 231, 256
Time 11, 12, 13, 14, 15, 17, 18, 20, 21, 22, 26, 27, 28, 30, 31, 32, 38, 40, 43, 54, 60, 61, 62, 63, 64, 65, 66, 68, 69, 70, 72, 73, 74, 75, 76, 77, 78, 79, 80, 82, 84, 85, 87, 88, 89, 90, 91, 94, 95, 96, 97, 98, 99, 101, 102, 104, 106, 107, 108, 109, 128, 129, 204, 205, 206, 208, 224, 226, 228, 231, 240, 241, 245, 247, 248, 252, 253, 254, 256
  'pure' 69, 70, 79
  as a form of distinctness 40, 64, 68, 69
  irreversibility of 21, 72, 75, 76, 78, 80, 81, 82, 84, 85, 86, 87, 88, 89, 91, 94, 95, 96, 97, 205, 206, 231, 237
  successiveness of 21, 75, 76, 77, 78, 79, 82, 89, 91, 95
  transitiveness of 21, 75, 76, 78, 81, 82, 84, 85, 86, 87, 88, 89, 90, 92, 95, 147, 205, 206, 231, 234
togetherness 21, 61, 62, 66, 67, 68, 69, 70, 75, 236

totality 45, 99, 102, 156, 157, 172, 174, 261
  or system 157, 174, 175, 176
transactions 238, 244, 254
transitiveness
  as betweenness ... 84, 85, 203
unit 41, 85, 99, 100, 102, 104, 106, 163, 185, 187, 191, 196, 197, 199, 200, 201, 202, 203, 209, 210, 212, 213, 214, 215
Universality 18, 23, 24, 27, 28, 64, 121, 122, 124, 126, 127, 155, 156, 160, 165, 167, 171, 172, 173, 174, 182, 183, 184, 192, 196, 207, 229, 230, 231, 234, 235, 242, 245, 247, 260
  abstract universal 160, 161, 177
  category of 23, 24, 127, 183, 207
  concrete universal 155, 157, 160, 161, 166, 169, 171, 172, 173, 175, 176, 177, 178
Universals 50, 108, 114, 155, 157, 160, 161, 164, 165, 166, 167, 168, 169, 170, 171, 172, 176, 178, 179, 199
vagueness 50, 53, 172, 180
Weber's Law 212, 213, 215
Zeno 30, 31, 68, 100